Dictionary of XML Technologies and the Semantic Web

Springer
London
Berlin
Heidelberg
New York
Hong Kong
Milan
Paris
Tokyo

Vladimir Geroimenko

Dictionary of XML Technologies and the Semantic Web

 Springer

Vladimir Geroimenko, PhD, DSc
School of Computing, University of Plymouth, Plymouth PL4 8AA, UK

British Library Cataloguing in Publication Data
A catalogue record for this book is available from the British Library

Library of Congress Cataloging-in-Publication Data
Geroimenko, Vladimir, 1955-
    Dictionary of XML technologies and the semantic Web / Vladimir Geroimenko
        p. cm. – (Springer professional computing)
    Includes bibliographical references.
    ISBN 1-85233-768-0 (alk paper)
        1. XML (Document markup language)—Dictionaries. 2. Semantic Web—Dictionaries. I.
    Title. II. Series.
    QA76.76.H94G47 2003
    006.7'4--dc22

                                                        2003061883

ISBN 1-85233-768-0 Springer-Verlag London Berlin Heidelberg
Springer-Verlag is part of Springer Science+Business Media
springeronline.com

Typesetting: Ian Kingston Editorial Services, Nottingham, UK
Printed and bound at The Cromwell Press, Trowbridge, Wiltshire
34/3830-543210 Printed on acid-free paper SPIN 10942680

Contents

Preface

The emerging Second-Generation Web is based entirely on XML and related technologies. It is intended to result in the creation of the Semantic Web, on which computers will be able to deal with the meaning ("semantics") of Web data and hence to process them in a more effective and autonomous way. This new version of the Web introduces a multitude of novel concepts, terms, and acronyms.

Purpose, Scope and Methods

This dictionary is an effort to specify the terminological basis of emerging XML and Semantic Web technologies. The ultimate goal of this dictionary is even broader than just to define the meaning of new words – it aims to develop a proper understanding of these leading-edge technologies. To achieve this, comprehensible definitions of technical terms are supported by numerous diagrams and code snippets, clearly annotated and explained.

The main areas covered in this dictionary are: (1) XML syntax and core technologies, such as Namespaces, Infoset and XML Schema; (2) all the major members of the XML family of technologies, such as XSLT, XPath and XLink; (3) numerous XML-based domain-specific languages, such as NewsML (News Markup Language); (4) the concept and architecture of the Semantic Web; (5) key Semantic Web technologies, such as RDF (Resource Description Framework), RDF Schema and OWL (Web Ontology Language); and (6) Web services, including WSDL (Web Services Description Language) and SOAP (Simple Object Access Protocol).

Some areas are not included in this edition of the dictionary, but they are planned to be covered in its next editions. These areas are: (1) software for editing and processing XML documents and data; (2) programming languages that can be used with XML, such as Java, Perl and ActionScript; (3) the historical aspect of the XML-related technologies; (4) the theoretical, philosophical and interdisciplinary foundations of the Semantic Web; (5) XML databases; and (6) XML-based multimedia in detail.

A variety of sources have been used to produce this dictionary. The major ones include: (1) the latest specifications published by the W3C and other organizations; (2) authoritative books, research articles and conference proceedings; and (3) online information, especially the Web sites of domain-specific markup languages.

The production of this dictionary was not only the process of "compiling" different sources; a unique research-based approach has been taken, which includes the use of a set of methods from the methodology of science, such as conceptual, logical and methodological analysis and synthesis.

The area covered in this dictionary is under extremely rapid development. This means that it is rather unstable and fluid. To try to conceptualize it in a dictionary is a really hard task. On the other hand, such conceptualization is apparently greatly needed for such a fast-moving area. The dictionary is intended to include the terms and concepts which seem to be the most stable and which would be unlikely to be changed in the very near future. The choice of such terms was not an easy job, and was based partly on logic and partly on intuition. Notice, however, that it is always a good idea to check for the latest specifications and news available on the Web sites listen in Appendix A and in appropriate entries.

Features and Organization of the Dictionary

The dictionary includes over 1,800 terms and definitions from a newly emerging area and also 264 illustrations to promote an understanding of the latest technologies. Clear and accessible definitions and a unique writing style bridge the gap between definition and explanation. Extensive cross-referencing of terms and a CD-ROM containing a fully searchable version of the dictionary make it ease to read and navigate.

The organization of the dictionary is intended to be clear and self-explanatory. Entries in the dictionary are of two types:

1. Main entries that contain full definitions. Their entry names are mostly in the format *acronym (full name)* and look like this:

XML (Extensible Markup Language)

2. Synonymous cross-references, which contain *See* references to appropriate main entries and look like this:

Extensible Markup Language *See* XML.

The dictionary uses the following types of references and cross-references:

- All capitalized words and acronyms in a sans serif font are references that point to appropriate main entries, for example: XML, UNABBREVIATED SYNTAX, XML-BASED MARKUP LANGUAGE.
- Many entries include references to online resources that offer additional or more detailed information about a topic, for example: "For more details, see http://www.w3.org/".
- *See* – A cross-reference that points to the main entry.
- *See also* – A cross-reference that is used to point to one or more main entries that contain some additional or supplementary information about a topic.
- *Contrast* – A cross-reference to another main entry that has a clearly apposite usage or meaning.
- *Compare* – A cross-reference to another main entry that is worth comparing with the current entry.

CD-ROM

The dictionary has an accompanying CD-ROM that contains a *searchable* version of the dictionary in PDF format. Clicking on any cross-references in the PDF file will take you straight to the referenced entry. The Adobe Reader can be downloaded free of charge from the Adobe Web site at http://www.adobe.com/.

Review Process

The choice of terms and, in many cases, the content of the Dictionary has been carefully checked by a distinguished board of experts to ensure that there are no glaring omissions. A list containing the names and short biographies of the members of the Technical Advisory Board can be found following this preface.

Acknowledgements

First of all, I would like to thank the members of the Advisory Board for helping me to make the dictionary much better. I would also like to express very special thanks to the team at Springer London Ltd, including Beverly Ford (Editorial Director) and Rebecca Mowat (Assistant Editor – Computing Science).

Trademarks

Some of the words used in this dictionary are registered trademarks. There was no attempt made to determine and report their legal status. For further information about any product name, consult the manufacturer's literature. Use of a word in this dictionary should not be regarded as affecting the validity of any trademark.

Future Editions

Although I have done my best to make this first edition of the dictionary as complete and error-free as possible, there is no doubt plenty of room for improvement. If you have an idea about a missing entry or find an error, please email me at vgeroimenko@plymouth.ac.uk.

Advisory Board

Jens Allwood (Sweden)

Professor at the Department of Linguistics and Chairman of The Interdisciplinary Center SSKKII for Cognitive Science, Göteborg University, Sweden. Guest professor at the Department of Communication Studies, University of Texas at Austin. Site leader for 28 externally funded research projects, including: Anthropological Linguistics, Director (HSFR); Better Terminal Use, Director (IBM); Text Comprehension, Co-director (Valand); Semantics and Spoken Interaction, Director (HSFR); A Pragmatic Language Understanding System, National Co-director (ESPRIT); Trust as a resource in achieving rationality, Co-director (RJ); Databases for Communication and Cooperation, Co-director (AMFO); Intelligent Instruments for Information, Co-director (NUTEK); Information Visualization and Exploration Systems, Director (NUTEK). Head of the research group 'Semantics and spoken language'. Author of 99 publications and coauthor of 55 publications on semantics and pragmatics. Member of editorial boards: of *Journal of Pragmatics*, 1976–; *Journal of Semantics*, 1982–88; *Linguistics*, 1976–85; *Systems Research*, 1984–; *Language and Context*, 1986–; *Pragmatics and Cognition*, 1991–. Editor in Chief: *Journal of Intercultural Communication*, 2000–. PhD (1976) from Göteborg University, Sweden.

Kurt Cagle (USA)

Author and President of Cagle Communications, an XML-oriented training and consulting firm located in Kirkland, Washington, with clients including Microsoft, Onyx Software, QMedia, Real Networks and AT&T, among others. Published books (authored or co-authored) include *Introducing Sparkle* (Microsoft 2003, Pending), *XSLT2 Handbook* (SAMS 2003, Pending), *XQuery Kick Start* (SAMS 2003), *SVG Programming* (Apress 2002), *XQuery Early Adopter* (2002, Wrox), *Professional XSLT* (2002, Wrox), bestseller *Beginning XML* (2001 and 2002, Wrox, 1st and 2nd editions), *XML Bible* (2000, Sybex), *Visual Basic Gold: Data Access Programming* (1999, Coriolis), *Understanding XML* (1998, Barron's), *Macromedia Director Bible* (1997, IDG), and others. Wrote monthly columns on XML and web industry standards for *Tech Republic* (CNet, 2003), *XML and Web Services Magazine* (Fawcette), *Java Pro* (Fawcette), *Visual Basic Programmers Journal* (Fawcette), and *XML Journal* (Sys-con). Technical Editor and Author for the *Macromedia Users Journal*. Papers accepted or presented at *SVG Open*, Vancouver (2003), *XML Web Services*, Boston (2003), *Knowledge Technologies Conference*, Seattle (2002), *Wrox XML*, the Netherlands (2002) and Las Vegas (2001), *XML One*, New York and San Jose (2001), *XML Connections*, New Orleans (2001) and Scottsdale, AZ (2001), *Macromedia Users Conference* (1995,1996, 1997,

1998). Member of OASIS and the National Writers Union.

Chaomei Chen (USA)

Associate Professor at the College of Information Science and Technology, Drexel University, USA. Founding director of the VIVID research centre at Brunel University, England. Author of *Mapping Scientific Frontiers* (Springer, 2002) and *Information Visualisation and Virtual Environments* (Springer, 1999). Co-editor of *Visualizing the Semantic Web* (Springer, 2002) and *Visual Interfaces to Digital Libraries* (Springer, 2002). Editor-in-Chief of *Information Visualization* (Palgrave Macmillan 2002–). Previously worked at Brunel University (England) and Glasgow Caledonian University (Scotland). PhD from the University of Liverpool (1995).

Lars Marius Garshol (Norway)

Development manager at Ontopia, a leading topic map software vendor. Co-editor of ISO 18048 (Topic Map Query Language), ISO 13250-2 (Topic Maps – Data Model) and ISO 13250-3 (Topic Maps – XML Syntax). Author of *Definitive XML Application Development* (Prentice Hall). Creator of several Semantic Web-related technologies, and a number of XML-related open source tools. MSc from University of Oslo (1999).

Christopher Hindle (UK)

Principal Lecturer in the School of Computing at the University of Plymouth. MA in Mathematics and PhD in Theoretical Physics from Cambridge were followed by research at Princeton and the ETH, Zurich. Subsequently taught at the UK Defence ADP Training Centre and Royal Naval Engineering College before taking up his current position as Computer Network and Systems Architecture Group Leader.

Ian Horrocks (UK)

Professor in the Department of Computer Science at the University of Manchester, UK. Designer and implementor of the FaCT DL reasoner, and a prime mover behind the OIL, DAML+OIL and OWL Web ontology languages. Has published widely (see http://www.cs.man.ac.uk/~horrocks/Publications/). Founding member of the Semantic Web Science Foundation, member of the Joint EU/US Committee on Agent Markup Languages, the Description Logic Steering Committee and of the editorial boards of *JAIR*, *ETAI* and the *Journal of Web Semantics*. Programme chair of ISWC2002 and the Semantic Web track of WWW2003. Coordinator of the EU IST WonderWeb project and consultant to the DARPA DAML program.

Tom Myers (USA)

Chief Technical Officer, N-Topus Software. Previously worked in the Department of Computer and Information Science of Colgate University in Hamilton, New York, and before that at the University of Delaware in Newark, Delaware. Author of *Equations, Models and Programs: A Mathematical Introduction to Computer Science* (Prentice Hall, 1988); coauthor of *JavaScript Objects* (Wrox, 1998), *Professional Java XML Programming* (Wrox, 2000) and *XML Programming* (APress, 2002), and related contributed chapters. PhD in Computer Science from the University of Pennsylvania.

Alexander Nakhimovsky (USA)

Associate Professor of Computer Science at Colgate University, USA; previously taught at SUNY Oswego and Cornell. Has been teaching computer science at Colgate since 1985. Co-author, jointly with Tom Myers, of *XML Programming* (Apress, 2002), *Professional Java XML Programming* (Wrox, 1999), and *Javascript Objects* (Wrox, 1998). Author of journal and conference articles. MA in mathematics from Leningrad University (1972), PhD from Cornell (1979).

Heinz Schweppe (Germany)

Professor of Computer Science at Free University Berlin, Database and Information Systems Group. Previously head of the AI department of Siemens Corporate Technology, Munich. Worked with Universities Bonn and Braunschweig. Member of the

Terms of XML Technologies and the Semantic Web

Abbreviated syntax In XPATH, shortened SYNTAX for a LOCATION STEP. See Figure A.1. *Contrast* UNABBREVIATED SYNTAX.

Absolute expression *See* ABSOLUTE LOCATION PATH.

Abbreviated syntax	Unabbreviated syntax
nothing	`child::`
@	`attribute::`
//	`/descendant-or-self::node()/`
.	`self::node()`
..	`parent::node()`

Figure A.1 Some examples of abbreviated syntax.

Absolute location path In XPATH, a LOCATION PATH that starts at the ROOT NODE of a NODE TREE. An absolute location path expression begins with a forward slash (which indicates the root node) and is followed by a RELATIVE LOCATION PATH. An absolute location path is a sequence of LOCATION STEPS, each separated by a forward slash. In the example shown in Figure A.2 the absolute location path selects all the "price" elements of all the "book" elements of the "catalog" element. Note that the "catalog" ELEMENT is the ROOT ELEMENT of the XML DOCUMENT and should not be confused with the ROOT NODE of the XPATH NODE TREE represented by the start forward slash. *Contrast* RELATIVE LOCATION PATH.

Action attribute *See* XFORMS MODEL.

Active intermediary *See* SOAP INTERMEDIARY.

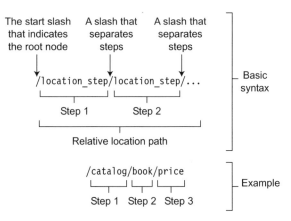

Figure A.2 Absolute location path.

Figure A.3 An example of an XLink "actuate" attribute.

Actuate attribute In XLINK, an ATTRIBUTE used to specify when and how the LINK should be activated. Its main ATTRIBUTE VALUES are: (1) onRequest – some user's action is required to activate the link, such as a mouse click (see Figure A.3); (2) onLoad – the link is activated automatically immediately on loading the STARTING RESOURCE.

ADML (Architecture Description Markup Language) An XML-BASED MARKUP LANGUAGE for the interchange of architectural descriptions between a variety of architectural design tools. More details about ADML are available at http://www.opengroup.org/architecture/adml/adml_home.htm.

aecXML (Architecture, Engineering and Construction XML) An XML-BASED MARKUP LANGUAGE for representing information in the Architecture, Engineering and Construction (AEC) industry. Details of aecXML can be found at http://www.iai-na.org/aecxml/mission.php.

Agent *See* INTELLIGENT AGENT.

Agent-Oriented Rule Markup Language *See* AORML.

Aggregation & Logging of User Requests for assistance Extensible Markup Language *See* ALUREXML.

AIML (Astronomical Instrument Markup Language) An XML-BASED MARKUP LANGUAGE for describing and controlling astronomical instruments. AIML is a domain-specific implementation of IML. More details about AIML can be obtained from http://pioneer.gsfc.nasa.gov/public/aiml/.

All Different statement In OWL, a statement that indicates all given INDIVIDUALS are different from each other. In the example shown in Figure A.4, "Mike", "Chris" and "Dan" are stated to be all different individuals of the CLASS "Person". *See also* SAME AS STATEMENT; DIFFERENT FROM STATEMENT.

all element In an XML SCHEMA, a special ELEMENT that is used as an INDICATOR that specifies by default that the CHILD ELEMENTS of the declared element may appear in any order, and also that each child element must occur once and only once. The QUALIFIED NAME of the "all" element can be either "xs:all" or "xsd:all", depending whether the XS NAMESPACE PREFIX or XSD NAMESPACE PREFIX is being used. See Figure A.5.

Figure A.4 Stating that individuals are all different.

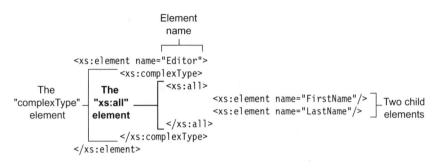

Figure A.5 The use of the "all" element.

all indicator *See* INDICATOR.

Alt (Alternative) *See* ALTERNATIVE CONTAINER.

Alt class In RDF SCHEMA, the rdf:Alt CLASS is the class of ALTERNATIVE CONTAINERS. It is a SUBCLASS of the CONTAINER CLASS.

Alternative container In RDF, the rdf:Alt CONTAINER is a container that is a collection of RESOURCES or LITERALS that represent alternative values, such as alternative language translations for the title of a book. See Figure A.6. Note that in the rdf:li ELEMENT, the "li" LOCAL PART stands for "a list item".

Alternative element *See* ALTERNATIVE CONTAINER.

ALUReXML (Aggregation & Logging of User Requests for assistance Extensible Markup Language) An XML-BASED MARKUP LANGUAGE that allows any Web-based "user assistance" product or system to log information on specific problems that customers have. For more details, see http://www.alurexml.org/alurexml.htm.

AML (Avatar Markup Language) An XML-BASED MARKUP LANGUAGE for describing avatar-based communication, including facial and body animation as well as text-to-speech content. (An avatar is the visual character you use to represent yourself in Virtual Reality). More details about AML are available at http://ligwww.epfl.ch/~aguye/AML/.

AnatML (Anatomical Markup Language) An XML-BASED MARKUP LANGUAGE for describing anatomy, especially for storing geometric information about the human musculoskeletal system. Details of AnatML are available at http://www.physiome.org.nz/sites/physiome/anatml/pages/.

Anatomical Markup Language *See* ANATML.

Ancestor In XPATH, an ancestor of the CONTEXT NODE, such as the PARENT of context node, the parent's parent, and so on. *See also* ANCESTOR AXIS.

ancestor axis In XPATH, an AXIS that selects the PARENT of the CONTEXT NODE, the parent's parent, and so on. The ancestor axis always includes the

```
<rdf:Description about="http://www.springer.de/spc/book1">
    <dc:Title>
        <rdf:Alt>
            <rdf:li xml:lang="en"> English Title</rdf:li>
            <rdf:li xml:lang="de"> Deutscher Titel</rdf:li>
        </rdf:Alt>
    </dc:Title>
</rdf:Description>
```

The "rdf:Alt" element

Figure A.6 An example of an RDF "Alternative" container.

5

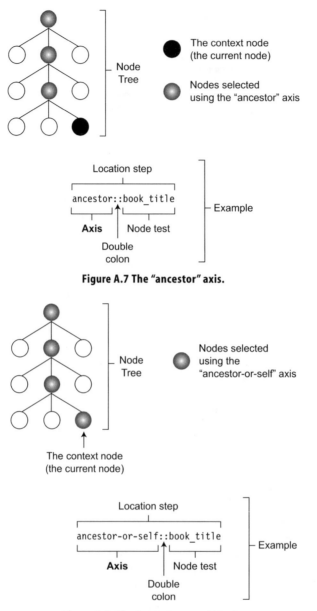

Figure A.7 The "ancestor" axis.

Figure A.8 The "ancestor-or-self" axis.

ROOT NODE, unless the context node is the root node. See Figure A.7.

ancestor-or-self axis In XPATH, an AXIS that selects the same NODES as the ANCESTOR AXIS and also the CONTEXT NODE itself. See Figure A.8.

Angle brackets Special signs used for delimiting a MARKUP TAG and differentiating it from the content

6

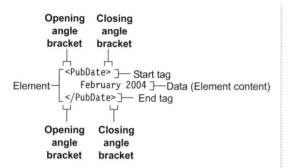

Figure A.9 Opening and closing angle brackets in XML.

of an XML, HTML or SGML document, as shown in Figure A.9. In this respect, angle brackets are a symbol of the so-called "XML revolution". The opening angle bracket (<) and the closing angle bracket (>) are also often called the "less-than" sign (<) and the "greater-than" (>) sign respectively. Because the signs (<) and (>) are used in XML MARKUP not for comparing numbers and values, but as paired DELIMITERS, the use of the term "angle brackets" is probably preferable. See Figure A.9.

Annotated XML The specification of XML, annotated by Tim Bray. More information is available at http://www.xml.com/axml/axml.html.

annotation element A special ELEMENT of the XML SCHEMA language that is intended for commenting XML schemas and also for adding information for applications similar to PROCESSING INSTRUCTIONS. To this end, it has two children, as shown in Figure A.10: (1) the DOCUMENTATION ELEMENT and (2) the APPINFO ELEMENT.

ANY keyword In a DTD, a keyword used in the ELEMENT TYPE DECLARATION to specify that elements of this type may contain all kinds of MARKUP and XML DATA, in any mixture.

Anonymous data type In an XML SCHEMA, a DATA TYPE that has no name and therefore cannot be explicitly referenced. *Contrast* NAMED DATA TYPE.

AORML (Agent-Oriented Rule Markup Language) An XML-BASED MARKUP LANGUAGE for describing agent-oriented business rules in the context of Agent Object Relationship (AOR) models. More details of AORML may be obtained from http://tmitwww.tm.tue.nl/staff/gwagner/AORML/. *See also* RULEML.

Apache Software Foundation *See* ASF.

API (Application Programming Interface) A standardized set of functions and commands that allows any developer to interface an APPLICATION program with other applications.

appinfo element A special ELEMENT of the XML SCHEMA language, used for inserting instructions for applications similar to PROCESSING INSTRUCTIONS into an XML SCHEMA. This element must be NESTED within of the ANNOTATION ELEMENT, as shown in Figure A.11. The "appinfo" abbreviation stands for "application information".

Application An application (also called an application program) is a computer software program that allows the user either to perform useful work not related to the computer itself (for example, a

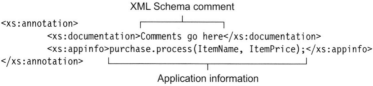

Figure A.10 The structure and use of the "annotation" element.

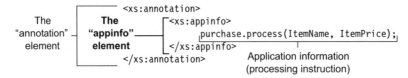

Figure A.11 The "appinfo" element.

word processor or an XML EDITOR), or to develop other software. This differs from the system software that is used by the computer for its own purposes. Any XML-BASED MARKUP LANGUAGE is officially called an XML APPLICATION, though such terminology is perhaps somewhat misleading.

Application information *See* APPINFO ELEMENT.

Application program *See* APPLICATION.

Application Programming Interface *See* API.

Application services *See* WEB SERVICES.

Application software *See* APPLICATION.

Arc In XLINK, navigable connections between LOCATORS participating in an EXTENDED LINK. It defines the direction of TRAVERSAL and optionally application behavior. There are three types of arc: (1) OUTBOUND ARC; (2) INBOUND ARC; and (3) THIRD-PARTY ARC. Figure A.12 shows an arc between two RESOURCES specified by their locator. This arc connects a particular book to the biography of its author. *See also* ARC-TYPE ELEMENT.

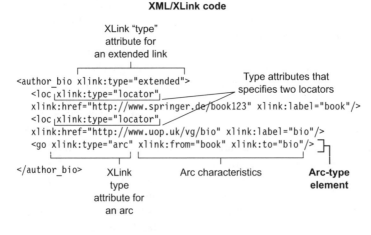

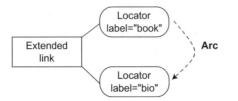

Figure A.12 An example of an XLink arc.

Archaeological Markup Language *See* ARCHAEOML.

ArchaeoML (Archaeological Markup Language) An XML-BASED MARKUP LANGUAGE for describing archaeological and geographical data as well as the epigraphic and linguistic features of ancient texts. More details of ArchaeoML may be obtained from http://www.oi.uchicago.edu/OI/PROJ/ XSTAR/ArchaeoML.html.

Architecture Description Markup Language *See* ADML.

Architecture, Engineering and Construction XML *See* AECXML.

Arc-type element In XLINK, the ELEMENT of an XML DOCUMENT that has a TYPE ATTRIBUTE with the "arc" ATTRIBUTE VALUE and therefore can be used to specify traversal rules among the link's PARTICIPATING RESOURCES. For more details, see ARC; TYPE ATTRIBUTE.

Article Extensible Markup Language *See* AXML.

ASF (The Apache Software Foundation) A not-for-profit corporation that hosts OPEN SOURCE software projects, including the Apache XML project. For more details, see http://www.apache.org/.

Associating style sheets with XML documents A W3C RECOMMENDATION that describes the mechanism of attaching of a STYLE SHEET to an XML DOCUMENT using a special XML style sheet PROCESSING INSTRUCTION. In an XML DOCUMENT, this processing instruction usually follows the XML DECLARATION. The ATTRIBUTE VALUES of its ATTRIBUTES are used to specify whether the attaching style sheet is an XSL STYLE SHEET or a CSS STYLE SHEET, as shown in Figure A.13. This RECOMMENDATION is available at http://www.w3.org/TR/xml-stylesheet/.

Astronomical Instrument Markup Language *See* AIML.

Atomic data type In an XML SCHEMA, a DATA TYPE that is considered to be the type that cannot be subdivided into other data types.

ATTLIST declaration (Attribute-list declaration) A DTD DECLARATION used for specifying the ATTRIBUTES of an ELEMENT. It defines: (1) The number of attributes; (2) ATTRIBUTE NAMES; (3) attribute types, such as CDATA or ENTITY; (4) attribute DEFAULT VALUES, such as "REQUIRED" or "IMPLIED". See Figure A.14 for an example.

ATTLIST keyword *See* ATTLIST DECLARATION; DTD DECLARATION.

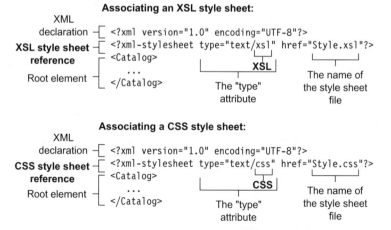

Figure A.13 Examples of associating style sheets with XML documents.

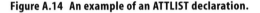

DTD:
```
<!ELEMENT Editor EMPTY >
```
Declaration of empty "Editor" element

"ATTLIST" keyword   Element name

```
<!ATTLIST Editor
    title    CDATA #IMPLIED  ←——This attribute is optional
    name     CDATA #REQUIRED ←——This attribute is required
    surname  CDATA #REQUIRED >
```
Declaration of its attributes

Attribute name   Attribute type   Attribute default

XML document:
```
<Editor name="Chaomei" surname="Chen"/>
```
Valid XML code

Figure A.14 An example of an ATTLIST declaration.

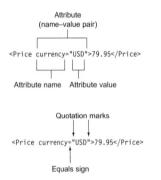

Attribute (name–value pair)

```
<Price currency="USD">79.95</Price>
```

Attribute name   Attribute value

Quotation marks

```
<Price currency="USD">79.95</Price>
```

Equals sign

Figure A.15 The anatomy of an attribute.

Attribute A STRUCTURAL CONSTRUCT of XML that consists of a NAME–VALUE PAIR enclosed within the START TAG of an ELEMENT, as shown in Figure A.15. As a property of an element, an attribute provides additional information about the element and modifies certain features of it. Accordingly, an attribute is not as autonomous as an element and makes sense only in the context of the element it belongs to. Attributes can contain any CHARACTER DATA, including WHITE SPACE. Unlike in HTML, ATTRIBUTE VALUES in XML must be surrounded by either double or single quotes. An element can have any number of attributes providing all of them have a unique attribute name. *See also* ATTRIBUTE NAME; ATTRIBUTE VALUE; ATTRIBUTE TYPE; ELEMENT; NAME–VALUE PAIR; START TAG.

attribute axis In XPATH, an AXIS that selects the ATTRIBUTE NODES of the CONTEXT NODE. See Figure A.16.

Attribute declaration An XML SCHEMA COMPONENT used to declare an ATTRIBUTE of an XML DOCUMENT element. All attributes are SIMPLE TYPES, since their ATTRIBUTE VALUES can contain only CHARACTER DATA. On the other hand, each ELEMENT that has one or more attributes is a COMPLEX DATA TYPE. An attribute declaration always appears as the very last part of a COMPLEX TYPE DECLARATION after everything else has been declared. Figure A.17 shows the ELEMENT DECLARATION of the PlanState element, which is an EMPTY ELEMENT. It is of a complex data type and has one attribute named "agreed". *See also* XML SCHEMA COMPONENT; BOOLEAN DATA TYPE.

Attribute declaration *See* ATTLIST DECLARATION.

Attribute default value *See* DEFAULT VALUE.

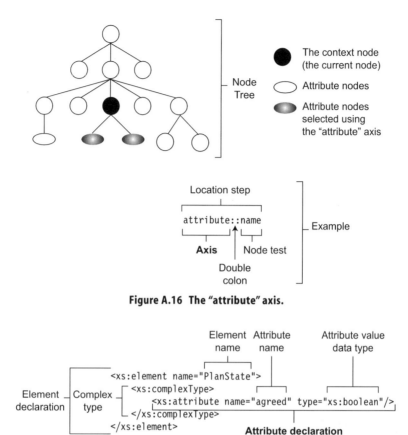

Figure A.16 The "attribute" axis.

Figure A.17 An example of an attribute declaration.

attribute element The "attribute" element is a special ELEMENT of the XML SCHEMA used in ATTRIBUTE DECLARATION for declaring ATTRIBUTES.

Attribute information item One of the eleven types of INFORMATION ITEMS in the INFORMATION SET. Like all of them, it is an abstract description of a STRUCTURAL CONSTRUCT of an XML DOCUMENT. This description is intended for use in other XML-related specifications, which need to conform to the information set. There is an attribute information item in the information set for each ATTRIBUTE of the document. The attribute information item has eight properties, as shown in Figure A.18. For more details, see http://www.w3.org/TR/xml-infoset/.

Attribute name The identifier of an ATTRIBUTE. See Figure A.19. An attribute name is the first part of a NAME–VALUE PAIR. An attribute name must be a VALID XML NAME. This, in particular, means: (1) Attribute names must begin with a letter (but not a number), an underscore (_) or a colon (:); (2) They may not begin with the letters x, m or l in any combination of upper and lower cases, since these are reserved by the W3C for a special use; (3) The use of names that start with a colon (such as :BookTitle) should be avoided, since colons are used only to separate the NAMESPACE PREFIX of a QUALIFIED NAME from its LOCAL PART. *See also* ATTRIBUTE VALUE.

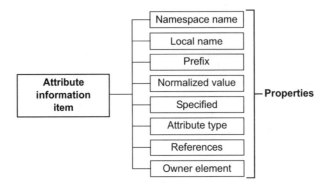

Figure A.18 The attribute information item and its properties.

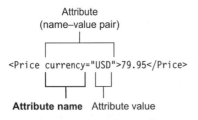

Figure A.19 An example of an attribute name.

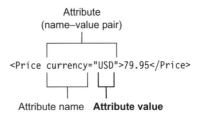

Figure A.20 An example of an attribute value.

Attribute node One of the seven NODE TYPES of the XPATH DATA MODEL that represents an ATTRIBUTE. Note that in XPATH, an ELEMENT NODE is the PARENT of an ATTRIBUTE NODE, but an attribute node is *not* the CHILD of its parent ELEMENT NODE.

Attribute specification A term that is sometimes used to refer to the individual listing for an ATTRIBUTE in an ATTLIST DECLARATION.

Attribute value In XML, a value assigned to an ATTRIBUTE. An attribute value must be enclosed in either double (" ") or single (' ') quotation

marks and can contain any CHARACTER DATA, including WHITE SPACE. See Figure A.20. *See also* ATTRIBUTE VALUE; NAME–VALUE PAIR; STRING LITERAL.

attributeGroup element In an XML SCHEMA, a special ELEMENT that is used as an INDICATOR that declares a named group of ATTRIBUTES, as shown in Figure A.21.

attributeGroup indicator *See* INDICATOR.

Attribute-list declaration *See* ATTLIST DECLARATION.

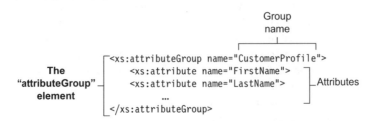

Figure A.21 The "attributeGroup" element.

Authentication In XML messaging, a security term that refers to the possibility to sign a message in a special way, to ensure that the person you are communicating with is indeed that person and that the message has not been change after having been signed. *See also* XML SIGNATURE.

Authentication and Authorization Extensible Markup Language *See* AUTHXML.

AuthXML (Authentication and Authorization Extensible Markup Language) AuthXML is a standard for encoding authentication and authorization information in transport-independent XML. (The "Auth" stands for both authentication and authorization). More details of AuthXML may be obtained from http://www.rsasecurity.com/.

Avatar Markup Language *See* AML.

Axes The plural of AXIS.

Axis In XPATH, the first part of a LOCATION STEP that specifies a NODE SET relative to the CONTEXT NODE. It defines the NODE TREE relationship between the context node and one or more NODES that are selected by the location step as candidates for the next context node. There are 13 different axes: (1) SELF AXIS; (2) CHILD AXIS; (3) DESCENDANT AXIS; (4) DESCENDANT-OF-SELF AXIS; (5) PARENT AXIS; (6) ANCESTOR AXIS; (7) ANCESTOR-OF-SELF AXIS; (8) FOLLOWING-SIBLING AXIS; (9) PRECEDING-SIBLING AXIS; (10) FOLLOWING AXIS; (11) PRECEDING AXIS; (12) ATTRIBUTE AXIS; (13) NAMESPACE AXIS.

AXML (Article Extensible Markup Language) An XML-based language for electronic markup of pages intended for hard copy. Details of AXML can be found at http://xml.gsfc.nasa.gov/article/.

B2B (Business to Business) E-commerce between enterprises over the Internet.

B2C (Business to Consumer) E-commerce between an enterprise and an individual over the Internet.

B2G (Business to Government) The exchange of products, services or information between businesses and government agencies over the Internet.

Bag class In RDF SCHEMA, the rdf:Bag CLASS is the class of BAG CONTAINERS. It is a SUBCLASS of the CONTAINER CLASS.

Bag container In RDF, the rdf:Bag CONTAINER is a container that is an unordered collection of RESOURCES or LITERALS, as shown in Figure B.1. Note that in the rdf:li ELEMENT, the "li" LOCAL PART stands for a "list item".

Bag element See BAG CONTAINER.

Balanced region See WELL-BALANCED REGION.

Banner Markup Language See BANNERML.

BannerML (Banner Markup Language) An XML-BASED MARKUP LANGUAGE for attaching additional text information to Internet banners. More details about BannerML can be obtained from http://www.cogitum.com/BannerML/.

base attribute The ATTRIBUTE of the XS:RESTRICTION ELEMENT that is used to specify the base DATA TYPE for a facet. For more details, see FACET.

Base URI See XML:BASE ATTRIBUTE; XML BASE SPECIFICATION.

bcXML (Building-Construction Extensible Markup Language) An XML-BASED MARKUP LANGUAGE for the building and construction industry. More information is available at http://www.econstruct.org/.

```
<rdf:Description about="http://www.springer.de">
        <SPC_Book>
          ┌ <rdf:Bag>
          │     <rdf:li resource="http://www.springer.de/spc/book1"/>
The "Bag" ┤     <rdf:li resource="http://www.springer.de/spc/book2"/>
element   │     <rdf:li resource="http://www.springer.de/spc/book3"/>
          └ </rdf:Bag>
        </SPC_Book>
      </rdf:Description>
    </rdf:RDF>
```

Figure B.1 An example of an RDF "Bag" container.

Bean Markup Language *See* BML.

Beginning tag *See* START TAG.

Berners-Lee, Tim The inventor of the WWW, Director of the W3C, and originator of the idea of the SEMANTIC WEB. More information about Tim Berners-Lee can be found at http://www.w3.org/People/Berners-Lee/.

Bibliography Markup Language *See* BIBLIOML.

BiblioML (Bibliography Markup Language) An XML-BASED MARKUP LANGUAGE for the interchange of bibliographic records. For more details, see the information at http://www.culture.fr/BiblioML/.

Binding component In the WSDL COMPONENT MODEL, a component that describes a binding of a PORT TYPE COMPONENT to a particular protocol, such as SOAP. The XML representation of the binding component is the wsdl:binding ELEMENT.

Binding operation component In the WSDL COMPONENT MODEL, a component that describes a binding for a PORT TYPE OPERATION to a message format. The XML representation of the port type operation component is the wsdl:operation ELEMENT.

Bioinformatic Sequence Markup Language *See* BSML.

BIOML (Biopolymer Markup Language) An XML-BASED MARKUP LANGUAGE for the annotation of biopolymer sequence information. For more details, see the information at http://www.bioml.com/BIOML/.

Biopolymer Markup Language *See* BIOML.

biz A FILENAME EXTENSION that indicates that the file is a BIZTALK document (file format). For example, "Catalog.biz".

BML (Bean Markup Language) An XML-based component configuration language for describing JavaBeans. For more details, see http://www.alphaworks.ibm.com/formula/bml/.

Body One of three XML DOCUMENT SECTIONS that may consist of (1) the ROOT ELEMENT and NESTED ELEMENTS; (2) CHARACTER DATA; (3) XML COMMENTS; (4) PROCESSING INSTRUCTIONS; (5) WHITE SPACE. A body is the main and also compulsory part of an XML DOCUMENT. See Figure B.2. *See also* PROLOG; EPILOG.

Body element A required STRUCTURAL CONSTRUCT of the SOAP MESSAGE STRUCTURE that contains the actual

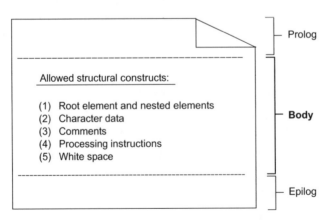

Figure B.2 The body as a section of an XML document.

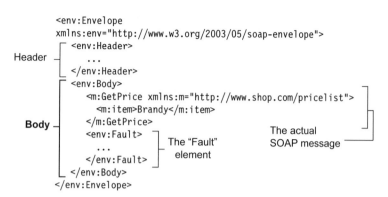

```
<env:Envelope
xmlns:env="http://www.w3.org/2003/05/soap-envelope">
        <env:Header>
            ...
        </env:Header>
        <env:Body>
            <m:GetPrice xmlns:m="http://www.shop.com/pricelist">
                <m:item>Brandy</m:item>
            </m:GetPrice>
            <env:Fault>
                ...
            </env:Fault>
        </env:Body>
</env:Envelope>
```

Header

Body

The "Fault" element

The actual SOAP message

Figure B.3 The SOAP Body.

SOAP MESSAGE. In the example shown in Figure B.3, the SOAP message requests the price of brandy.

Bolero Extensible Markup Language *See* BOLEROXML.

BoleroXML (Bolero Extensible Markup Language) A set of XML-based cross-industry languages that are intended for the secure and automated exchange of information between all parties in a trade chain. More details about BoleroXML can be obtained from http://www.bolero.net/boleroxml/.

Boolean data type In an XML SCHEMA, a BUILT-IN PRIMITIVE DATA TYPE that is used to specify a true or false value, as shown in Figure B.4. This data type is also used in other XML technologies, such as XPATH.

Box model *See* CSS BOX MODEL.

Box properties In CSS, the collection of properties and values that control the formatting of the margins, padding, height, width, and border aspects of any element. *See* CSS BOX MODEL.

BPEL (Business Process Execution Language) *See* BPEL4WS.

BPEL4WS (Business Process Execution Language for Web Services) An XML-BASED MARKUP LANGUAGE for describing business processes including multiple WEB SERVICES and for standardizing message exchange internally and between partners. It has superseded XLANG and WSFL. BPEL4WS is also sometimes identified as BPELWS or BPEL. For more details, see the information at http://www-106.ibm.com/developerworks/webservices/library/ws-bpel/.

BPELWS *See* BPEL4WS.

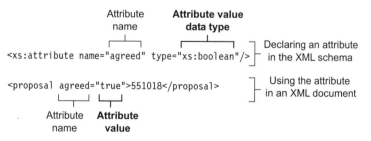

Attribute name

Attribute value data type

```
<xs:attribute name="agreed" type="xs:boolean"/>
```

Declaring an attribute in the XML schema

```
<proposal agreed="true">551018</proposal>
```

Attribute name

Attribute value

Using the attribute in an XML document

Figure B.4 An attribute with a value of the Boolean data type.

BPML (Business Process Modeling Language)
An XML-based METALANGUAGE for modeling business processes. It provides an abstract domain-neutral model and XML grammar for expressing genetic processes and supporting entities. More details of BPML may be obtained from http://www.bpmi.org/bpml.esp.

Browser *See* WEB BROWSER.

BSML (Bioinformatic Sequence Markup Language) An XML-BASED MARKUP LANGUAGE that describes gene sequences or annotations. Details of BSML are available at http://www.labbook.com/products/xmlbsml.asp.

BTP (Business Transaction Protocol) An XML-based protocol for managing complex B2B transactions over the Internet. Details of BTP can be found at http://www.oasis-open.org/committees/business-transactions/documents/specification/2002-06-03.BTP_cttee_spec_1.0.pdf.

Building-Construction Extensible Markup Language *See* BCXML.

Built-in data type In an XML SCHEMA, a term that is sometimes used to refer to a DATA TYPE available to

all authors, such as "xs:string" or "xs:boolean" (*see* BOOLEAN DATA TYPE).

Built-in derived data type In an XML SCHEMA, a DATA TYPE available to all authors, defined by restricting existing data types. *See also* BUILT-IN DATA TYPE; DERIVED DATA TYPE.

Built-in internal general entities In XML, five predefined ENTITIES used to represent SPECIAL SYMBOLS.

Built-in primitive data type In an XML SCHEMA, a DATA TYPE available to all authors that cannot be defined using other data types, such as string or date. *See also* BUILT-IN DATA TYPE; PRIMITIVE DATA TYPE.

Business to Business *See* B2B.

Business to Consumer *See* B2C.

Business to Government *See* B2G.

Business Process Execution Language for Web Services *See* BPEL4WS.

Business Process Modeling Language *See* BPML.

Business Transaction Protocol *See* BTP.

Call Control Extensible Markup Language *See* CCXML.

Call Processing Language *See* CPL.

Candidate recommendation *See* W3C CANDIDATE RECOMMENDATION.

Caption element *See* FORM CONTROLS.

Card *See* WML.

Cascading Style Sheets *See* CSS.

Cascading Style Sheets Level 1 *See* CSS1.

Cascading Style Sheets Level 2 *See* CSS2.

Cascading Style Sheets Level 3 *See* CSS3.

Case Based Markup Language *See* CBML.

Case-insensitive A term that indicates that no distinction is to be made between uppercase and lowercase letters, such as "G" and "g". Unlike XML, HTML syntax is case-insensitive. For example, the TAGS <HTML>, <html>, and <Html> are identical. *Contrast* CASE-SENSITIVE.

Case-sensitive A term that indicates that the distinction between uppercase and lowercase letters (such as "Q" and "q") must be maintained. Unlike HTML, XML SYNTAX is case-sensitive. For example,

<book>, <BOOK>, and <Book> are three different TAGS since their ELEMENT NAMES are not equivalent. *Contrast* CASE-INSENSITIVE.

CaveScript XML An XML-based data format for storing information about a cave survey or a cave map. More information is available at http://www.speleonics.com.au/cavescript/.

CBML (Case Based Markup Language) An XML-based language for marking up cases in XML, to enable distributed computing and case-based reasoning. More details about CBML can be obtained from http://www.cs.tcd.ie/Lorcan.Coyle/CBML/.

CCXML (Call Control Extensible Markup Language) An XML-BASED MARKUP LANGUAGE that provides telephony call control support for VOICEXML and some more traditional dialog systems. Although CCXML is intended to be integrated with VoiceXML, the two languages are separate and neither is required an implementation of the other. More information about CCXML is available at http://www.w3.org/TR/ccxml/.

CDA (Clinical Document Architecture) An XML-BASED MARKUP LANGUAGE for exchanging clinical documents such as discharge summaries and progress notes. CDA was initially known as the Patient Record Architecture (PRA). More details are available at http://www.hl7.org/Library/standards_non1.htm.

CDATA *See* CDATA SECTION.

CDATA section A STRUCTURAL CONSTRUCT of an XML DOCUMENT for including blocks of text that contain many special characters that would otherwise be interpreted as MARKUP. CDATA sections begin with the string (<![CDATA[) and end with the string (]]>), as shown in Figure C.1. The use of CDATA sections allows developers to avoid replacing each of a large number of SPECIAL SYMBOLS with their corresponding ENTITY REFERENCE. CDATA sections are

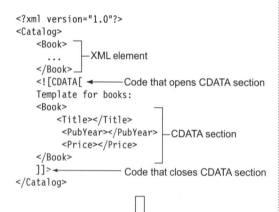

Figure C.1 The code and browser views of a CDATA section.

especially useful for including: (1) examples of XML MARKUP code; (2) code in JavaScript and other scripting languages; and (3) internal CSS.

The example XML code, shown in Figure C.1, includes not only an entry of a book catalogue but also a CDATA section that contains a template for creating an unlimited number of entries. This CDATA section is displayed in Internet Explorer as regular text. Note that all the advantages of XML are lost, because the XML parser has not checked the text but has just displayed it "as is". At the same time, including a catalogue template may be very helpful for a catalogue developer.

CDF (Channel Definition Format) An XML-BASED MARKUP LANGUAGE for organizing a set of related Web documents into a logical hierarchy (or a Web "channel") for automatic delivery via the Internet. For more details, see the information at http://msdn.microsoft.com/workshop/delivery/cdf/reference/CDF.asp.

Cell Markup Language *See* CELLML.

CellML (Cell Markup Language) An XML-BASED MARKUP LANGUAGE for storing and exchanging computer-based biological models. It includes information about model structure, mathematics (which describes the underlying biological processes using MATHML) and RDF metadata (which allows scientists to search for specific models or their components). See http://www.cellml.org/ for more details.

CFML (ColdFusion Markup Language) An XML-based server-side markup language used by Macromedia's application server ColdFusion. Details of CFML can be found at http://www.macromedia.com/v1/cfdocs/cfml_language_reference/contents.htm.

Channel Definition Format *See* CDF.

Character An atomic unit of text, which can be a letter, number, punctuation mark, symbol, white space etc.

Character data An XML STRUCTURAL CONSTRUCT that refers to PLAIN TEXT other than MARKUP contained in an XML DOCUMENT. In other words, character data are the text content of an ELEMENT or ATTRIBUTE. Not all elements necessarily contain character data. Character data are not processed by an XML PARSER and may therefore contain any character sequence, with the exception of SPECIAL SYMBOLS that must be escaped using corresponding ENTITY REFERENCES. *Compare* CDATA SECTION.

Character information item One of the 11 types of INFORMATION ITEM in the INFORMATION SET. Like all of them, it is an abstract description of a STRUCTURAL CONSTRUCT of an XML DOCUMENT. This description is intended for use in other XML-related specifications, which need to conform to the information set. There is a character information item in the information set for each character in the document's CHARACTER DATA or within a CDATA SECTION. This information item has three properties, as shown in Figure C.2. For more details, see http://www.w3.org/TR/xml-infoset/.

Character Mapping Markup Language *See* CHARMAPML.

Character reference In XML, a special numeric ENTITY for representing single displayable characters or symbols that are beyond the first 127 characters of UNICODE. A character reference can use a decimal or hexadecimal number and special characters as the opening DELIMITER (&# and &#x

respectively) and a semicolon as the closing delimiter. See Figure C.3.

Character Set Names *See* IANA CHARACTER SET NAMES.

Character string In programming, a sequence of characters interpreted by the computer as text rather that numbers.

CharMapML (Character Mapping Markup Language) An XML-BASED MARKUP LANGUAGE for the interchange of mapping data for character encoding. More details are available at http://www.unicode.org/unicode/reports/tr22/.

Chemical Markup Language *See* CHEMML; CML.

ChemML (Chemical Markup Languages) An XML-BASED MARKUP LANGUAGE for describing high-level chemical objects like atoms and links. More details about ChemML are available at http://www.ot-software.com/second/chemml.html.

Chess Game Markup Language *See* CHESSGML.

ChessGML (Chess Game Markup Language) An XML-BASED MARKUP LANGUAGE that is intended for the exchange and publication of any kind of chess data. More information is available at http://www.saremba.de/chessgml/.

Child An ELEMENT, a NODE or another STRUCTURAL CONSTRUCT of a HIERARCHICAL TREE STRUCTURE that is a sub-element, a sub-node or another sub-construct of an element, node etc. from an immediate higher level of the hierarchy. The concept of a child is based on the PARENT–CHILD METAPHOR. See

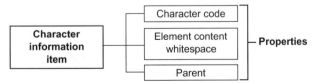

Figure C.2 The character information item and its properties.

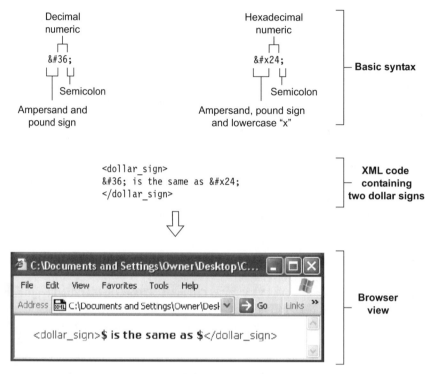

Figure C.3 The syntax and an example of the character reference.

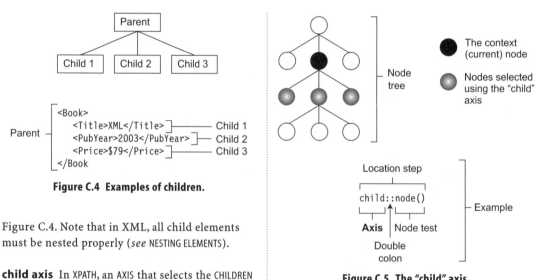

Figure C.4 Examples of children.

Figure C.4. Note that in XML, all child elements must be nested properly (*see* NESTING ELEMENTS).

child axis In XPATH, an AXIS that selects the CHILDREN of the CONTEXT NODE. See Figure C.5.

Figure C.5 The "child" axis.

Child element An ELEMENT that is nested (contained) within another element. *See* CHILD; HIERARCHICAL TREE STRUCTURE; NESTING ELEMENTS.

Child node *See* CHILD.

Children *See* CHILD.

Choice element In an XML SCHEMA, a special ELEMENT that is used as an INDICATOR that specifies that either one CHILD ELEMENT or another may occur in XML DOCUMENTS. The QUALIFIED NAME of the "choice" element can be either "xs:choice" or "xsd:choice", depending whether the XS NAMESPACE PREFIX or XSD NAMESPACE PREFIX is being used. See Figure C.6.

choice indicator *See* INDICATOR.

Chord Markup Language *See* CHORDML.

ChordML (Chord Markup Language) An XML-BASED MARKUP LANGUAGE for representing chords, lyrics, repetition and information about music. More details of ChordML may be obtained from http://www.cifranet.org/xml/ChordML.html.

Class 1. The fundamental concept of any object-oriented programming languages used in several XML-based languages, such as RDF SCHEMA and OWL. Generally, it is a prototype that describes the properties and behavior of all the objects (also known as "instances") that are or can be created from it.

2. A STRUCTURAL CONSTRUCT of RDF SCHEMA. Classes are groups that RESOURCES may be divided into. Classes are themselves resources that may be identified using a URI and described using an RDF PROPERTY. A class can have members (known as "instances" of the class) that can be declared using the TYPE PROPERTY.

3. A structural construct of OWL. OWL extends RDF SCHEMA with new classes that make it possible to express ONTOLOGIES in a much more sophisticated way. Figure C.7 shows a CLASS of dogs defined as a SUBCLASS of the SUPERCLASS of pets in both RDF schema and OWL.

Class class In RDF SCHEMA, the CLASS of RESOURCES that are RDF SCHEMA CLASSES. In other words, the rdfs:Class class is the class of all classes. Note that this class is an INSTANCE of itself.

OWL has its own "class" class. The owl:Class class is a SUBCLASS of the rdfs:Class class, as shown in Figure C.8. Note that OWL has a SUPERCLASS of all OWL classes named "owl:Thing" that is also the class of all INDIVIDUALS. *See also* THING CLASS.

Class definition An informal term for an owl:Class ELEMENT. *See* CLASS.

Class instance *See* INSTANCE; CLASS.

Class name An informal term for the rdf:ID ATTRIBUTE VALUE of an owl:Class ELEMENT. *See also* CLASS.

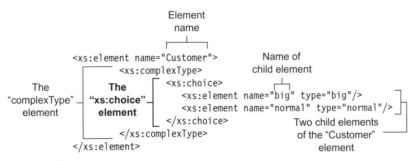

Figure C.6 The use of the "choice" element.

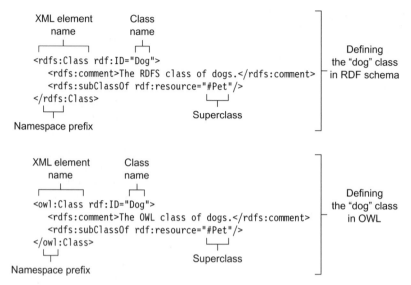

Figure C.7 The "dog" class in RDF Schema and OWL.

Figure C.8 The relationship between the "RDFS class" class and the "OWL class" class.

Clinical Document Architecture *See* CDA.

Close tag *See* END TAG.

Closing angle bracket *See* ANGLE BRACKETS.

Closing tag *See* END TAG.

CML (Chemical Markup Language) An XML-BASED MARKUP LANGUAGE that describes chemistry formulas and data. Details of CML can be found at `http://www.xml-cml.org/`.

ColdFusion Markup Language *See* CFML.

Color property In CSS, one of the TEXT PROPERTIES. There are four ways of specifying the value of the color property: (1) by RGB (an acronym for Red–Green–Blue) hexadecimal value (for example, navy is #000080); (2) by RGB decimal value (for example, red is RGB(255,0,0)); (3) by RGB percentage value (for example, blue is RGB(0%,0%,100%)); (4) by name using the following 16 named colors: aqua, black, blue, fuchsia, gray, green, lime, maroon, navy, olive, purple, red, silver, teal, white, yellow.

Comics Markup Language *See* COMICSML.

ComicsML (Comics Markup Language) An XML-BASED MARKUP LANGUAGE for describing digital comics. More information about ComicsML is available at `http://www.jmac.org/projects/comics_ml/`.

Comment A special part of computer code that is typically ignored by the computer and is intended to explain the code to human readers in order to improve its readability, maintenance and debugging. *See also* CSS COMMENT; DTD COMMENT; XML COMMENT.

24

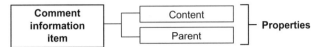

Figure C.9 The comment information item and its properties.

```
The          <rdfs:Class rdf:ID="Dog">
"rdfs:comment" ─┌ <rdfs:comment>The class of pet dogs.</rdfs:comment>
element         <rdfs:subClassOf rdf:resource="#Pet"/>
            </rdfs:Class>
```

Figure C.10 An example of the comment property.

Comment information item One of the 11 types of INFORMATION ITEMS in the INFORMATION SET. Just like the others, it is an abstract description of a STRUCTURAL CONSTRUCT of an XML DOCUMENT. This description is intended for use in other XML-related specifications, which need to conform to the information set. There is one comment information item in the information set for each XML COMMENT in the document's CHARACTER DATA or within a CDATA SECTION. This information item has two properties, as shown in Figure C.9. For more details, see http://www.w3.org/TR/xml-infoset/.

Comment node One of seven NODE TYPES of XPATH DATA MODEL that represents an XML COMMENT.

Comment property In RDF SCHEMA, the rdfs:comment PROPERTY that is used to provide a human-readable description of a RESOURCE, as shown in Figure C.10.

Commerce XML *See* CXML.

Common Warehouse Metamodel *See* CWM.

Communication protocol A set of rules and standards that regulates data transmission between computers.

Complex element A term that is sometimes used to refer to an ELEMENT of a COMPLEX TYPE.

Complex type In an XML SCHEMA, an ELEMENT is a complex type if it can contain other elements and/or ATTRIBUTES. There are four basic kinds of complex type element: (1) elements that contain only other elements; (2) elements that contain only CHARACTER DATA; (3) elements that contain both other elements and text; (4) EMPTY ELEMENTS. A complex type can be defined in an XML SCHEMA using COMPLEX TYPE DEFINITION. *Contrast* SIMPLE TYPE.

Complex type definition An XML SCHEMA COMPONENT that is a definition of an ELEMENT of a COMPLEX TYPE using a special XML schema element called "complexType". Its QUALIFIED NAME can be either "xs:complexType" or "xsd:complexType", depending whether the XS NAMESPACE PREFIX or XSD NAMESPACE PREFIX is being used. Figure C.11 shows the complex type definition of the "Editor" element, which specifies that the element can contain two other elements. *Contrast* SIMPLE TYPE DEFINITION.

Complex type element *See* COMPLEX TYPE.

complexType element A special ELEMENT of the XML SCHEMA language that is used in COMPLEX TYPE DEFINITIONS for defining COMPLEX TYPES. For more information, see COMPLEX TYPE DEFINITION.

Complex type indicator *See* INDICATOR.

Component model *See* WSDL COMPONENT MODEL.

Constraining facet *See* FACET.

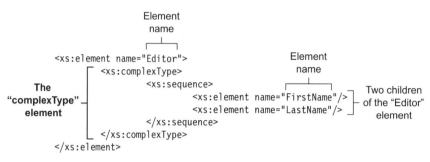

Figure C.11 An example of a complex type definition.

Construction rule A term that is sometimes used to refer to a TEMPLATE.

Container In RDF, a collection of RESOURCES. There are three different types of container: (1) BAG CONTAINER; (2) SEQUENCE CONTAINER; (3) ALTERNATIVE CONTAINER.

Container class In RDF SCHEMA, the rdfs:Container CLASS is a SUPERCLASS of the RDF schema container classes, such as BAG CLASS, SEQ CLASS and ALT CLASS.

Content *See* ELEMENT CONTENT.

Content model In a DTD, a form of the ELEMENT TYPE DECLARATION used for describing the allowed structure and content of ELEMENTS.

Context In linguistics, the words surrounding a word or sentence that may affect its meaning. For example, the meaning of "funny" often depends on its context. Compare "The film is funny" (i.e. amusing) and "The equation is funny" (i.e. strange). *See also* CONTEXT NODE.

Context information In XFI, an abstract set of information sent to a receiver to describe the structural position of a FRAGMENT within the original XML DOCUMENT. Usually, context information is contained in a FRAGMENT CONTEXT SPECIFICATION file.

Context node In XPATH, the node the XSLT PROCESSOR is currently working on. Also known as the "current node". The context node defines the starting point for evaluation of a LOCATION PATH.

Contributor element One of the 15 ELEMENTS of the DUBLIN CORE METADATA ELEMENT SET. The <dc:contributor> element specifies someone who has provided content to the RESOURCE other then the creator. Note that "dc" is the NAMESPACE PREFIX of the DUBLIN CORE NAMESPACE. *See also* CREATOR ELEMENT.

Controlled Trade Markup Language *See* CTML.

Core XML technologies Key members of the XML FAMILY OF TECHNOLOGIES. They include: (1) XML; (2) NAMESPACES IN XML; (3) XINCLUDE; (4) INFORMATION SET; (5) XFI; (6) XML BASE SPECIFICATION; (7) ASSOCIATING STYLE SHEETS WITH XML DOCUMENTS. For more details, see the information at http://www.w3.org/XML/Core/.

Country Codes An ISO standard (ISO 3166) for the representation of names of the countries of the world using their two- and three-character abbreviations. Country Codes are one of the NON-NORMATIVE REFERENCES of the XML 1.0 RECOMMENDATION. For more details, see the information at http://www.din.de/gremien/nas/nabd/iso3166ma/codlstp1/.

Coverage element One of the 15 ELEMENTS of the DUBLIN CORE METADATA ELEMENT SET. The <dc:coverage> element specifies the spatial locations and temporal durations characteristics of the RESOURCE. Note that "dc" is the NAMESPACE PREFIX of the DUBLIN CORE NAMESPACE.

CPExchange (Customer Profile Exchange) An XML-based standard for the privacy-enabled exchange of customer profile information among enterprise applications and partners. More details about CPExchange can be obtained from http://www.cpexchange.org/.

CPL (Call Processing Language) An XML-BASED MARKUP LANGUAGE for describing and controlling Internet telephony services. More details about CPL can be obtained from http://www.ietf.org/internet-drafts/draft-ietf-iptel-cpl-06.txt.

CR (Candidate Recommendation) *See* W3C CANDIDATE RECOMMENDATION.

Creator element One of the 15 ELEMENTS of the DUBLIN CORE METADATA ELEMENT SET. The <dc:creator> element specifies the person or organization primary responsible for the RESOURCE. Note that "dc" is the NAMESPACE PREFIX of the DUBLIN CORE NAMESPACE.

CSS (Cascading Style Sheets) A simple technology that allows the author to define how the content of certain ELEMENTS of an XML DOCUMENT should be formatted and displayed, including typeface, font size and color, margins and spacing. This technology was originally used for styling HTML documents and does not use XML SYNTAX. Its main advantages are that it is: (1) easy to use; (2) well established; and (3) implemented in many HTML authoring tools. However, the use of CSS has many serious disadvantages, such as: (1) CSS display only the data that an XML document already contains. No other text can be added; (2) CSS display the document data only in the order in which the data appear in the document; (3) CSS STYLE SHEETS do not use the XML syntax and hence cannot be processed by XML-compliant software; (4) CSS do not allow the display of the ATTRIBUTE

data; (5) CSS do not provide mechanisms for transforming one XML document into another, or into other popular formats. The current implementations of the CSS technology include CSS1, CSS2 and CSS3. More details of CSS may be obtained from http://www.w3.org/Style/CSS/. *See also* CSS STYLE; CSS STYLE SHEET.

CSS1 (Cascading Style Sheets Level 1) A W3C RECOMMENDATION that defines the first, elementary, level of CSS as a simple technology that allows the author to define how the content of certain ELEMENTS of an XML DOCUMENT should be formatted and displayed, including typeface, font size and color, margins and spacing. This technology was originally used for styling HTML documents and does not use XML SYNTAX. This RECOMMENDATION is available at http://www.w3.org/TR/REC-CSS1/. *See also* CSS; CSS2; CSS3.

CSS2 (Cascading Style Sheets Level 2) A W3C RECOMMENDATION that defines the second, more advanced, level of CSS technology. CSS2 is built on CSS1 with the addition of some new features, such as support for media-specific style sheets (e.g. visual and aural browsers, printers and Braille devices), content positioning and table layout. In other words, CSS2 allows developers to use the style sheet technology for presenting documents across multiple devices and media types. This RECOMMENDATION is available at http://www.w3.org/TR/1998/REC-CSS2-19980512/. *See also* CSS; CSS1; CSS3.

CSS3 (Cascading Style Sheets Level 3) The third level of CSS technology, currently under development. More information is available at http://www.w3.org/Style/CSS/current-work/. *See also* CSS; CSS1; CSS2.

CSS box model A concept of CSS that is intended to define how the content of an XML ELEMENT will be displayed on a Web page in terms of the page layout. Each element is considered to be enclosed

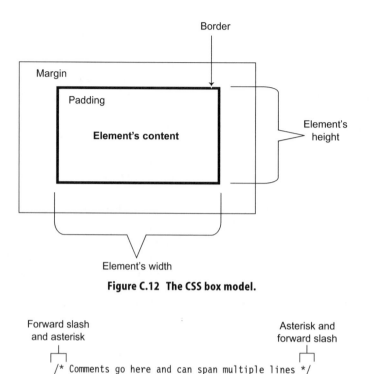

Figure C.12 The CSS box model.

Figure C.13 CSS comment syntax.

in an invisible box surrounded by padding, borders and margins, as shown in Figure C.12.

CSS comment A COMMENT that can be inserted into a CSS STYLE SHEET using the syntax shown in Figure C.13. CSS comments: (1) begin with (/*) and end with (*/); (2) can appear anywhere within CSS code but not inside a CSS STYLE SHEET REFERENCE; (3) can span multiple lines; (4) cannot be NESTED.

CSS declaration A term sometimes used to refer to CSS STYLE SHEET REFERENCE.

CSS Mobile Profile A W3C SPECIFICATION that defines a subset of CSS2 intended for use with mobile devices such as wireless phones. For more

information, see http://www.w3.org/TR/css-mobile/.

CSS rule *See* CSS STYLE.

CSS selector *See* SELECTOR.

CSS style A CSS style (also sometimes called a CSS rule) is the main STRUCTURAL CONSTRUCT of a CSS STYLE SHEET. It defines how the content of an XML DOCUMENT will be presented in a Web browser in terms of font size, color, placement and other details. A CSS style consists of two parts, as shown in Figure C.14: (1) the selector is the part before the left brace. It specifies the name of one or more XML ELEMENTS that the style should be applied to; (2) the declaration is one of many structural constructs within the braces made up of

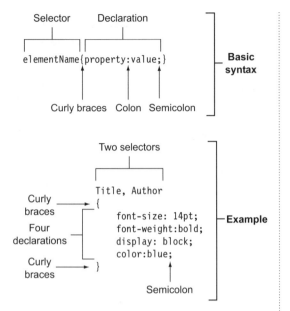

Figure C.14 The anatomy of a CSS style.

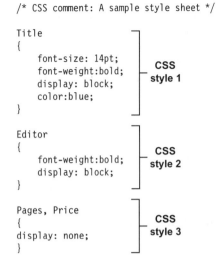

Figure C.15 An example of a CSS style sheet.

property–value pairs. A CSS declaration defines how the chosen element should be displayed.

A property is one of many available display properties of the selected XML elements, and each property can take an appropriate value. If more that one declaration is used, each property–value pair must end with a semicolon. *See also* GROUPING SELECTORS; HIDING ELEMENTS.

CSS style sheet A CSS style sheet is a list made up of several CSS STYLES that defines how XML data will be formatted and displayed, including text appearance (formatting, size, color) and page layout (background, borders, margins). See Figure C.15. *See also* GROUPING SELECTORS; HIDING ELEMENTS.

CSS style sheet reference A special PROCESSING INSTRUCTION inserted into an XML DOCUMENT in order to attach a CSS STYLE SHEET to this document. It includes two attributes: (1) the type attribute that specifies the MIME type of the style sheet; (2) the href attribute that defines the name of a CSS file to attach. See Figure C.16. *See also* ASSOCIATING STYLE SHEETS WITH XML DOCUMENTS; CSS STYLE SHEET.

CSS text properties *See* TEXT PROPERTIES.

CTML (Controlled Trade Markup Language) An XML-BASED MARKUP LANGUAGE for describing an

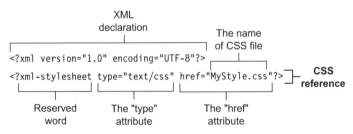

Figure C.16 An example of a CSS file reference in an XML document.

international collection of business documents (such as trade applications or delivery verification certificates) by means of the extension and expansion of an existing XML vocabulary. More information about CTML is available at `http://www.oasis-open.org/committees/controlled-trade/documents/vocabulary/CTML_Vocabulary.pdf`.

Current node *See* CONTEXT NODE.

Custom XML vocabulary *See* VOCABULARY.

Customer Profile Exchange *See* CPEXCHANGE.

CWM (Common Warehouse Metamodel) An XML-based metadata standard that describes metadata interchange among data warehousing, business intelligence, knowledge management and portal technologies. Details of CWM can be found at `http://www.omg.org/cwm/`.

cXML (Commerce XML) An XML-BASED MARKUP LANGUAGE for exchanging business transaction information in common formats over the Internet. More information about cXML is available at `http://www.cxml.org/`.

daliML (Data Link for Intermediaries Markup Language) An XML-based protocol for the exchange of withholding and payment information. For more details, see the information at `http://www.dali1441.com/dali/dalihome.nsf/daliML?openframeset`.

DAML (DARPA Agent Markup Language) A language for expressing ONTOLOGIES that extends RDF. The latest version of DAML incorporates OIL and is called DAML+OIL. DAML+OIL forms the basis of OWL and are expected to be superseded by it. Details of DAML can be found at `http://www.daml.org/`.

DAML-based Web Service Ontology *See* DAML-S.

DAML+OIL (DARPA Agent Markup Language + Ontology Inference Layer) A semantic markup language for Web RESOURCES that extends RDF and RDF SCHEMA with richer modeling primitives. It was built from the original DAML ontology language, DAML-ONT, with the inclusion of many components of OIL. Currently DAML+OIL is being superseded by OWL. Details of DAML+OIL are available at `http://www.daml.org/language/` and `http://www.w3.org/TR/daml+oil-reference/`.

DAML-ONT (DAML Ontology) The original DAML ontology language that was replaced by DAML+OIL. For more details, see the information at `http://www.daml.org/2000/10/daml-ont.html`.

DAML Ontology *See* DAML-ONT.

DAML-S (DAML-based Web Service Ontology) An ONTOLOGY and semantic MARKUP for describing WEB SERVICES that is based on DAML and is built on top of DAML+OIL. It is intended to support tools and INTELLIGENT AGENT technology to enable automation of services on the SEMANTIC WEB. More details about DAML-S can be obtained from `http://www.daml.org/services/`.

DARPA (Defense Advanced Research Projects Agency) The central research and development organization for the Department of Defense, USA. DARPA is developing DAML. Details of DARPA are available at `http://www.darpa.mil/`.

DARPA Agent Markup Language *See* DAML.

DARPA Agent Markup Language + Ontology Inference Layer *See* DAML+OIL.

Data Definition Markup Language *See* DDML.

Data interoperability *See* INTEROPERABILITY.

Data Link for Intermediaries Markup Language *See* DALIML.

Data model A fundamental concept of the development of information systems (especially computer databases) utilized by many members of the XML FAMILY OF TECHNOLOGIES, such as XML, RDF or WSDL. Generally, a data model is an abstract structure that specifies types of its STRUCTURAL CONSTRUCTS and also types of relationships between them. The data model of an XML DOCUMENT can have a variety of (slightly) different representations, such as an INFORMATION SET, XML SCHEMA, DTD, XPATH, XML DOM, SAX etc. The data model of a particular class of XML DOCUMENT (also known as DOCUMENT TYPE) is formally defined in an XML SCHEMA or a DTD and consists of the allowable ELEMENT NAMES and ATTRIBUTE NAMES and optional structural and occurrence constrains.

Data type In programming, a definition of the range of possible values that a data item can have, such as STRING, integer or Boolean. The XML SCHEMA provides authors with a mechanism for specifying data types of the content of an ELEMENT or ATTRIBUTE. Data types can be divided into three different groups: (1) PRIMITIVE DATA TYPES and DERIVED DATA TYPES; (2) ATOMIC DATA TYPES, LIST DATA TYPES and UNION DATA TYPES; (3) BUILT-IN DATA TYPE and USER-DERIVED DATA TYPE. For more details, see http://www.w3.org/TR/xmlschema-2/.

Datatype property A type of OWL property that is used to relate RESOURCES to LITERALS or to data values that may be typed using an XML SCHEMA built-in DATA TYPE. A datatype property can be defined using the owl:DatatypeProperty ELEMENT,

as shown in Figure D.1. *Contrast* OBJECT PROPERTY. *See also* LITERAL CLASS; OWL VOCABULARY.

Datatypes for DTDs *See* DT4DTD.

Date data type In an XML SCHEMA, a DATA TYPE that is used for specifying a value that is a date, as shown in Figure D.2.

Date element One of the 15 ELEMENTS of the DUBLIN CORE METADATA ELEMENT SET. The <dc:date> element specifies the date of the creation or publication of the RESOURCE. Note that "dc" is the NAMESPACE PREFIX of the DUBLIN CORE NAMESPACE.

DC (Dublin Core) *See* DUBLIN CORE.

dc:contributor element *See* CONTRIBUTOR ELEMENT.

dc:coverage element *See* COVERAGE ELEMENT.

dc:creator *See* CREATOR ELEMENT.

dc:date element *See* DATE ELEMENT.

dc:description element *See* DESCRIPTION ELEMENT.

dc:format element *See* FORMAT ELEMENT.

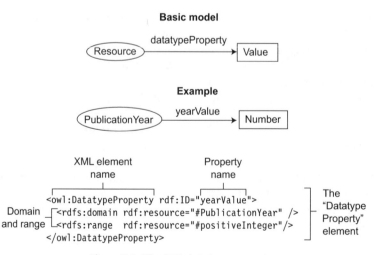

Figure D.1 The OWL datatype property.

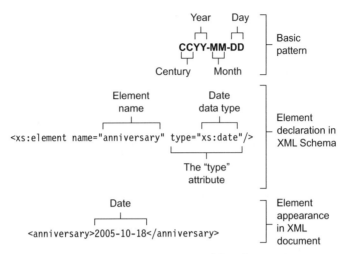

Figure D.2 The syntax and use of date data type.

dc:identifier element *See* IDENTIFIER ELEMENT.

dc:language element *See* LANGUAGE ELEMENT.

dc:publisher element *See* PUBLISHER ELEMENT.

dc:relation element *See* RELATION ELEMENT.

dc:rights element *See* RIGHTS ELEMENT.

dc:source element *See* SOURCE ELEMENT.

dc:subject element *See* SUBJECT ELEMENT.

dc:title element *See* TITLE ELEMENT.

dc:type element *See* TYPE ELEMENT.

DCD (Document Content Description) One of the early SCHEMA language proposals. More details of DCD may be obtained from http://www.w3.org/TR/NOTE-dcd/. *See also* XML SCHEMA.

DCES (Dublin Core Element Set) *See* DUBLIN CORE METADATA ELEMENT SET.

DCMES *See* DUBLIN CORE METADATA ELEMENT SET.

DCMI (The Dublin Core Metadata Initiative) *See* DUBLIN CORE.

DDML (Document Definition Markup Language) One of the early SCHEMA language proposals that led to the current XML SCHEMA language. Also previously known as XSchema. Details of DDML can be found at http://www.w3.org/TR/NOTE-ddml/. *See also* DT4DTD; SOX; XML-DATA.

Deck *See* WML.

default attribute In an XML SCHEMA, the ATTRIBUTE of an ELEMENT DECLARATION or ATTRIBUTE DECLARATION that is used for specifying the DEFAULT VALUE of the ELEMENT or ATTRIBUTE. For more details, see DEFAULT VALUE.

Default content *See* DEFAULT VALUE.

Default element content *See* DEFAULT VALUE.

Default namespace An UNPREFIXED NAMESPACE declared for the ROOT ELEMENT or any other specified ELEMENT, and therefore applied by default to all the document's elements, or to all the elements contained in the specified element. A default namespace can be overridden by specifying a PREFIXED NAMESPACE and then using a QUALIFIED NAME

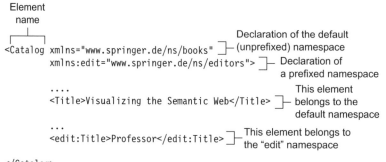

Figure D.3 An example of a default namespace.

for an individual element, as shown in Figure D.3. An XML DOCUMENT can have multiple default namespaces. *See also* OVERRIDING NAMESPACES; NAMESPACE; NAMESPACE DECLARATION; NAMESPACE NAME.

Default value 1. In an XML SCHEMA, the ATTRIBUTE VALUE that is automatically assigned to the ATTRIBUTE in an XML DOCUMENT if no other value is specified explicitly. See Figure D.4.

2. In XML schema, the text-only value of the ELEMENT CONTENT that is automatically assigned to the ELEMENT in an XML document if no other textual content is specified explicitly. See Figure D.4.

3. In a DTD, the ATTRIBUTE VALUE that is defined using the ATTLIST DECLARATION. In an XML document based on the DTD, this predefined value will be the value for the attribute if none is specified explicitly.

Defense Advanced Research Projects Agency
See DARPA.

Defense Logistics Format *See* DLF.

Definitions component The top-level component of the WSDL COMPONENT MODEL that serves as a container for WSDL COMPONENTS and system type components. The definitions component is represented in XML by the DEFINITIONS ELEMENT, which is the ROOT ELEMENT of any WSDL document. See Figure D.5.

Definitions element The XML representation of the DEFINITIONS COMPONENT of the WSDL COMPONENT MODEL is the wsdl:definitions ELEMENT, as shown in Figure D.6. This element is the ROOT ELEMENT of every WSDL document. The ELEMENT NAME comprises the NAMESPACE PREFIX "wsdl" and the LOCAL PART "definitions". The wsdl:definitions element can also have one or more attributes, such as the NAMESPACE DECLARATION of the NAMESPACE for WSDL.

Delimiter A special character that marks the beginning or end of a text string. The main types of delimiter used in XML are shown in Figure D.7: (1) START TAG and END TAG are delimiters for an ELEMENT and also ELEMENT CONTENT; (2) ANGLE BRACKETS (<>) are delimiters for a START TAG. An OPENING ANGLE BRACKET followed by a forward slash and a CLOSING ANGLE BRACKET are used as a delimiter for an END TAG; (3) quotation marks ("") are delimiters for an ATTRIBUTE VALUE; (4) an ampersand (&) and a semicolon (;) are used as delimiters for an XML ENTITY including SPECIAL SYMBOLS; (5) A forward slash followed by a closing angle bracket (/>) is the delimiter that marks the end of an EMPTY ELEMENT tag.

Derived data type In an XML SCHEMA, a DATA TYPE that is defined by restricting existing data types. Also called "user-derived data type".

Derived type *See* DERIVED DATA TYPE.

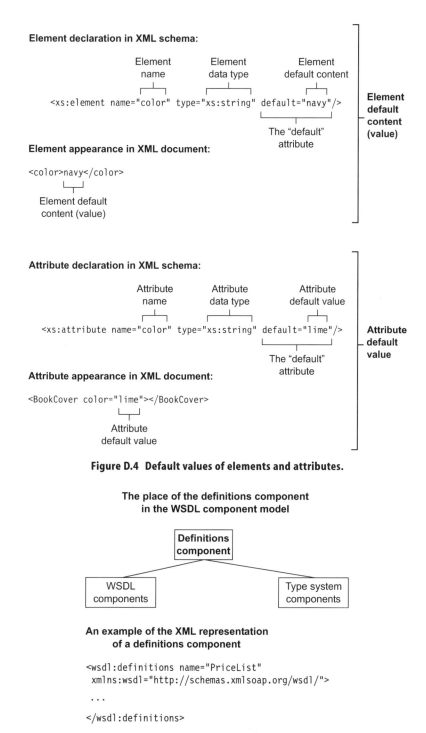

Figure D.4 Default values of elements and attributes.

**The place of the definitions component
in the WSDL component model**

```
                 Definitions
                 component

    WSDL                        Type system
    components                  components
```

**An example of the XML representation
of a definitions component**

```
<wsdl:definitions name="PriceList"
 xmlns:wsdl="http://schemas.xmlsoap.org/wsdl/">

 ...

</wsdl:definitions>
```

Figure D.5 The WSDL "definitions" component.

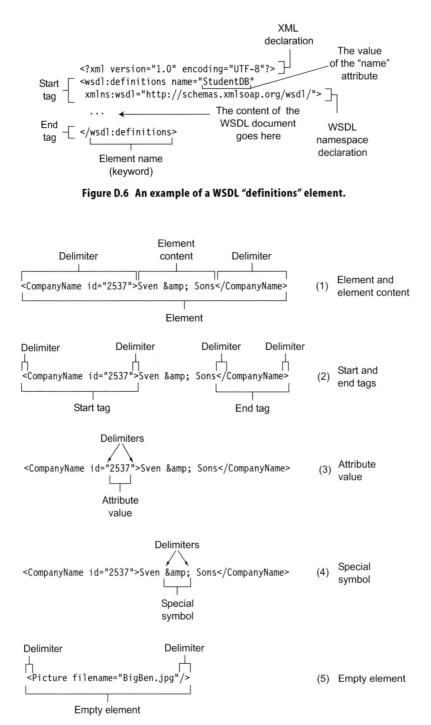

Figure D.6 An example of a WSDL "definitions" element.

Figure D.7 Different types of delimiters.

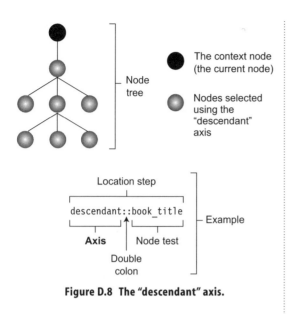

Figure D.8 The "descendant" axis.

Descendant In XPATH, a CHILD of the CONTEXT NODE, or a child of a child, and so on. *See also* DESCENDANT AXIS.

descendant axis In XPATH, an AXIS that selects the CHILDREN of the CONTEXT NODE, the children of children (i.e. "grandchildren" of the context node), and so on. The descendant axis never contains ATTRIBUTE NODES or NAMESPACE NODES. See Figure D.8.

descendant-or-self axis In XPATH, an AXIS that selects the same NODES as the DESCENDANT AXIS and also the CONTEXT NODE itself. See Figure D.9.

Description In RDF, a collection of STATEMENTS about a RESOURCE. *See also* RDF:DESCRIPTION ELEMENT.

Description element One of the 15 ELEMENTS of the DUBLIN CORE METADATA ELEMENT SET. The `<dc:description>` element specifies a textual description of the content of the RESOURCE. Note the "dc" is the NAMESPACE PREFIX of the DUBLIN CORE NAMESPACE.

Description Logic Markup Language *See* DLML.

Dialogue Moves Markup Language *See* DMML.

Different From statement In OWL, a statement that indicates that an INDIVIDUAL is different from other individuals. In the example shown in Figure D.10, a person known as "George W. Bush" is stated to be different from "George Bush". *See also* ALL DIFFERENT STATEMENT; SAME AS STATEMENT; OWL VOCABULARY.

DIG35 *See* DIG35 METADATA SPECIFICATION.

DIG35 Metadata Specification An XML-based metadata standard for the imaging industry developed by the Digital Imaging Group (DIG). It describes additional information about images to make them rich, completely self-contained sources of information. More details is available at `http://www.i3a.org/i_dig35.html`.

Digital Signature *See* XML SIGNATURE.

Directed labeled graph *See* RDF DATA MODEL.

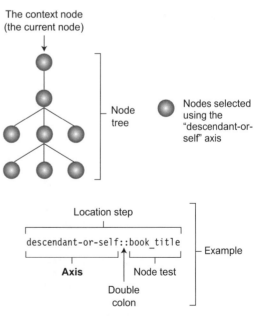

Figure D.9 The "descendant-or-self" axis.

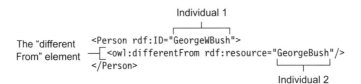

Figure D.10 **Stating that one individual is different from another.**

Directory Services Markup Language *See* DSML.

Directory XML *See* DIRXML.

DirXML (Directory XML) XML-based directory interchange software for keeping different directories synchronized. DirXML enables the universal flow of information across the different systems and applications within an enterprise and partner systems. More information is available at http://www.novell.com/products/edirectory/dirxml/.

DISCO (Discovery of Web Services) An XML-BASED MARKUP LANGUAGE for publishing and discovering WEB SERVICES, developed by Microsoft. Using DISCO, the information about Web services can be embedded in web documents and then recovered by an INTELLIGENT AGENT. More information can be found at http://uddi.microsoft.com/.

Discovery of Web Services *See* DISCO.

Disjoint classes In OWL, a CLASS is said to be disjoint with another class if the two classes have no common INSTANCES. In the example shown in Figure D.11, the "Dog" class is defined as a SUBCLASS of the "Pet" class that is disjoint with the "Cat" class and the "Rabbit" class. The owl:disjointWith ELEMENT is a means of defining disjoint classes. *See also* OWL VOCABULARY.

Display property In CSS, a property for specifying how and whether the content of an XML ELEMENT will be displayed in the browser window. The most common values of the Display property are: (1) display:block; – the element data will be displayed like a new paragraph, that is with a line break placed before and after it; (2) display:inline; – the element data will be

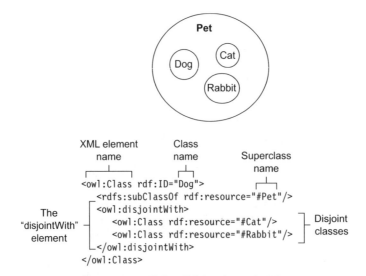

Figure D.11 **Defining disjoint classes in OWL.**

displayed directly after the preceding element, with no line breaks. This is the default value of the Display property; (3) display:none; – the specified XML element will not be displayed at all.

DLF (Defense Logistics Format) An XML-BASED MARKUP LANGUAGE for the interchange of defense logistics forms. More details about DLF are available at http://www.milpac.com/specs/.

DLG (Directed labeled graph) *See* RDF DATA MODEL.

DLML (Description Logic Markup Language) An XML-BASED MARKUP LANGUAGE for encoding description logic expressions. Details of DLML can be found at http://co4.inrialpes.fr/xml/dlml/.

DML (Dynamic Markup Language) An XML-BASED MARKUP LANGUAGE for object based graphics construction and the development of user interfaces. More information about DML is available at http://www.rocklyte.com/dml/.

DMML (Dialogue Moves Markup Language) An XML-BASED MARKUP LANGUAGE for interacting with multimodal dialog systems. For more details, see http://www.cs.columbia.edu/~radev/publication/aisb.ps.

DocBook (Documentation Book) An XML/SGML-based markup language for describing books and papers about computer hardware and software. More information is available at http://www.oasis-open.org/committees/docbook/.

DOCTYPE declaration (Document Type Declaration) A special PROCESSING INSTRUCTION embedded within the PROLOG of an XML DOCUMENT in order to associate an EXTERNAL DTD with the document. Note that the term "Document Type Declaration" is always abbreviated to DOCTYPE, not to its proper acronym, to avoid confusion with DTD (Document Type Definition). The DOCTYPE declaration is used to attach a DTD to an XML file.

A DOCTYPE declaration can be constructed in two different ways, as shown in Figure D.12: (1) using the SYSTEM keyword in order to explicitly define the Internet location of the DTD; or (2) using the PUBLIC keyword to indicate that the DTD is a publicly available (usually corporate)

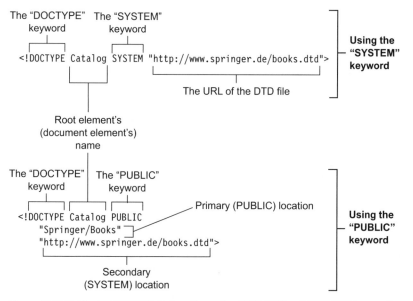

Figure D.12 Writing a DOCTYPE declaration using "SYSTEM" and "PUBLIC" keywords.

standard. In both cases, the name of the ROOT ELEMENT (also called the DOCUMENT ELEMENT) must be specified and this associates a DTD with all children of this element (i.e. with the entire XML DOCUMENT). Note that the DOCTYPE declaration can also contain an INTERNAL DTD within itself (i.e. as part of the XML document).

Document A structured unit of recorded information (in electronic form or hard copy) that is managed as a discrete item in information systems.

Document Content Description *See* DCD.

Document Definition Markup Language *See* DDML.

Document element An official term for the ROOT ELEMENT.

Document entity A term used to refer to the DOCUMENT ROOT.

Document fragment *See* FRAGMENT.

Document fragment body *See* FRAGMENT BODY.

Document information item One of the 11 types of INFORMATION ITEM. Like all of them, it is an abstract description of a STRUCTURAL CONSTRUCT of an XML DOCUMENT. This description is intended for use in other XML-related specifications, which need to conform to the INFORMATION SET. There is one and only one document information item in the information set and all other information items are accessible from its property. The document information item has nine properties, as shown in Figure D.13. For more details, see http://www.w3.org/TR/xml-infoset/.

Document instance An individual XML DOCUMENT in relation to the DOCUMENT TYPE to which it belongs, and which is specified in a particular SCHEMA. Also known as an "instance document".

Document Object Model *See* DOM.

Document order In XPATH, a set of rules that define the occurrence ordering of NODE in an XML DOCUMENT. Some of these rules are: (1) the ROOT NODE is the first node; (2) ELEMENT NODES occur before their CHILDREN; (3) the ATTRIBUTE NODES and NAMESPACE NODES of an ELEMENT occur before the children of the element; (4) the namespace nodes occur before the attribute nodes.

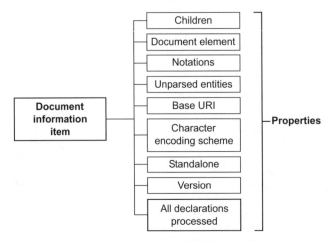

Figure D.13 The document information item and its properties.

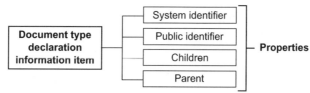

Figure D.14 The document type declaration information item and its properties.

Document parts *See* XML DOCUMENT SECTIONS.

Document root The top-level node in the abstract XML DOCUMENT STRUCTURE (also known as the document entity) that contains three XML DOCUMENT SECTIONS: (1) an optional PROLOG; (2) BODY, which contains the ROOT ELEMENT (also known as the document element); and (3) an optional EPILOG. The document root should not be confused with the ROOT ELEMENT (also known as the document element). The document root is the starting point for an XML PARSER. Since it has no name, it cannot be referenced. See Figure X.17 at the XML DOCUMENT STRUCTURE entry.

Document Schema Definition Languages *See* DSDL.

Document structure *See* XML DOCUMENT STRUCTURE; HIERARCHICAL TREE; XML DOCUMENT; XML DOCUMENT SECTIONS.

Document Structure Description *See* DSD.

Document Style Semantics and Specification Language *See* DSSSL.

Document tree *See* XML DOCUMENT STRUCTURE.

Document type A group of XML DOCUMENTS that share a common XML VOCABULARY defined in a SCHEMA or DTD.

Document Type Declaration *See* DOCTYPE DECLARATION.

Document Type Declaration information item One of the 11 types of INFORMATION ITEM in the INFORMATION SET. Like all of them, it is an abstract description of a STRUCTURAL CONSTRUCT of an XML DOCUMENT. This description is intended for use in other XML-related specifications, which need to conform to the information set. If the XML document contains a DTD, there is a single document type declaration information item in the information set. This information item has four properties, as shown in Figure D.14. For more details, see http://www.w3.org/TR/xml-infoset/.

Document Type Definition *See* DTD.

Documentation Book *See* DOCBOOK.

documentation element A special ELEMENT of the XML SCHEMA language used for inserting COMMENTS into an XML schema. This element must be a CHILD ELEMENT of the ANNOTATION ELEMENT, as shown in Figure D.15.

```
<xs:annotation>
    ┌   <xs:documentation>
The        │       An XML Schema comment  ┐
"documentation"─┤       looks like this.      ├ Comment
element    │   </xs:documentation>        ┘
    └   </xs:annotation>
```

Figure D.15 The "documentation" element and a comment.

DOM (Document Object Model) A programming interface that allows programs and scripts to dynamically assess and manipulate the content and structure of HTML, XML and other documents. More details about DOM can be found at http://www.w3.org/DOM/. *See also* XML DOM.

DOM API *See* API; DOM; XML DOM.

Domain A particular area of activity or interest, especially one that a particular company, organization or person deals with. XML allows anyone to create custom XML-BASED MARKUP LANGUAGES for describing their specific domain, such as the Holy Scriptures or beer production.

Domain property In RDF SCHEMA, the rdfs:domain PROPERTY is a property that is used to state that any RESOURCE that has a given property is an INSTANCE of one or more CLASSES. In the example shown in Figure D.16, the domain of the "age" property is the "dog" class.

DOM tree *See* DOM; XML DOM.

Dot NET Framework *See* .NET FRAMEWORK.

DSD (Document Structure Description) A SCHEMA language for XML that may be seen as a less complex alternative to XML SCHEMA. It is written in XML SYNTAX and has some further features that are not available in XML schema. More details about DSD can be obtained from http://www.brics.dk/DSD/. *See also* RELAX; RELAX NG; SCHEMATRON; TREX.

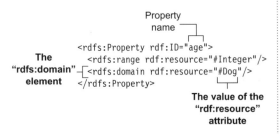

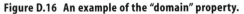

Figure D.16 An example of the "domain" property.

DSDL (Document Schema Definition Languages) An XML-based framework that allows multiple validation tasks and technologies to be applied to an XML document to achieve more complete validation results. More details about DSDL are available at http://www.dsdl.org/.

DSig *See* XML DIGITAL SIGNATURE

DSML (Directory Services Markup Language) An XML-BASED MARKUP LANGUAGE for expressing computer network directory queries and updates in a common format shared by different directory systems. See http://www.dsml.org/ for more details.

DSSSL (Document Style Semantics and Specification Language) A standard for the processing of SGML documents, especially for their visual presentation and also transformation. More information about DSSSL is available at http://www.jclark.com/dsssl/.

DT4DTD (Datatypes for DTDs) One of the early SCHEMA language proposals that led to the current XML SCHEMA language. See http://www.w3.org/TR/dt4dtd/ for more information. *See also* DDML; SOX; XML-DATA.

dtd The FILENAME EXTENSION of a DTD (Document Type Definition) file; for example "Catalog.dtd".

DTD (Document Type Definition) In XML or SGML, a set of declarations that describe the components and structure of a class of documents (DOCUMENT TYPE) or a specific document. A DTD for XML allows authors to declare the ELEMENTS and ATTRIBUTES of an XML DOCUMENT and also to define how those elements relate to each other. As a result, a VALIDATING PARSER can use a DTD to check whether all necessary elements and attributes are presented in an XML document, no illegal elements or attributes are included, and the elements are organized in a specified HIERARCHICAL TREE STRUCTURE. This process is called VALIDATION and an

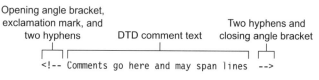

Figure D.17 The basic syntax for DTD comments.

XML document that complies with its associated DTD is called a VALID XML DOCUMENT.

DTDs are also used for describing common XML VOCABULARIES in order to enable their sharing between many companies and organizations. The DTD for XML is specified in Sections 3 and 4 of the XML 1.0 RECOMMENDATION, which is available at http://www.w3.org/TR/REC-xml. *See also* SCHEMA; XML SCHEMA.

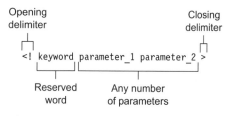

Figure D.18 The syntax of a DTD declaration.

DTD comment A DTD document can be commented using the syntax shown in Figure D.17. A DTD comment: (1) cannot contain a double hyphen (--); (2) cannot be placed inside another DTD comment (i.e. cannot be NESTED).

DTD declaration The main STRUCTURAL CONSTRUCT of a DTD. A DTD declaration is a statement used to specify ELEMENT NAMES, ELEMENT CONTENT, ELEMENT ATTRIBUTES, and other structural constructs of a particular type of XML DOCUMENT. The basic syntax of a DTD declaration is shown in Figure D.18. Four basic keywords: (1) the "ELEMENT" keyword used in the ELEMENT TYPE DECLARATION for declaring ELEMENTS; (2) the "ATTLIST" keyword used in the ATTLIST DECLARATION for declaring ATTRIBUTES; (3) the "ENTITY" keyword used for declaring ENTITIES; and (4) the "NOTATION" keyword used to declare external NON-TEXT DATA.

DTD-less XML document The term "DTD-less" is sometimes used to refer to an XML DOCUMENT that is used without a DTD or SCHEMA. A DTD-less document must be a WELL-FORMED XML DOCUMENT.

Dublin Core (The Dublin Core Metadata Initiative) An open forum engaged in developing interoperable online METADATA standards and specialized metadata vocabularies that support a broad range of purposes and business models. Dublin Core is primarily intended for use with RDF. The DUBLIN CORE METADATA ELEMENT SET is a standard set of 15 ELEMENTS for cross-domain description of generalized Web RESOURCE.

Note that the initiative takes its name from a workshop on metadata semantics that took place in 1995 in Dublin, Ohio, USA. More details are available at http://dublincore.org/.

Dublin Core Metadata Element Set A standard set of 15 ELEMENTS for cross-domain description of generalized Web RESOURCES as well as any other documents and resources: (1) TITLE ELEMENT; (2) CREATOR ELEMENT; (3) SUBJECT ELEMENT; (4) DESCRIPTION ELEMENT; (5) PUBLISHER ELEMENT; (6) CONTRIBUTOR ELEMENT; (7) DATE ELEMENT; (8) TYPE ELEMENT; (9) FORMAT ELEMENT; (10) IDENTIFIER ELEMENT; (11) SOURCE ELEMENT; (12) LANGUAGE ELEMENT; (13) RELATION ELEMENT; (14) COVERAGE ELEMENT; (15) RIGHTS ELEMENT. Also known as DCMES and DCES (Dublin Core Element Set). For more information, see http://www.dublincore.org/documents/dces/.

Dublin Core Metadata Initiative *See* DUBLIN CORE.

Dublin Core Metadata Standard A term that is sometimes used to refer to the DUBLIN CORE METADATA ELEMENT SET. *See also* DUBLIN CORE.

Dublin Core namespace The NAMESPACE of the DUBLIN CORE METADATA ELEMENT SET. The NAMESPACE DECLARATION of this namespace is shown in Figure D.19. Note that the NAMESPACE PREFIX is "dc". *See also* DUBLIN CORE.

Dynamic Markup Language *See* DML.

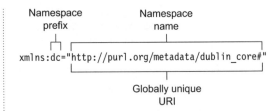

Figure D.19 The declaring of the Dublin Core namespace.

Earth Science Markup Language *See* ESML.

EBNF (Extended Backus–Naur Form) A formal notation used to define XML 1.0 in a precise and concise manner. *See also* XML 1.0 RECOMMENDATION.

e-Business (Electronic Business) A term used to refer to conducting business on the Internet that includes not only buying and selling (i.e. E-COMMERCE), but also collaborating with other business partners and servicing customers. However, the terms "e-Business" and "e-Commerce" are often used interchangeably.

ebXML (Electronic Business XML) A standard framework and a set of specifications that are intended to facilitate open and global business transactions using XML. It enables enterprises of any size and in any geographical location to conduct business with each other through the exchange of XML-based messages. More details of ebXML may be obtained from http://www.ebxml.org/.

ECML (Electronic Commerce Modeling Language) An XML-based specification for describing and exchanging payment transaction information for both electronic wallets and B2B payment types, such as credit card, electronic check, mobile phone and PDA payments. More details of ECML may be obtained from http://rfc3505.x42.com/.

Ecological Metadata Language *See* EML.

e-Commerce (Electronic Commerce) A term that refers to buying and selling on the Internet. Often this term is used interchangeably with the term E-BUSINESS.

eCX (Electronic Catalog XML) An XML-BASED MARKUP LANGUAGE for exchanging product information and catalog structure between different catalog systems. More details about eCX can be obtained from http://www.ecx-xml.org/.

Edge Side Includes *See* ESI.

EDI (Electronic Data Interchange) A standard for exchanging business data between two companies via the Internet or telephone lines. The traditional EDI uses complicated and expensive data formats and networks. XML complements EDI because it can be used to exchange business-to-business information in a more effective and inexpensive manner. An XML DOCUMENT can be easily transformed into EDI using an XSLT STYLE SHEET and an XSLT PROCESSOR, as shown in Figure E.1.

EFS (Electronic Form System) An XML-BASED MARKUP LANGUAGE for describing electronic forms and surveys. More information is available at http://www.electronicform.org/efs.html.

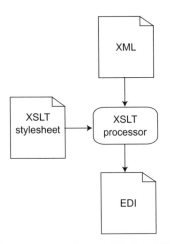

Figure E.1 Transforming XML into EDI.

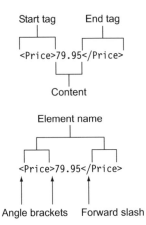

Figure E.2 The anatomy of a non-empty XML element.

e-GIF (electronic-Government Interoperability Framework) An XML-based framework that sets out the UK e-government's technical standards for achieving interoperability and information systems coherence across the public sector. Details of e-GIF are available at http://www.govtalk.gov.uk/schemasstandards/egif.asp.

e-Government A term that refers to the delivery of local government service through electronic means, especially over the Internet.

e-Government Interoperability Framework *See* E-GIF.

Election Markup Language *See* EML.

Electronic Business *See* E-BUSINESS.

Electronic Business XML *See* EBXML.

Electronic Catalog XML *See* ECX.

Electronic Commerce *See* E-COMMERCE.

Electronic Commerce Modeling Language *See* ECML.

Electronic Data Interchange *See* EDI.

Electronic Form System *See* EFS.

Electronic government *See* E-GOVERNMENT.

Element The main building block of an XML DOCUMENT. A typical non-empty element is composed of the START TAG (also called the opening tag, open tag, beginning tag, or starting-tag), the END TAG (also called the closing tag, close tag or ending tag) and the ELEMENT CONTENT, enclosed within this pair of tags, as shown in Figure E.2. Each element can be identified by ELEMENT NAME (sometimes also called its GENERIC IDENTIFIER) and may have one or more ATTRIBUTES. *See also* EMPTY ELEMENT.

Element attribute A term used to refer to an ATTRIBUTE of an ELEMENT.

Element content Any data placed between the START TAG and the END TAG of an ELEMENT. Element content may include (1) other elements; (2) CHARACTER DATA; (3) CHARACTER REFERENCES; (4) ENTITY REFERENCES; (5) XML COMMENTS; (6) PROCESSING INSTRUCTIONS; (7)

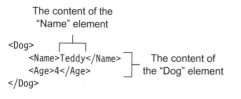

The content of the
"Name" element

```
<Dog>
    <Name>Teddy</Name>      The content of
    <Age>4</Age>            the "Dog" element
</Dog>
```

Figure E.3 Different types of element content.

CDATA SECTIONS; (8) WHITE SPACE. The specific element content is defined for each element within the document's SCHEMA or DTD. See Figure E.3.

Element declaration An XML SCHEMA COMPONENT used to declare an ELEMENT for use in XML DOCUMENTS. See Figure E.4. *See also* EMPTY ELEMENT DECLARATION; MAXOCCURS ATTRIBUTE; MINOCCURS ATTRIBUTE.

element element The "element" element is a special ELEMENT of the XML SCHEMA used in ELEMENT DECLARATION for declaring elements.

Element group indicator *See* INDICATOR.

Element information item One of the 11 types of INFORMATION ITEMS in the INFORMATION SET. Like all of them, it is an abstract description of a STRUCTURAL

CONSTRUCT of an XML DOCUMENT. This description is intended for use in other XML-related specifications, which need to conform to the information set. There is an element information item in the information set for each ELEMENT of the document. One of the element information items forms the root of the element tree – it is the value of the document element property of the DOCUMENT INFORMATION ITEM. The element information item has nine properties, as shown in Figure E.5. For more details, see http://www.w3.org/TR/xml-infoset/.

ELEMENT keyword *See* DTD DECLARATION; ELEMENT TYPE DECLARATION.

Element name The label which is given to the START TAG and END TAG that make up an ELEMENT. In Figure E.6, "sale_price" is the name of the element marked up with the <sale_price> and </sale_price> tags. Everyone is free to invent names of XML ELEMENTS for creating their own domain-specific languages, such as NEWSML or MUSICXML. As a rule, the element name should describe the element's content in an explicit and easily understandable way. The names of XML

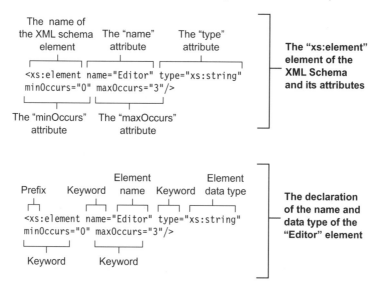

Figure E.4 An example of an element declaration.

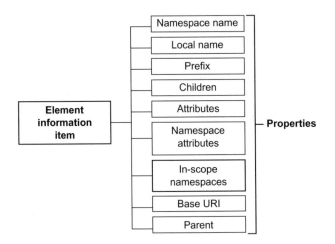

Figure E.5 The element information item and its properties.

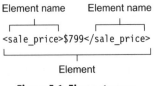

Figure E.6 Element name.

elements are CASE-SENSITIVE and must match exactly in start and end tags. Also they must begin with a letter (but not a number), an underscore (_) or a colon (:). They may not begin with the letters x, m and l in any combination of upper and lower cases, since this is reserved by the W3C for a special use. Here are some examples of acceptable element names: booktitle, BookTitle, _bookTitle, _2Book_title. The following element and attribute names *are not allowed*: 2Book_title, xmlBookTitle, XMLbookTitle and XmL_book_title. No WHITE SPACE is permitted for separating parts of an element name, or before and after the name inside a TAG. For instance, element names <Book Title> and < BookTitle > are illegal. Note that it is better to avoid using names that start with a colon (such as :BookTitle or :2bookTitle), since colons are used only to separate a NAMESPACE PREFIX from the LOCAL PART of a QUALIFIED NAME.

Element node One of the seven NODE TYPES of the XPATH DATA MODEL. An element note represents an ELEMENT of the source XML DOCUMENT. A special element note (which is a CHILD of the ROOT NODE) represents the ROOT ELEMENT of the XML document. Note that in XPATH, an ELEMENT NODE is the PARENT of an ATTRIBUTE NODE, but an attribute node is *not* the CHILD of its parent element node.

Element root *See* XPATH DATA MODEL.

Element tree A hierarchical tree-like structure make up of ELEMENTS, that has one and only one top-level element called the ROOT ELEMENT, and PARENT-CHILD as the only direct element-to-element relationship. *See also* HIERARCHICAL TREE STRUCTURE; PARENT-CHILD METAPHOR; XML DOCUMENT SECTIONS; XML DOCUMENT STRUCTURE; XML DOM.

Element type declaration A DTD DECLARATION for specifying an ELEMENT NAME and the allowed ELEMENT CONTENT. It has two forms related to (1) element content categories and (2) element content models, as shown in Figure E.7. See also ELEMENT DECLARATION.

Element type name A term used to refer to an ELEMENT NAME in a SCHEMA to emphasize that the

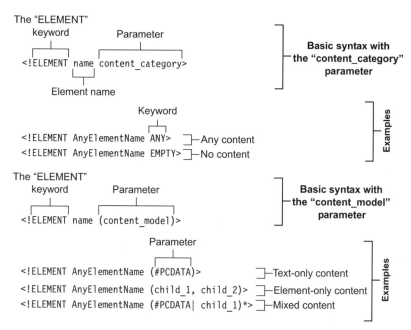

Figure E.7 Two different forms of the element type declaration.

schema defines an element not as one single instance, but as a class of elements that can have many instances.

Embedded metadata A type of METADATA that is stored and maintained within the object it describes. *Contrast* STANDALONE METADATA.

EML (Ecological Metadata Language) An XML-BASED MARKUP LANGUAGE for the ecology discipline. Details of EML are available at `http://knb.ecoinformatics.org/software/eml/`.

EML (Election Markup Language) An XML-BASED MARKUP LANGUAGE for the electronic exchange of election and voter services information. For more details, see the information at `http://www.oasis-open.org/committees/election/`.

Empty element An ELEMENT that has no ELEMENT CONTENT and contains data only in its ATTRIBUTES. There are two equivalent types of empty element in XML. (1) Type 1 uses a special all-in-one

empty-element tag, in which the START TAG and END TAG are combined into a single tag and the forward slash is placed just before the (>) sign at the end of the tag, as shown in Figure E.8. (2) Type 2 uses a start tag immediately followed by an end tag. The difference between these two equally legal types of empty element is as follows: Type 1 is a "proper" empty element that will *never* have any element content. In the case of Type 2, it is

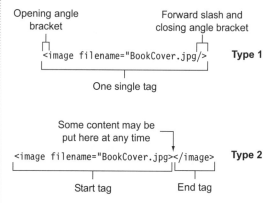

Figure E.8 Two types of empty element in XML.

Empty element declaration in XML schema:

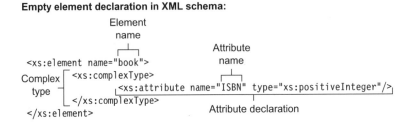

Empty element appearance in XML document:

Figure E.9 Empty element declaration.

supposed that the element is empty at the moment, but later some content might be entered between its tags. The use of the empty element syntax allows developers to distinguish between elements that they do not need to worry about because they are empty by definition and elements that may require content data to be entered.

Empty element declaration In an XML SCHEMA, an ELEMENT DECLARATION used to declare an EMPTY ELEMENT. This is a normal element declaration of the COMPLEX TYPE with one or more (or none) ATTRIBUTES. Since an ELEMENT declared in this way may not have any ELEMENT CONTENT, the element is an empty element. See Figure E.9.

Empty-element tag *See* EMPTY ELEMENT.

Encoding attribute An optional property of an XML DECLARATION that specifies the character-encoding method. The default encoding value (that XML processors use if this attribute is omitted) is the UTF-8 character set. Some other possible values are shown in Figure E.10. *See also* IANA CHARACTER SET NAMES; STANDALONE ATTRIBUTE; VERSION ATTRIBUTE; XML DOCUMENT.

Encryption The process of encoding data to prevent unauthorized access, especially during transmission.

End tag A TAG that is used as a DELIMITER to show the end of an ELEMENT and the ELEMENT CONTENT. It consists of a forward slash followed by an ELEMENT NAME, enclosed within ANGLE BRACKETS, as shown in Figure E.11. In XML, each START TAG (except the EMPTY-ELEMENT TAG) must have a matching end tag that has the same element name. The end tag is also called the closing tag, close tag or ending tag. *Contrast* START TAG.

Ending resource *See* TRAVERSAL.

Ending tag *See* END TAG.

Enterprise XML A term that sometimes refers to the implementation of XML in enterprise applications such as e-commerce, data warehousing, databases, and data retrieval. For more details see, for example, http://www.elsevier-international.com/catalogue/title.cfm?ISBN=012663355X.

Entity A STRUCTURAL CONSTRUCT of an XML DOCUMENT, an SGML document or a DTD. Generally, it is a

XML declaration

```
<?xml version="1.0" encoding="UTF-8" standalone="yes"?>
```

Version
attribute

**Encoding
attribute**

Standalone
attribute

VALUE	DESCRIPTION
UTF-8	Compressed Unicode (the XML default)
UTF-16	Compressed UCS (Universal Character System) (provides some support for non-English characters)
ISO-8859-1	Latin-1: Western European languages
ISO-8859-2	Latin-2: Eastern European languages
ISO-8859-3	Latin-3: Southern European languages
ISO-8859-4	Latin-4: Northern European languages
ISO-8859-5	Cyrillic: Russian, Bulgarian, Serbian etc.
ISO-8859-6	Arabic
ISO-8859-7	Greek
ISO-8859-8	Hebrew
ISO-2022-JP	Japanese

Figure E.10 The encoding attribute and some of its possible values.

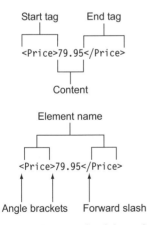

Start tag   End tag

```
<Price>79.95</Price>
```

Content

Element name

```
<Price>79.95</Price>
```

Angle brackets   Forward slash

Figure E.11 An example of the end tag.

special sequence of characters (called the entity name) used to represent another sequence of characters (called entity content). In XML and DTDs, entities provide a mechanism that enables the use of replaceable content. First, an entity must be declared in a DTD. Then, it can be referred to by an ENTITY REFERENCE in order to insert the entity's contents into an XML document or the DTD. In XML DTDs, there are several types of entities, as shown in Figure E.12. *See also* ENTITY REFERENCE; EXTERNAL ENTITY; EXTERNAL GENERAL ENTITY; GENERAL ENTITY; INTERNAL ENTITY; INTERNAL GENERAL ENTITY; PARAMETER ENTITY; PARSED ENTITY; SPECIAL SYMBOLS; UNPARSED ENTITY.

ENTITY keyword *See* DTD DECLARATION; INTERNAL GENERAL ENTITY.

Entity reference A STRUCTURAL CONSTRUCT of an XML DOCUMENT that is a reference to a previously

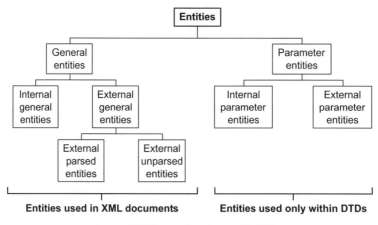

Figure E.12 Types of entity used in DTDs.

declared ENTITY on this document. Entity references can be used for (1) inserting STRING LITERALS of any size into ELEMENT CONTENT or (2) ATTRIBUTE VALUES; and (3) offering easy to remember alternatives to CHARACTER REFERENCES. In XML, all entities must be declared in a DTD or XML SCHEMA before being used, with the exception of five built-in entity references for representing SPECIAL SYMBOLS. Note that an entity reference is used in much the same way as a macro. See Figure E.13.

enumeration facet In an XML SCHEMA, a FACET that restricts a simple data type by assigning a set of acceptable values, such as "Winter", "Spring",

"Summer", and "Autumn" for the "Season" attribute. Fore more details, see FACET.

env:Body element *See* BODY.

env:Envelope element *See* ENVELOPE.

env:Fault element *See* FAULT ELEMENT.

env:Header element *See* HEADER.

Envelope A required STRUCTURAL CONSTRUCT of the SOAP MESSAGE STRUCTURE that is the ROOT ELEMENT of a SOAP document. It is used to identify the

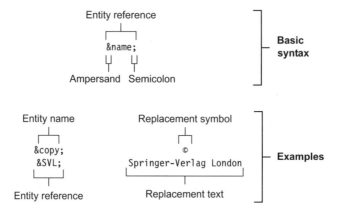

Figure E.13 Entity reference.

Namespace

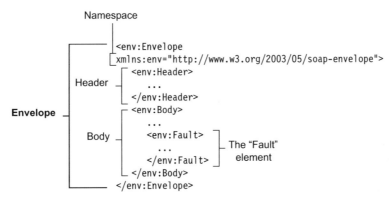

Figure E.14 SOAP Envelope.

XML DOCUMENT as a SOAP MESSAGE and to declare the NAMESPACE of SOAP. All other ELEMENTS of a soap message are CHILDREN of the "Envelope" element. See Figure E.14.

Envelope element *See* ENVELOPE.

eosML (Equation of State Markup Language)
An XML-BASED MARKUP LANGUAGE for describing fluid system properties using compositional equation of state (EOS) models. More details are available at http://www.posc.org/ebiz/eosML/.

Epilog One of three XML DOCUMENT SECTIONS that may consist of (1) XML COMMENTS; (2) PROCESSING INSTRUCTIONS; and (3) WHITE SPACE. A epilog is an optional part of an XML DOCUMENT. See Figure E.15. *See also* PROLOG; BODY.

EPP (Extensible Provisioning Protocol) An XML-based protocol that allows multiple service providers to perform object provisioning operations using a shared central object repository. Details of EPP are available at http://www.verisign.com/developer/xml/epp.html.

Equation of State Markup Language *See* EOSML.

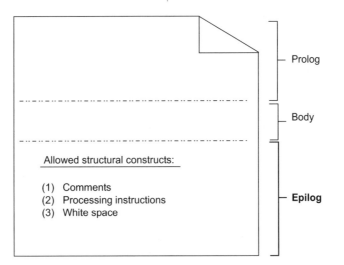

Figure E.15 The epilog as a section of an XML document.

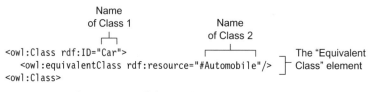

Figure E.16 Defining equivalent classes in OWL.

Equivalent class In OWL, a CLASS is said to be equivalent to another class if the two classes have the same INSTANCES. In the example shown in Figure E.16, the "Car" class in defined to be the equivalent class to the "Automobile" class using the `owl:equivalentClass` ELEMENT. *See also* OWL VOCABULARY.

ESI (Edge Side Includes) An XML-BASED MARKUP LANGUAGE for defining Web page components for dynamic assembly and delivery of Web applications at the edge of the Internet. More details about ESI are available at `http://www.edge-delivery.org/`.

ESML (Earth Science Markup Language) An XML-BASED MARKUP LANGUAGE for exchanging information within the Earth science community. See `http://esml.itsc.uah.edu/` for more details.

Event-based parser *See* EVENT-DRIVEN PARSER.

Event-based parsing A data-centric method of parsing XML DOCUMENTS that is employed in EVENT-DRIVEN PARSERS.

Event-driven parser An XML PARSER that processes XML data sequentially, handling components one at a time. It uses an event-based method of parsing in which an event is fired whenever an XML ELEMENT is encountered. This method is not memory-intensive and is thus useful for processing large documents. SAX is the best-known example of an API for event-driven parsers. Note that an event-driven parser can be either a VALIDATING PARSER or a NON-VALIDATING PARSER. *Contrast* TREE-BASED PARSER.

Exchangeable Faceted Metadata Language *See* XFML.

Exchangeable Routing Language *See* XRL.

Expanded name In XPATH, the name of a NODE that is modeled as a pair consisting of a local part and a (possibly null) namespace URI, as shown in

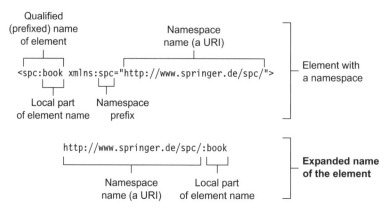

Figure E.17 An example of an expanded name.

Figure E.17. Note that instead of using the NAMESPACE PREFIX, an expanded name uses the NAMESPACE NAME (i.e. namespace URI). Also called "expanded-name".

Expanded-name *See* EXPANDED NAME.

Exploration and Mining Markup Language *See* XMML.

Expression The main STRUCTURAL CONSTRUCT of XPATH. There are two types of XPath expression: (1) ABSOLUTE EXPRESSION; (2) RELATIVE EXPRESSION. An expression can return one of four DATA TYPES: NODE SET, STRING, Boolean or number. The most important kind of expression is the LOCATION PATH that returns a NODE SET.

Extended link In XLINK, a type of LINK that provides full XLink functionality, such as INBOUND ARCS and THIRD-PARTY ARCS. It also can have an arbitrary number of PARTICIPATING RESOURCES in any combination of REMOTE RESOURCES and LOCAL RESOURCES. Any ELEMENT of an XML DOCUMENT can be used as a container element for an extended link after adding the "xlink:type" ATTRIBUTE with the ATTRIBUTE VALUE "extended". In the example shown in Figure E.18, an extended link is an ARC between two RESOURCES specified by their LOCATORS. This arc connects a particular book to the biography of its author. *Contrast* SIMPLE LINK.

Extended-type element In XLINK, the ELEMENT of an XML DOCUMENT that has a TYPE ATTRIBUTE with the "extended" ATTRIBUTE VALUE and therefore can be used as a PARENT ELEMENT for other elements that specifies an EXTENDED LINK. For more details, see EXTENDED LINK; TYPE ATTRIBUTE.

Extensibility A term that refers to the ability of XML to provide SYNTAX for creating XML-BASED MARKUP LANGUAGES instead of defining the actual tags. It is intended to stress that fact that anyone can "extend" XML by creating their own languages, specifically tailored for their businesses, domains, and purposes. Note that there is some contradiction in the use of this term. Since the XML SYNTAX, as defined in the XML 1.0 RECOMMENDATION, can be extended or changed only by the W3C, XML is, strictly speaking, a METALANGUAGE for creating and describing extensible XML-BASED MARKUP LANGUAGES.

Extensible *See* EXTENSIBILITY.

Extensible 3D *See* X3D.

Extensible Access Control Markup Language *See* XACML.

Extensible Address Language *See* XAL.

Extensible Business Reporting Language *See* XBRL.

Extensible Communications Protocol A COMMUNICATION PROTOCOL that is based on XML and uses its SYNTAX. *See* SOAP; XML-RPC; XMP.

```
         Element     Attribute   Attribute
          name         name        value
        ┌────┴───┐   ┌───┴──┐    ┌───┴──┐
<author_bio xlink:type="extended">
    <loc xlink:type="locator"
    xlink:href="http://www.springer.de/book123" xlink:label="book"/>
    <loc xlink:type="locator"
    xlink:href="http://www.uop.uk/vg/bio" xlink:label="bio"/>
    <go xlink:type="arc" xlink:from="book" xlink:to="bio"/>
</author_bio>
```

Figure E.18 An example of an extended link in XLink.

Extensible Customer Information Language *See* XCIL.

Extensible Customer Relationships Language *See* XCRL.

Extensible Data Format *See* XDF.

Extensible Forms Description Language *See* XFDL.

Extensible Graphics Library *See* XGL.

Extensible Graph Markup and Modeling Language *See* XGMML.

Extensible Hypertext Markup Language *See* XHTML.

Extensible Inter-Nodes Constraint Markup Language *See* XINCAML.

Extensible Linking Language *See* XLL.

Extensible Markup Language *See* XML.

Extensible Markup Language 1.1 *See* XML 1.1.

Extensible Media Commerce Language *See* XMCL.

Extensible Metadata Platform *See* XMP.

Extensible Name and Address Language *See* XNAL.

Extensible Name Language *See* XNL.

Extensible Name Service *See* XNS.

Extensible Provisioning Protocol *See* EPP.

Extensible Rights Markup Language *See* XRML.

Extensible Scientific Interchange Language *See* XSIL.

Extensible Style Sheet Language *See* XSL.

Extensible Style Sheet Language Family *See* XSL.

Extensible Style Sheet Language Transformations *See* XSLT.

Extensible Telephony Markup Language *See* XTML.

Extensible Virtual Reality Modeling Language *See* X-VRML.

Extension *See* FILENAME EXTENSION.

External DTD A DTD or a subset of a DTD that is located in a separate file with the "dtd" FILENAME EXTENSION and is associated with an XML DOCUMENT using a DOCTYPE DECLARATION. An external DTD and an INTERNAL DTD can supplement each other. Note that the internal DTD has priority over the external DTD, meaning that its declarations will override similar declarations of the external DTD. Also called "external subset". *Contrast* INTERNAL DTD.

External entity An ENTITY defined in an external file. External entities can contain text, binary data or CHARACTER DATA. *Contrast* INTERNAL ENTITY.

External general entity An ENTITY defined in a separate external document (i.e. outside of the XML DOCUMENT's DTD) and used in the body of an XML document.

External parameter entity An ENTITY defined in an external file and used exclusively within a DTD.

External subset One of two subsets into which a DTD may be divided. *See* EXTERNAL DTD.

extref attribute In XFI, the ATTRIBUTE of the FCS ELEMENT that specifies a URI reference to the external subset in a FRAGMENT CONTEXT SPECIFICATION.

f:fcs element *See* FCS ELEMENT.

f:fragbody element *See* FRAGMENT CONTEXT SPECIFICATION.

Facet In an XML SCHEMA, a restriction on a DATA TYPE that is used to control acceptable values for ELEMENTS and ATTRIBUTES. There are two types of facet: (1) fundamental facets that cannot be omitted; (2) constraining facets that set optional limits on the allowed values. Some of the most useful facets: ENUMERATION FACET; LENGTH FACET; MAXLENGTH FACET; MINLENGTH FACET; PATTERN FACET.

As shown in Figure F.1, the base attribute of a special xs:restriction element is used to specify the base data type that is going to be

restricted. All elements that specify facets are CHILDREN of the xs:restriction element. The example also shows how the four enumeration facets specified in the XML schema provide possible choices for the ELEMENT CONTENT of the Season element when using an IDE such as XMLSpy.

Fallback element In XINCLUDE, the ELEMENT that provides a mechanism for recovering if RESOURCES are missing. This element must be a CHILD of the INCLUDE ELEMENT.

Fault element An optional STRUCTURAL CONSTRUCT of the SOAP MESSAGE STRUCTURE that provides information about errors that occurred while processing

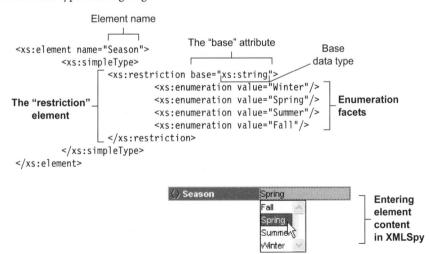

Figure F.1 The use of facets in an XML Schema and an IDE.

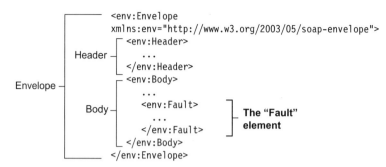

Figure F.2 The SOAP "Fault" element.

the SOAP MESSAGE. It is a CHILD of the BODY ELEMENT, as shown in Figure F.2.

fcs An acronym sometimes used for "FRAGMENT CONTEXT SPECIFICATION".

FCS document An acronym that is sometimes used to refer to a FRAGMENT CONTEXT SPECIFICATION DOCUMENT.

fcs element In XFI, the ROOT ELEMENT of a FRAGMENT CONTEXT SPECIFICATION DOCUMENT. It includes the NAMESPACE DECLARATION of the XFI NAMESPACE and some other ATTRIBUTES.

FieldML An XML-BASED MARKUP LANGUAGE for specifying spatially and/or temporally varying quantities in biological models in a form that is both computer and human readable. More details are available at http://www.physiome.org.nz/sites/physiome/fieldml/pages/.

File extension See FILENAME EXTENSION.

Filename extension In filenames, the group of letters after the dot (period) in a filename that indicates the type (or format) of the file. For example, if the filename is "Catalog.xml", the extension is ".xml". Operating systems use filename extensions to choose which application to launch when a user clicks on a file. See Figure F.3.

Financial Extensible Markup Language *See* FINXML.

Financial Information Exchange Markup Language *See* FIXML.

Financial Products Markup Language *See* FPML.

Financial Services Markup Language *See* FSML.

FinXML (Financial Extensible Markup Language) An XML-based framework for supporting a single universal standard for the integration and exchange of digital information in capital markets. More details about FinXML can be obtained from http://www.finxml.org/.

First-Generation Web The current version of the Web, based on HTML, which is gradually evolving into the Second-Generation Web, known as the SEMANTIC WEB. On the HTML-based Web, only humans were able to understand the content of Web documents and to deal with them. Computers played a passive and inadequate role in this process. They had no real access to the content of a presentation because they were not able to understand the meaning of information on HTML Web pages.

fixed attribute In an XML SCHEMA, the ATTRIBUTE of an ELEMENT DECLARATION or ATTRIBUTE DECLARATION that is

EXTENSION	DOCUMENT TYPE	EXAMPLES
.biz	BizTalk document	Catalog.biz
.cml	CML (Chemical Markup Language) document	Catalog.cml
.dcd	DCD (Document Content Description)	Catalog.dcd
.dtd	DTD (Document Type Definition)	Catalog.dtd
.ent	External entity	Catalog.ent
.fo	XSL-FO document	Catalog.fo
.htm .html	HTML document	Catalog.htm Catalog.html
.math	MathML document	Catalog.math
.rdf	RDF document	Catalog.rdf
.smil	SMIL document	Catalog.smil
.svg	SVG document	Catalog.svg
.vml .vxml	VoiceXML document	Catalog.vml Catalog.vxml
.wml	WML document	Catalog.wml
.xdr	XDR (XML-Data Reduced) Schema	Catalog.xdr
.xhtml	XHTML document	Catalog.xhtml
.xml	XML document	Catalog.xml
.xsd	XML Schema document	Catalog.xsd
.xsl	XSL stylesheet	Catalog.xsl
.xslt	XSLT document	Catalog.xslt

Figure F.3 Main types of XML-related documents and their filename extensions.

used for specifying the FIXED VALUE of the ELEMENT or ATTRIBUTE. For more details, see FIXED VALUE.

Fixed content *See* FIXED VALUE.

Fixed element content *See* FIXED VALUE.

Fixed value 1. In an XML SCHEMA, the ATTRIBUTE VALUE that is automatically assigned to the ATTRIBUTE in an XML DOCUMENT in such a way that no other value can be specified. A document with any other attribute value will not be a VALID XML DOCUMENT. See Figure F.4.

2. In an XML SCHEMA, the text-only ELEMENT CONTENT that is automatically assigned to the ELEMENT in an XML DOCUMENT in such a way that no other textual content can be specified. A document with any other ELEMENT CONTENT will not be a VALID XML DOCUMENT. See Figure F.4.

3. In a DTD, the attribute value that is defined using the ATTLIST DECLARATION. In an XML document based on the DTD, this predefined value will be the only legal value for the attribute. A document with any other attribute value will not be a VALID XML DOCUMENT.

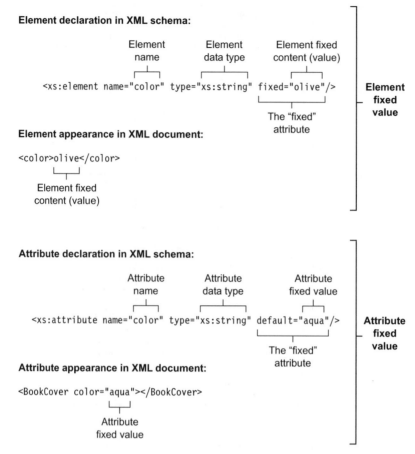

Figure F.4 Fixed values of elements and attributes.

FIXML (Financial Information Exchange Markup Language) An XML-BASED MARKUP LANGUAGE for the Financial Information Exchange (FIX) Protocol that is intended for embedding FIXML messages within traditional FIX headers and trailers to minimize the impact on existing implementations. More details are available at http://www.fixprotocol.org/.

Flavor of XML *See* XML FLAVOR.

fo A FILENAME EXTENSION that indicates that the file is an XSL-FO (XSL Formatting Objects) document. For example, "Catalog.fo".

FO (Formatting Objects) *See* XSL-FO.

fo:layout-master-set element *See* XSL-FO.

fo:root element *See* XSL-FO.

fo:sequence-specification element *See* XSL-FO.

following axis In XPATH, an AXIS that selects all NODES that are after the CONTEXT NODE. See Figure F.5.

following-sibling axis In XPATH, an AXIS that selects sibling NODES of the CONTEXT NODE that are after the context node. See Figure F.6.

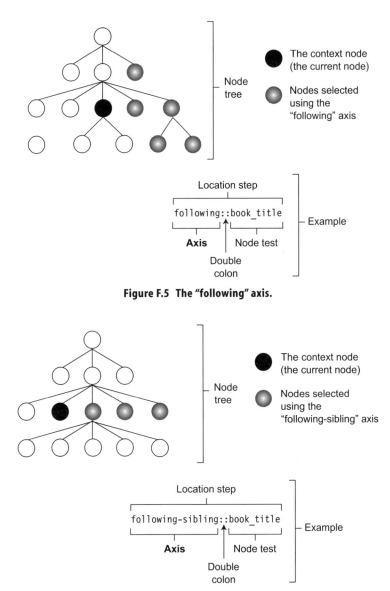

Figure F.5 The "following" axis.

Figure F.6 The "following-sibling" axis.

Font properties In CSS, the collection of properties and values that control the fonts used to display an XML DOCUMENT.

FOP (Formatting Objects Processor) Apache's print formatter driven by XSL-FO. FOP is output format independent. It is an open-source Java implementation of XSL. More details about FOP can be obtained from http://xml.apache.org/fop/.

for-each element An ELEMENT of an XSLT STYLE SHEET that is used in a TEMPLATE to select every XML ELEMENT of a specified NODE SET. In the example shown in

Element name   The "select" attribute

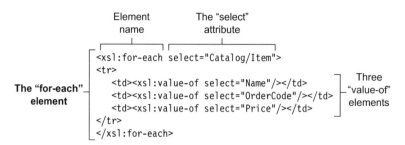

The "for-each" element

Three "value-of" elements

Figure F.7 An example of an XSLT "for-each" element.

Figure F.7, the xsl:for-each element selects each "Item" element of the "Catalog" element (i.e. the first "Item" element, the second "Item" element, and so on).

Format element One of the 15 ELEMENTS of the DUBLIN CORE METADATA ELEMENT SET. The <dc:format> element specifies the data representation of the RESOURCE, such as text/html, executable application, or GIF image. Note the "dc" is the NAMESPACE PREFIX of the DUBLIN CORE NAMESPACE.

Formatting Objects Processor *See* FOP.

Form controls Special ELEMENTS of the XFORMS language that are used to create and control the USER INTERFACE of XForms. Figure F.8 shows two XForms controls defined using the "input" and "submit"

elements. Note that both form controls have a "caption" element as their CHILD ELEMENT.

Forwarding intermediary *See* SOAP INTERMEDIARY.

FpML (Financial Products Markup Language) An XML-based protocol for complex financial products that supports e-commerce activities in the field of financial derivatives. Details of FpML can be found at http://fpml.org/.

fragbody element *See* FRAGMENT CONTEXT SPECIFICATION.

fragbodyref attribute *See* FRAGMENT CONTEXT SPECIFICATION.

Fragment In XFI, part of an XML DOCUMENT (called the FRAGMENT BODY) together with some extra

The "input" control

The "submit" control

Figure F.8 Samples of XForms controls.

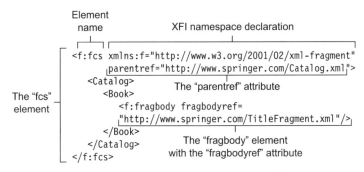

Figure F.9 An example of a fragment context specification.

information (called CONTEXT INFORMATION). This information can possibly be added in order to enable the use and interchange of the fragment in the absence of the rest of the XML DOCUMENT.

Fragment body In XFI, a WELL-BALANCED REGION of an XML DOCUMENT considered separately from the rest of the document for the purposes of defining it as a FRAGMENT.

Fragment context information *See* CONTEXT INFORMATION.

Fragment context specification In XFI, an XML DOCUMENT (also called "fragment context specification document") that describes the CONTEXT INFORMATION of a FRAGMENT. "Fragment context specification" is sometimes abbreviated as "fcs". Figure F.9 shows an example of a fragment context specification document that specifies the context information for a fragment that is actually the "Title" ELEMENT. The specification is used to describe the structural position of the FRAGMENT BODY within the original XML DOCUMENT, namely: the "Title" element is a CHILD of the "Book" element and a grandchild

of the "Catalog" element. The "parentref" ATTRIBUTE specifies the URI of the original XML document. Note that the "fragbody" element is inserted into the XML DOCUMENT TREE exactly at the position where the fragment body is located. It references the file that contains the actual fragment using the "fragbodyref" attribute.

Fragment context specification document In XFI, an XML DOCUMENT that contains a FRAGMENT CONTEXT SPECIFICATION defined using the "fcs" ROOT ELEMENT.

Fragment entity In XFI, the storage object in which the FRAGMENT BODY is transmitted.

Fragment interchange In XFI, the process of receiving and parsing of a FRAGMENT by a fragment-aware application.

Fragment Interchange namespace The NAMESPACE for XFI. Figure F.10 shows its NAMESPACE DECLARATION, which is the "xmlns:f" ATTRIBUTE of the "f:fcs" ROOT ELEMENT. The NAMESPACE PREFIX of the XFI NAMESPACE is usually "f".

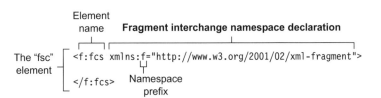

Figure F.10 Declaring the XFI namespace.

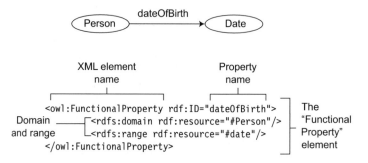

Figure F.11 An example of an OWL functional property.

FSML (Financial Services Markup Language)
An SGML-based markup language for interchanging financial documents over the Internet. More details of FSML may be obtained from http://www.echeck.org/library/ref/fsml15-brief.html.

Functional property In OWL, a property that has no more that one value for each individual, i.e. its value is unique. In the example shown in Figure F.11, the "dateOfBirth" property is defined to be functional. This means that a person has only one date of birth. A functional property can be defined using the owl:FunctionalProperty ELEMENT. *See also* OWL VOCABULARY.

Fundamental facet *See* FACET.

gbXML (Green Building XML) An XML-BASED MARKUP LANGUAGE that describes building information stored in Computer-Aided Design (CAD) digital models, in order to make it available for designing resource efficient and environmentally responsible buildings. Details of gbXML can be found at http://www.gbxml.org/.

GDML (Geometry Description Markup Language) An XML-BASED MARKUP LANGUAGE for defining geometric data. More information about GDML is available at http://gdml.web.cern.ch/gdml/.

GEML (Gene Expression Markup Language) An XML-BASED MARKUP LANGUAGE for exchanging gene expression data between different systems including web-based genome databases. Details of GEML can be found at http://www.geml.org/.

Genealogical Information Markup Language *See* GENIML.

Gene Expression Markup Language *See* GEML.

General entity An ENTITY for the use in the body of an XML DOCUMENT. *Contrast* PARAMETER ENTITY. *See also* ENTITY REFERENCE; INTERNAL GENERAL ENTITY; SPECIAL SYMBOLS.

Generalized Markup Language *See* GML.

Generic identifier *See* GI.

GeniML (Genealogical Information Markup Language) An XML-BASED MARKUP LANGUAGE for recording and exchanging genealogical data. See http://www.geniml.org/ for more details.

Geography Markup Language *See* GML.

Geometry Description Markup Language *See* GDML.

Geophysical Markup Language *See* GEOPHYSICALML.

GeophysicalML (Geophysical Markup Language) An XML-BASED MARKUP LANGUAGE for exchanging geophysical data. More details of GeophysicalML may be obtained from http://www.posc.org/ebiz/Geophysics/.

GI (Generic identifier) Another term for ELEMENT NAME that emphasizes that each element is of a type, identified by name.

Global attribute *See* GLOBAL DECLARATION.

Global declaration An ELEMENT DECLARATION or ATTRIBUTE DECLARATION that appears at the top level of an XML SCHEMA as CHILDREN of the SCHEMA ELEMENT. ELEMENTS and ATTRIBUTES declared in this way are called "Global elements" and "Global attributes" respectively. All global element declaration, with the exception of the declaration of the ROOT ELEMENT, must explicitly be referenced to allow them to appear in an XML DOCUMENT. *Contrast* LOCAL DECLARATION.

Global element *See* GLOBAL DECLARATION.

Global Positioning System Exchange Format *See* GPX.

Global Positioning System/Location Markup Language *See* GPSML.

Global Uniform Interoperable Data Exchange *See* GUIDE.

Global XML Web Services Architecture *See* GXA.

Glossary Extensible Markup Language *See* GLOSSXML.

GlossXML (Glossary Extensible Markup Language) An XML-BASED MARKUP LANGUAGE for describing and interchanging dictionaries of words and phrases. Details of GlossXML can be found at `http://www.creativyst.com/Prod/Glossary/Doc/XMLOut.htm`.

GML (Generalized Markup Language) The precursor of SGML.

GML (Geography Markup Language) An XML-BASED MARKUP LANGUAGE for the transport and storage of geographic information. Details of GML are available at `http://www.opengis.net/gml/01-029/GML2.html`.

GPSML (Global Positioning System/Location Markup Language) An XML-BASED MARKUP LANGUAGE for sharing GPS (Global Positioning System) location information. More details are available at `http://www.chaeron.com/gps.html`. *See also* GPX.

GPX (Global Positioning System Exchange Format) An XML-BASED MARKUP LANGUAGE for the interchange of GPS (Global Positioning System) data such as waypoints, routes, and tracks. For more details, see `http://www.topografix.com/gpx.asp`. *See also* GPSML.

Graph data model *See* RDF DATA MODEL.

Graph Exchange Language *See* GXL.

Graphical User Interface *See* GUI.

Graph syntax *See* RDF DATA MODEL.

Greater-than sign *See* ANGLE BRACKETS.

Green Building XML *See* GBXML.

group element In an XML SCHEMA, a special ELEMENT that is used as an INDICATOR that declares a named group of elements. ELEMENT DECLARATIONS of the group members cannot be placed directly within the "group" element tags. First, an ALL ELEMENT, a CHOICE ELEMENT or a SEQUENCE ELEMENT must be declared. The QUALIFIED NAME of the "group" element can be either "xs:group" or "xsd:group",

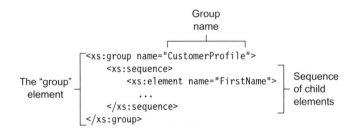

Figure G.1 The "group" element.

```
first_name, last_name, id_number ─┤─Three grouped selectors
{
     color: red; ─┤─Shared property
}
```

Figure G.2 Grouping selectors.

depending whether the XS NAMESPACE PREFIX or XSD NAMESPACE PREFIX is being used. See Figure G.1.

group indicator *See* INDICATOR.

Grouping selectors In CSS, a technique used to display several XML ELEMENTS identically by assigning the same declarations to a group of ELEMENT NAMES (SELECTORS) separated by a comma. In the example shown in Figure G.2, the content of all the three elements (first_name, last_name, id_number) will be displayed as red in a WEB BROWSER.

GUI (Graphical User Interface) In computing, an interface that employs visual metaphors and uses icons, symbols, dialog boxes, windows and other screen objects to represent programs, files, commands etc. It allows the user to interact with the computer in an intuitive way, usually with a mouse.

GUIDE (Global Uniform Interoperable Data Exchange) An XML-BASED MARKUP LANGUAGE for describing business information interchanges between a set of endpoints. For more details, see the information at http://www.bizcodes.org/GUIDE/.

Guideline XML *See* GXML.

GXA (Global XML Web Services Architecture) Microsoft's open architecture for enhancing the current XML WEB SERVICES standards, which addresses the issues of security, reliability and multi-party agreement. Details of GXA can be found at http://msdn.microsoft.com/library/en-us/dngxa/html/gloxmlws500.asp.

GXL (Graph Exchange Language) An XML-BASED MARKUP LANGUAGE for exchanging graphs that enable INTEROPERABILITY between different graph-based tools. More details about GXL may be obtained from http://www.gupro.de/GXL/.

gXML (Guideline XML) An XML-BASED MARKUP LANGUAGE for exchanging E-COMMERCE guidelines. Guidelines (also known as EDI Transaction Sets and Schemas) are used to define business documents such as purchase orders, invoices and catalog requests. More information is available at http://www.edifecs.com/b2b_resources_guideline.jsp.

Header An optional STRUCTURAL CONSTRUCT of the SOAP MESSAGE STRUCTURE that contains application-specific information about the SOAP MESSAGE, such as directives or contextual information. See Figure H.1. *See also* SOAP INTERMEDIARY.

Header element *See* HEADER.

Helper component *See* XML SCHEMA COMPONENT.

HEML (Historical Event Markup and Linking) An XML-BASED MARKUP LANGUAGE for describing historical events. More details about HEML can be obtained from http://www.heml.org/.

Hiding elements In CSS, a method of preventing specified XML ELEMENTS from being displayed using the DISPLAY PROPERTY with the value "none", as shown in Figure H.2. This feature of CSS can be very useful for creating an XML-based Web site that has to display dissimilar content to different users. By default, each element of an XML DOCUMENT is displayed by a Web browser. If no STYLE SHEET is attached, the browser uses its own default style sheet to show the content of all the elements in a document.

Hierarchical tree *See* HIERARCHICAL TREE STRUCTURE.

Hierarchical tree structure An abstract structure in the form of a hierarchical element tree that

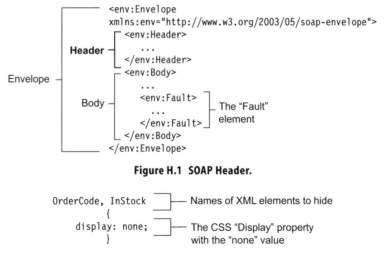

Figure H.1 SOAP Header.

Figure H.2 Example CSS code used for hiding XML elements.

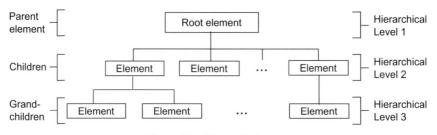

Figure H.3 Hierarchical tree.

has one and only one top-level element called the ROOT ELEMENT that is the PARENT of all other elements in the tree. PARENT–CHILD is the only direct element-to-element relationship. The hierarchical tree structure is the underlying structure of all XML DOCUMENTS and their constructs. See Figure H.3. *See also* NODE TREE; XML DOCUMENT SECTIONS; XML DOCUMENT STRUCTURE; XML DOM; XPATH DATA MODEL.

Hierarchical way of thinking A term that is sometimes used to refer to a new way of thinking about the structure of XML-based Web documents that will totally dominate on the SECOND-GENERATION WEB. Since every XML DOCUMENT is organized as a HIERARCHICAL TREE STRUCTURE, the proper understanding and effective use of XML requires a novel non-linear way of thinking. It is based on a number of metaphorical concepts, such as "tree-like structure", "one and only one ROOT ELEMENT", "PARENT–CHILD relationship", "PROPERLY NESTED ELEMENTS" and others. *See also* HIERARCHICAL TREE STRUCTURE; PARENT–CHILD; XML DOCUMENT SECTIONS; XML DOCUMENT STRUCTURE; XML DOM.

Historical Event Markup and Linking *See* HEML.

HR-XML (Human Resources XML) Consortium A non-profit, vendor-neutral organization for the development and promotion of standardized XML vocabularies for human resources. See http://www.hr-xml.org/ for more details.

htm/html FILENAME EXTENSIONS identifying a Web page written in HTML (Hypertext Markup Language). For example, "Catalog.htm" or "Catalog.html".

HTML (Hypertext Markup Language) An SGML-based markup language for describing HYPERTEXT documents (WEB PAGES and WEB SITES) on the FIRST-GENERATION WEB. HTML has played a central role in the enormous success of the WWW, but it has had several limitations. It deals only with the ways of presenting Web pages (defining their spatial layout and styling fonts and paragraphs) and also has a predefined set of tags that is unable to satisfy the particular needs of the millions of e-businesses in marking up the content of their Web documents in a meaningful way.

Note that although XML will form the basis of the SECOND-GENERATION WEB, it is not a replacement for HTML. They are designed for different purposes: XML for describing data, HTML for displaying data. XML cannot push HTML aside because it needs HTML as a means of presenting the data it describes. At the same time, XML forces HTML to change itself. A new generation of HTML called XHTML began its life as a reformulation of the latest version of HTML, namely HTML 4.0, in XML. This means that HTML will be replaced by XHTML, not by XML. The latter two languages will complement one another very well in the future Web. XML will be used to structure and describe the Web data, while XHTML pages will be used to display it.

Figure H.4 shows the difference in marking up the same text "John Smith" using HTML and XML. The HTML code indicates that this text should be displayed in a WEB BROWSER as bold and red. The

```
<b><font color ="red">John Smith</font></b>   ⎤⎯ HTML code

<VIP_Customer shop="Green Superstore">
        <First_Name>John</First_Name>               ⎤
        <Last_Name>Smith</Last_Name>                ⎬⎯ XML code
</VIP_Customer>                                      ⎦
```

Figure H.4 A comparison between HTML code and XML code.

XML code describes the meaning of the words "John" and "Smith" and requires some additional CSS or XSLT files to define how to display this text. More details about HTML are available at http://www.w3.org/MarkUp/.

HTML-based Web *See* FIRST-GENERATION WEB.

HTTP (Hypertext Transfer Protocol) A protocol for distributed, collaborative, hypermedia information systems. It is the main protocol used to transmit and receive all data over the World Wide Web. HTTP is a set of instructions for communications between a web server and a client (WEB BROWSER). Every web address begins with http://. More information about HTTP is available at http://www.w3.org/Protocols/Specs.html. *See also* URL.

Human Markup Language *See* HUMANML.

Human Resources XML Consortium *See* HR-XML CONSORTIUM.

HumanML (Human Markup Language) An XML-BASED MARKUP LANGUAGE for describing uniquely human characteristics including physical, cultural, social, psychological and intentional features. See http://www.humanmarkup.org/ for more details.

Hyperlink In a WEB PAGE or other HYPERTEXT document, an embedded cross-reference in the form of highlighted text or images that (when clicked with the mouse) allows the computer to display

another section of the same document or a different document, as well as to automatically download other files such as sounds and video clips. A word or phrase that contains a hyperlink is usually in blue and underlined. *See also* HTTP; XLINK.

Hypermedia/Time-based Structuring Language *See* HYTIME.

Hypertext A method of organizing computer-based information in which readers can choose their own paths through the document, usually by clicking on a HYPERLINK. A typical WEB PAGE is the best-known example of a hypertext document. The WWW is a global hypertext system. *See also* HTTP.

Hypertext Markup Language *See* HTML.

Hypertext Transfer Protocol *See* HTTP.

HyTime (Hypermedia/Time-based Structuring Language) An SGML-based ISO/IEC standard (ISO/IEC 10744) for marking up hypertext and multimedia. XML is not based on HyTime, but uses some of its concepts for the design of XML VOCABULARIES and DATA MODELS. HyTime is one of the NON-NORMATIVE REFERENCES of the XML 1.0 RECOMMENDATION. More details of HyTime may be obtained from http://www.iso.ch/cate/d29303.html and http://www.hytime.org/.

71

i18n (internationalization) An acronym for "internationalization" that consists of the first letter ("i") and the last letter ("n") of the word "internationalization" and also of the number of letters located between "i" and "n", namely "18". *See* INTERNATIONALIZATION; L10N.

IANA (Internet Assigned Numbers Authority) An organization that is responsible for the registry for character sets, port numbers, MIME types etc, and also oversees the allocation of IP (Internet Protocol) addresses to ISPs (Internet Service Providers). Details of IANA can be found at http://www.iana.org/.

IANA Character Set Names A standard of official names for character set that can be used as ATTRIBUTE VALUES for the ENCODING ATTRIBUTE of the XML DECLARATION. This is one of the NORMATIVE REFERENCES of the XML 1.0 RECOMMENDATION. More details are available at http://www.iana.org/assignments/character-sets/.

ICE (Information and Content Exchange Protocol) An XML-based protocol that is intended to automate Web content syndication (i.e. information reuse, integration and sharing between Web sites) in both publishing and e-commerce. More details about ICE are available at http://www.icestandard.org/.

IDE (Integrated Development Environment) An advanced software package for creating specialist applications that usually consists of several specialized parts, including those that enable a visual design of an application or its GUI. XMLSpy is a well-known example of an IDE for XML.

Identifier element One of the 15 ELEMENTS of the DUBLIN CORE METADATA ELEMENT SET. The <dc:identifier> element specifies a STRING or number used to uniquely identify the RESOURCE. Examples include URL, URN, and ISBN. Note that "dc" is the NAMESPACE PREFIX of the DUBLIN CORE NAMESPACE.

IDML (International Development Markup Language) An XML-BASED MARKUP LANGUAGE for exchanging information that is specific to international development. More details about IDML are available at http://www.idmlinitiative.org/.

IEC (International Engineering Consortium) An international organization responsible for technical standards for electrical and electronic engineering. See http://www.iec.org/ for more details.

IETF (Internet Engineering Task Force) An open international community concerned with the evolution of the Internet architecture. It defines standards for Internet operating PROTOCOLS that are expressed in the form of RFCS. More details about IETF are available at http://www.ietf.org/.

```
<?xml version="1.0" encoding="UTF-8"?>
<book xmlns:xi="http://www.w3.org/2001/XInclude">
    <title>Visualizing the Semantic Web</title>
    <xi:include href="subtitle.xml"/>
</book>
```

The "include" element

Figure I.1 An example of an "include" element.

IETF Language Tags An RFC (RFC 3066) that specifies the syntax of tags for describing textual data that can be used to represent human languages. The RFC 3066 format is used for creating valid LANGUAGE CODES (ISO 639) used as ATTRIBUTE VALUES of the XML:LANG ATTRIBUTE. This is one of the NORMATIVE REFERENCES of the XML 1.0 RECOMMENDATION. More details are available at http:// www.ietf.org/rfc/rfc3066.txt/.

IFX (Interactive Financial Exchange) An XML-based messaging protocol and a scalable framework for the exchange of financial data that supports existing and emerging financial services. Details of IFX can be found at http:// www.ifxforum.org/.

Ill-formed document An ill-formed document is not a WELL-FORMED XML DOCUMENT.

IML (Instrument Markup Language) An XML-BASED MARKUP LANGUAGE that can be used for describing any kind of instrument that can be controlled by a computer. For more details, see http://pioneer.gsfc.nasa.gov/public/iml/.

Improperly nested elements ELEMENTS that are NESTED with overlapping, and not in accordance

with the RUSSIAN DOLL APPROACH. *Contrast* PROPERLY NESTED ELEMENTS. *See also* HIERARCHICAL TREE STRUCTURE; NESTING ELEMENTS; OVERLAPPING ELEMENTS.

Inbound arc In XLINK, an ARC that has a REMOTE STARTING RESOURCE and a LOCAL ENDING RESOURCE. *Compare* OUTBOUND ARC; THIRD-PARTY ARC.

Inbound link In XLINK, a LINK that is based on an INBOUND ARC.

Include element In XINCLUDE, the ELEMENT whose "href" ATTRIBUTE specifies the location of a RESOURCE to include, as shown in Figure I.1.

Indenting nested elements A development practice that consists in the indentation of NESTED ELEMENTS by putting extra WHITE SPACE around them. It makes an XML DOCUMENT easily readable for humans. Note that for computers it does not matter at all, because an XML PARSER ignores white space included in the ELEMENT CONTENT. The two pieces of XML code shown in Figure I.2 are identical for a computer, but the code written in line is less understandable for a human reader than the indented one (especially if a document contains thousands of ELEMENTS).

```
<pet>
    <dog>
        <name>Teddy</name>
    </dog>
</pet>
```
— Indented XML code

```
<pet><dog><name>Teddy</name></dog></pet>
```
The same code written in line

Figure I.2 Indenting XML elements.

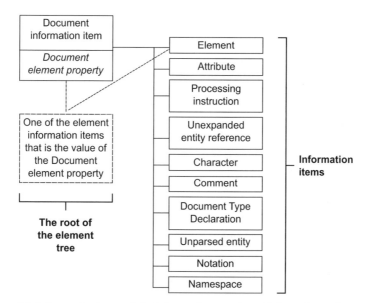

Figure I.3 Information items of the information set of a well-formed XML document.

Indicator In an XML SCHEMA, a special ELEMENT or ATTRIBUTE used to specify how elements of the COMPLEX TYPE are to be used in XML DOCUMENTS. There are seven indicators that can be divided into three groups. **Group 1, order indicators**, specify how elements should occur: (1) the "all" indicator, which uses the XS:ALL ELEMENT; (2) the "choice" indicator, which uses the XS:CHOICE ELEMENT; (3) the "sequence" indicator, which uses the XS:SEQUENCE ELEMENT. **Group 2, occurrence indicators**, specify how often an element may occur: (4) the "minOccurs" indicator, which uses the MINOCCURS ATTRIBUTE; (5) the "maxOccurs" indicator, which uses the MAXOCCURS ATTRIBUTE. **Group 3, group indicators**, are used to specify related sets of elements: (6) the "group" (element group) indicator, which uses the GROUP ELEMENT; (7) the "attributeGroup" indicator, which uses the ATTRIBUTEGROUP ELEMENT.

Individual In OWL, an INSTANCE of a CLASS. For example, an individual named Mike can be described as an instance of the class "Person". *See also* THING CLASS.

Information and Content Exchange Protocol *See* ICE.

Information item An abstract description of some part (or STRUCTURAL CONSTRUCT) of an XML DOCUMENT. An INFORMATION SET can consist of up to 11 types of information item: (1) the DOCUMENT INFORMATION ITEM; (2) ELEMENT INFORMATION ITEMS; (3) ATTRIBUTE INFORMATION ITEMS; (4) PROCESSING INSTRUCTION INFORMATION ITEMS; (5) UNEXPANDED ENTITY REFERENCE INFORMATION ITEMS; (6) CHARACTER INFORMATION ITEMS; (7) COMMENT INFORMATION ITEMS; (8) the DOCUMENT TYPE DECLARATION INFORMATION ITEM; (9) UNPARSED ENTITY INFORMATION ITEMS; (10) NOTATION INFORMATION ITEMS; (11) NAMESPACE INFORMATION ITEMS. See Figure I.3.

Although the Information Set is described as a HIERARCHICAL TREE, other types of interface are possible, such as event-based or query-based. Each information item has a set of associated properties. Details of information items are available at http://www.w3.org/TR/xml-infoset/.

Information resource *See* RESOURCE.

Information Set The Information Set (also known as the XML Information Set, XML Infoset, or Infoset) is an abstract DATA MODEL for XML. The main idea of the Information Set is to provide a set of consistent definitions for STRUCTURAL CONSTRUCTS of a WELL-FORMED XML DOCUMENT that can be used in other XML-related specifications in order to avoid terminological and conceptual confusions. An XML DOCUMENT has an Information Set if it is WELL-FORMED and also conforms to the NAMESPACE specification. Note that the document does not need to be VALID to have an Information Set. Figure I.4 shows that the Information Set specification is based on the XML and namespace syntax and is intended to be used as a basis for other specifications.

The Information Set of an XML DOCUMENT consists of 11 INFORMATION ITEMS. Each item has a set of

associated properties. The concepts "Information Set", "Information item", and "property" are similar to the well-known and more generic concepts "HIERARCHICAL TREE", "NODE", and "property". However, the new terms are intended to avoid confusion with other specific DATA MODELS. The W3C RECOMMENDATION "XML Information Set" is available at http://www.w3.org/TR/xml-infoset/.

Information Technology Markup Language *See* ITML.

Infoset *See* INFORMATION SET.

Inheriting and overriding properties In CSS, two complementary methods for assigning styles to specified child or individual ELEMENTS. If an XML ELEMENT has any CHILD ELEMENTS, all of them will inherit many of the parent's properties, such as font size and color. If an XML element has to have some individual display options, its inherited properties should be overridden by explicitly specifying their new values. See Figure I.5.

Initial SOAP sender *See* SOAP INTERMEDIARY.

Inline DTD A term sometimes used to refer to a INTERNAL DTD.

Input element *See* FORM CONTROLS.

Instance In an RDF SCHEMA, a member of a CLASS. An instance can be declared using the TYPE PROPERTY.

Instance data An XFORMS SECTION that is a skeleton XML DOCUMENT that gets updated as the user fills out the XFORM. In the example shown in Figure I.6, the "instance" element is used to define that the XML DOCUMENT containing the submitted data will includes the "payment" ELEMENT that has three CHILD ELEMENTS.

Instance document *See* DOCUMENT INSTANCE.

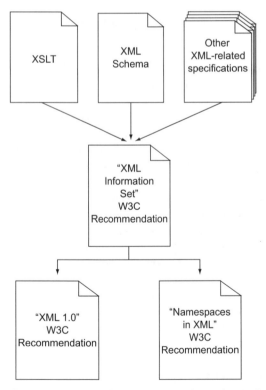

Figure I.4   Relationships of the "XML Information Set" to other specifications.

Instance element *See* INSTANCE DATA.

XML document

```
<?xml version="1.0" encoding="UTF-8"?>
<?xml-stylesheet type="text/css" href="Style.css"?>
<Customer>
    <Name>
        <FirstName>John</FirstName>
        <LastName>Wood</LastName>
    </Name>
    <Phone>274.35.76</Phone>
</Customer>
```

First child of the Customer element that has 2 children

Second child of the Customer element

CSS style sheet

```
Customer {font-size: 12pt;}
LastName {font-size: 20pt;}
```

Property inherited by all the children
Property that overrides the inherited property

Browser view

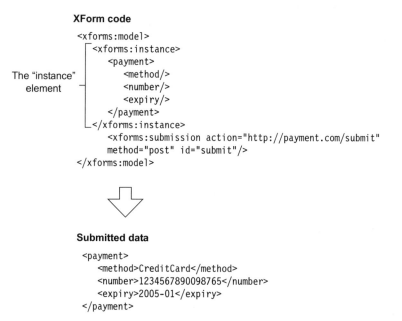

Figure I.5   An example of inheriting and overriding parent's properties.

XForm code

```
<xforms:model>
    <xforms:instance>
        <payment>
            <method/>
            <number/>
            <expiry/>
        </payment>
    </xforms:instance>
    <xforms:submission action="http://payment.com/submit"
    method="post" id="submit"/>
</xforms:model>
```

The "instance" element

Submitted data

```
<payment>
    <method>CreditCard</method>
    <number>1234567890098765</number>
    <expiry>2005-01</expiry>
</payment>
```

Figure I.6   The use of instance data.

Instrument Markup Language *See* IML.

Integrated Development Environment *See* IDE.

Intelligent agent A software tool that carries out a task on behalf of a user or computer, typically relatively autonomously. A well-known example is finding the best price for an item by scouring the Web. Also known as a "software agent", "Web agent", "Web bot" ("bot" is short for "robot") and "Internet robot".

Interaction Techniques Markup Language *See* INTML.

Interactive Financial Exchange *See* IFX.

Intermediary *See* SOAP INTERMEDIARY.

Internal DTD A DTD or a subset of a DTD that is embedded within the DOCTYPE DECLARATION of an XML DOCUMENT, as shown in Figure I.7. Square brackets are used as the opening and closing DELIMITERS of the internal DTD declarations. An internal DTD and an EXTERNAL DTD can supplement each other. Note that the internal DTD has priority over the external DTD that means that its declarations will override similar declarations of the external DTD. Also called "internal subset". *Contrast* EXTERNAL DTD.

Internal entity An ENTITY that is defined within a DTD. *Contrast* EXTERNAL ENTITY. *See also* ENTITY REFERENCE; INTERNAL GENERAL ENTITY; SPECIAL SYMBOLS.

Internal general entity An ENTITY defined within a DTD and used in the body of an XML DOCUMENT in order to provide shortcuts for replacement text, as shown in Figure I.8. In XML, there are five built-in internal general entities used to represent SPECIAL SYMBOLS. *Contrast* EXTERNAL GENERAL ENTITY. *See also* ENTITY REFERENCE.

Internal subset One of two subsets into which a DTD may be divided. *See* INTERNAL DTD.

International Development Markup Language *See* IDML.

International Engineering Consortium *See* IEC.

International Organization for Standardization *See* ISO.

International Standard Book Number *See* ISBN.

Internationalization The process of designing and developing software products for use with different languages and cultures. A commonly used acronym of the word "internationalization" is "i18n" (*see* I18N). For more information about

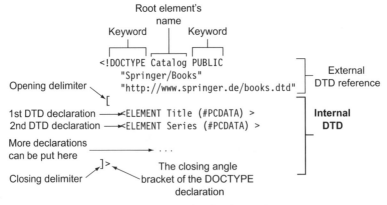

Figure I.7 An example of an internal DTD.

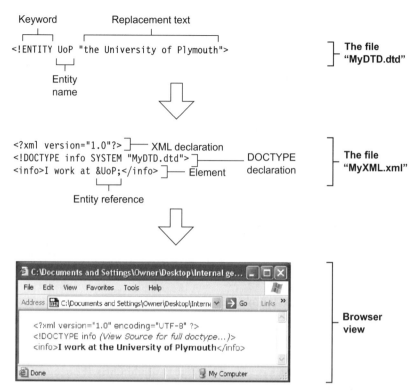

Figure I.8 The use of the internal general entity.

the W3C Internationalization activity, see http://www.w3.org/International/. *See also* LOCALIZATION.

Internet Assigned Numbers Authority *See* IANA.

Internet Engineering Task Force *See* IETF.

Internet robot *See* INTELLIGENT AGENT.

Interoperability The ability of different types of computers, applications, operating systems, and networks to exchange information in a useful and meaningful way without prior communication.

InTML (Interaction Techniques Markup Language) An XML-BASED MARKUP LANGUAGE for describing virtual reality applications, in particular input and output devices, interaction

techniques, application-specific behavior and VR objects. For more details, see the information at http://www.cs.ualberta.ca/%7Epfiguero/InTml/.

intref attribute The ATTRIBUTE of the FCS ELEMENT that specifies a URI reference to the internal subset in a FRAGMENT CONTEXT SPECIFICATION.

Invalid document An XML DOCUMENT that does not follow the rules defined in its SCHEMA (such as an XML SCHEMA or a DTD) and therefore is not a VALID XML DOCUMENT.

Inverse functional property In OWL, a property whose INVERSE PROPERTY is a FUNCTIONAL PROPERTY, i.e. has a unique value. In the example shown in Figure I.9, the "hasBirthPlace" property is defined to be an inverse functional property that is the

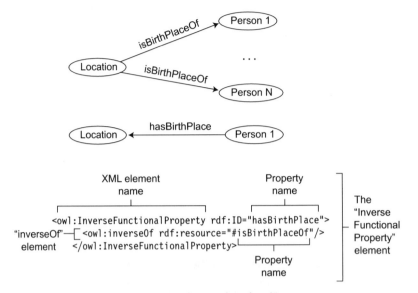

Figure I.9 The OWL "inverse functional" property.

inverse of the property "isBirthPlaceOf". This means that although a location can be the birthplace of many people, a person has only one birthplace. A inverse functional property can be defined using the `owl:InverseFunctionalProperty` ELEMENT. *See also* OWL VOCABULARY.

Inverse property In OWL, a property that is the inverse of another property. In the example shown

in Figure I.10, the "hasChild" property is defined to be the inverse of the property "hasParent". If Mike hasChild Chris, it can be inferred that Chris hasParent Mike. A inverse property can be defined using the `owl:inverseOf` ELEMENT. *See also* OWL VOCABULARY.

ISBN (International Standard Book Number)
An individual number assigned to every published book.

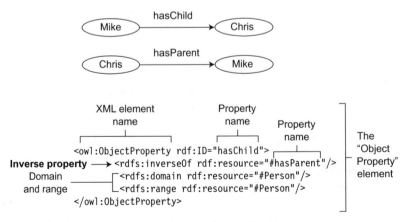

Figure I.10 The OWL "inverse" property.

isDefinedBy property In an RDF SCHEMA, the rdfs:isDefinedBy PROPERTY is a property that is used to indicate a RESOURCE defining the SUBJECT RESOURCE.

ISO (International Organization for Standardization) A non-governmental worldwide federation of national standards institutes from over 140 countries, one from each country, which is developing international standards for businesses, governments and society. Note that "ISO" is actually not an acronym but a word, which means "equal" (derived from the Greek "isos"). More details of ISO may be obtained from http://www.iso.ch/.

ISO 3166 Country Codes *See* COUNTRY CODES.

ISO 639 Language Codes *See* LANGUAGE CODES.

ISO/IEC 10646 *See* UCS.

ISO/IEC 10744 Standard *See* HYTIME.

ITML (Information Technology Markup Language) An XML-BASED MARKUP LANGUAGE and an HTTP-based protocol for the integration of partners and business processes in the Application Service Provider (ASP) and ASP aggregation market. Details of ITML can be found http://www.itml.org/.

J

Java Markup Language *See* JAVAML.

JavaML (Java Markup Language) An XML-BASED MARKUP LANGUAGE for describing Java source code. For more details, see `http://www.unizh.ch/home/mazzo/reports/www9conf/342/342.html`.

Java Speech API Markup Language *See* JSML.

JDF (Job Definition Format) An XML-BASED MARKUP LANGUAGE for describing and exchanging information about a printing job. It serves to bridge the communication gap between production services and Management Information Systems (MIS). Details of JDF can be found at `http://www.cip4.org/`.

Job Definition Format *See* JDF.

Job Survey Markup Language *See* JSML.

JSML (Java Speech API Markup Language) An XML-BASED MARKUP LANGUAGE for annotating text input to speech synthesizers that provides a speech synthesizer with detailed information on how to speak text. More details are available at `http://java.sun.com/products/java-media/speech/forDevelopers/JSML/`.

JSML (Job Survey Markup Language) An XML-BASED MARKUP LANGUAGE for describing a job survey. More information about JSML is available at `http://www.codap.com/job_survey_jobsur.htm`.

KBML (Koala Bean Markup Language) A Java library that enables the serialization of JavaBeans in XML. More details are available at `http://koala.ilog.fr/kbml/`. *See also* BML.

Koala Bean Markup Language *See* KBML.

L10n (Localization) An acronym for LOCALIZATION that consists of the first letter ("L") and the last letter ("n") of the word "localization" and also of a number that shows how many letters are located between "L" and "n", namely "10". *See* I18N.

L12y (Localizability) An acronym for LOCALIZABILITY that consists of the first letter ("L") and the last letter ("y") of the word "localizability" and also of the number of letters located between "i" and "n", namely "12".

Label property In an RDF SCHEMA, the `rdfs:label` PROPERTY is a property that is used to provide a human-readable version of the name of a RESOURCE.

Land Extensible Markup Language *See* LANDXML.

LandXML (Land Extensible Markup Language) An XML-BASED MARKUP LANGUAGE for storing and exchanging civil engineering and survey data. Details of LandXML are available at `http://www.landxml.org/`.

Language Codes An ISO standard (ISO 639) for the representation of names of human languages that can be used as ATTRIBUTE VALUES of the XML:LANG ATTRIBUTE, such as "en" for English and "en-US" for American English. These tags use the IETF LANGUAGE TAG syntax. Language Codes are one of the NON-NORMATIVE REFERENCES of the XML 1.0 RECOMMENDATION. More details are available at `http://`

`lcweb.loc.gov/standards/iso639-2/langcodes.html`.

Language element One of the 15 ELEMENTS of the DUBLIN CORE METADATA ELEMENT SET. The `<dc:language>` element specifies the language of the intellectual content of the RESOURCE. Note that "dc" is the NAMESPACE PREFIX of the DUBLIN CORE NAMESPACE.

Language Tags *See* IETF LANGUAGE TAGS.

Last Call Working Draft *See* W3C LAST CALL WORKING DRAFT.

Learning Material Markup Language Framework *See* LMML.

LegalXML (Legal Extensible Markup Language) A member section within OASIS that brings legal and technical experts together to create standards for the electronic exchange of legal data. More details of LegalXML may be obtained from `http://www.legalxml.org/`.

length facet In an XML SCHEMA, a FACET that restricts the length of a SIMPLE TYPE, such as the number of characters or the number of items in a list.

Less-than sign *See* ANGLE BRACKETS.

Link In XLINK, an explicit relationship between two or more RESOURCES or portions of resources. There two types of link in XLink: (1) SIMPLE LINK; (2) EXTENDED LINK. *See also* MULTIDIRECTIONAL LINK; TRAVERSAL.

Link database *See* LINKBASE.

Linkbase An XLINK document that contains a collection of INBOUND LINKS or/and THIRD-PARTY LINKS.

Linking element In XLINK, a term that is sometimes used to refer to an XML ELEMENT that asserts the existence and describes the characteristics of a LINK.

List data type In XML SCHEMA, a DATA TYPE that is a list of ATOMIC DATA TYPE values.

Literal In programming, a constant. *Contrast* VARIABLE.

Literal class In an RDF SCHEMA, the CLASS of literal values such as STRINGS or integers. The rdfs:Literal class is an INSTANCE of the CLASS CLASS and a SUBCLASS of the RESOURCE CLASS.

Literal string In programming, a sequence of characters that is a constant. *See also* LITERAL; STRING; STRING LITERAL.

LMML (Learning Material Markup Language Framework) A set of XML-BASED MARKUP LANGUAGES for various educational fields. More details about LMML are available at http://www.lmml.de/.

Local declaration An ELEMENT DECLARATION or ATTRIBUTE DECLARATION that appears at a level that is lower than the top level of an XML SCHEMA. *Contrast* GLOBAL DECLARATION.

Local ending resource In XLINK, a LOCAL RESOURCE that is the destination of TRAVERSAL.

Local name *See* LOCAL PART.

Local part The second part of a QUALIFIED NAME separated from the first part (a NAMESPACE PREFIX) by

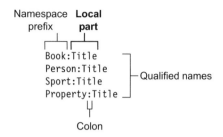

Figure L.1 Examples of local parts of qualified names.

a colon. In examples shown in Figure L.1, the word "Title" is the local part of four different QUALIFIED NAMES. *See also* NAMESPACE; OVERRIDING NAMESPACES; PREFIXED NAMESPACE.

Local resource In XLINK, an XML ELEMENT that participates in a LINK as the own content of the LINKING ELEMENT. *Contrast* REMOTE RESOURCE.

Local starting resource In XLINK, a LOCAL RESOURCE from with TRAVERSAL begins.

Localizability The degree to which a software product can be localized. *See also* LOCALIZATION; L12Y; L10N.

Localization Modifying or adapting a software product to fit the requirements of a particular foreign language and culture. This process may include translating the user interface, documentation and packaging, changing dialog box geometries, and the like. The word "localization" is often abbreviated as L10N. *See also* INTERNATIONALIZATION.

Location path In XPATH, the most important type of path EXPRESSIONS that returns a NODE SET rather than one of the other DATA TYPES (i.e. STRING, Boolean or number). A location path consists of one or more LOCATION STEPS. Basically, a location path selects a set of NODES relative to the CONTEXT NODE (also known as "the current node"). There are two kinds of location path: (1) ABSOLUTE LOCATION PATH and (2) RELATIVE LOCATION PATH. Note that the syntax of location path expressions is very similar to a

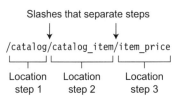

Figure L.2 An example of an location path.

computer file system. In the example shown in Figure L.2, the location path selects all the "item_price" elements of all the "catalog_item" elements of the "catalog" element. For more details, see LOCATION STEP.

Location path expression *See* LOCATION PATH.

Location step In XPATH, a STRUCTURAL CONSTRUCT of a LOCATION PATH. It consists of three parts: (1) an AXIS; (2) a NODE TEST; (3) zero or more PREDICATES. The axis and the node test are separated by double colon; each predicate must be placed in square brackets. A location step works in the following way: (1) the

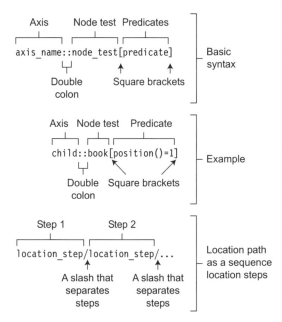

Figure L.3 The anatomy of the location step.

axis selects a node set relative to the current node (also called the CONTEXT NODE) that contains candidates for the next current node; (2) the node test filters the candidate NODES based on a NODE TYPE or node name; (3) predicates are intended to provide further mechanisms for refining and filtering the NODE SET selected by the first two parts.

A LOCATION PATH can consist of one or more location steps. Each step in turn selects a node set relative to a current node. In the example shown in Figure L.3, the location step selects the first "book" ELEMENT that is a CHILD of the current node.

Locator In XLINK, an ELEMENT that has the TYPE ATTRIBUTE with the "locator" ATTRIBUTE VALUE and is used for identifying a REMOTE RESOURCE that is a PARTICIPATING RESOURCE in the LINK. Figure L.4 shows two locators that specify REMOTE RESOURCES (a book and the biography of its author) to be connected by an ARC of an EXTENDED LINK. *See also* LOCATOR-TYPE ELEMENT.

Locator-type element In XLINK, the ELEMENT of an XML DOCUMENT that has a TYPE ATTRIBUTE with the "locator" ATTRIBUTE VALUE and therefore can be used to address the REMOTE RESOURCES participating in the LINK. For more details, see LOCATOR; TYPE ATTRIBUTE.

Log Graphics Markup Language *See* LOGGRAPHICSML.

Log Markup Language *See* LOGML.

LogGraphicsML (Log Graphics Markup Language) An XML-BASED MARKUP LANGUAGE for defining graphic presentations of well log data (related to drilling etc). For more details, see the information at http://www.posc.org/ebiz/LogGraphicsML/v1.0/.

LogML (Log Markup Language) An XML-BASED MARKUP LANGUAGE for describing log reports of Web servers. Details of LogML can be found at http://www.cs.rpi.edu/~puninj/LOGML/.

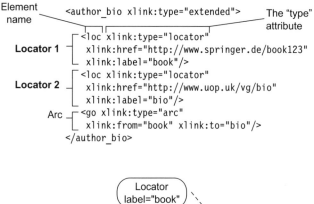

```
Element          <author_bio xlink:type="extended">       The "type"
name                                                       attribute
              ┌ <loc xlink:type="locator"
Locator 1  ─┤   xlink:href="http://www.springer.de/book123"
              └   xlink:label="book"/>
              ┌ <loc xlink:type="locator"
Locator 2  ─┤   xlink:href="http://www.uop.uk/vg/bio"
              └   xlink:label="bio"/>
       Arc ─┌ <go xlink:type="arc"
              └   xlink:from="book" xlink:to="bio"/>
            </author_bio>
```

Figure L.4 An example of XLink locators.

Machine and Human Readability One of the main features of XML. XML documents are easily readable by both machines and humans. Computers can easily "read" XML since it is a PLAIN TEXT format and almost all software and devices are able to process text. Individuals can open an XML DOCUMENT using any text editor or word processor and understand it even without any previous knowledge of XML since XML is SELF-DESCRIBING DATA. For example, it is not difficult to "read" the XML code, shown in Figure M.1, as a meaningful statement: "The price of a car is $29,995".

MAGE-ML (Microarray Gene Expression Markup Language) An XML-BASED MARKUP LANGUAGE for describing and communicating information about microarray based experiments, including microarray designs, gene expression data, and data analysis results. Details of MAGE-ML can be found at http://www.mged.org/Workgroups/ MAGE/introduction.html.

Main element A term that is sometimes used to refer to the ROOT ELEMENT.

Marine Trading Markup Language *See* MTML.

Figure M.1 An example illustrating human readability of XML.

Market Data Definition Language *See* MDDL.

Markup 1. A method of conveying METADATA using special symbols. Handwritten markup was used long before the computer era by writers and copy editors marking up the text of a book or journal article with special copy-editing symbols in order to indicate how to typeset the text. Markup is also sometimes called text encoding.

2. A sequence of characters or other symbols (such as TAGS) inserted at certain places in a text document to define how the document should be displayed or printed, as well as to show explicitly its logical structure and the meaning of the document data.

3. In an XML DOCUMENT, any text other than CHARACTER DATA, including START TAGS, END TAGS, EMPTY-ELEMENT TAGS, XML COMMENTS, PROCESSING INSTRUCTIONS, DTDS, ENTITY REFERENCES, CHARACTER REFERENCES, and CDATA SECTION delimiters. *See also* MARKUP LANGUAGE; PRESENTATIONAL MARKUP; STRUCTURAL MARKUP.

Markup language A type of computer language which is designed either to define how documents should be displayed (for example, HTML, which uses PRESENTATIONAL MARKUP), or to show explicitly their logical structure and the meaning of the document data (for example, XML, which uses STRUCTURAL MARKUP). Basically, markup languages add METADATA to the document data using a sequence of characters (such as TAGS, ANGLE BRACKETS and other DELIMITERS) inserted at certain places in a text document. *See also* XML-BASED MARKUP LANGUAGES. More details are available at `http://www.w3.org/MarkUp/` and `http://www.w3.org/XML/`.

Markup metalanguage A MARKUP LANGUAGE used for creating and describing other markup languages. Markup metalanguages include XML and SGML. *See also* METALANGUAGE.

Markup tag *See* MARKUP; TAG.

Match attribute In XSLT, the ATTRIBUTE of the TEMPLATE element that is used to associate the template with an XML ELEMENT. The ATTRIBUTE VALUE of the "match" attribute is an XPATH LOCATION PATH. Figure M.2 shows two examples of the XSLT "match" attribute. In Example 1, the "match" attribute is used to match the ROOT NODE of the XPATH NODE TREE. Note that the ROOT NODE represents not the ROOT ELEMENT but the DOCUMENT ROOT. In Example 2, the "match" attribute value specifies the "Book" ELEMENTS, which are CHILD ELEMENTS of the "Catalog" element. Note that the "Catalog" element is the root element of the XML DOCUMENT and should not be confused with the root node (i.e. with the DOCUMENT ROOT) represented by the start forward slash. The attribute value of the match attribute is also known as "a pattern".

MATE (Multilevel Annotation, Tools Engineering) Markup Framework An XML-BASED MARKUP LANGUAGE for describing spoken language dialogues. More information is available at `http://mate.nis.sdu.dk/information/d12/`.

Materials Property Data Markup Language *See* MATML.

math The FILENAME EXTENSION of MathML (Mathematical Markup Language) documents. For example, "Catalog.math".

Mathematical Markup Language *See* MATHML.

MathML (Mathematical Markup Language) An XML-BASED MARKUP LANGUAGE for describing mathematical notation and for capturing both its structure and content. Details of MathML are available at `http://www.w3.org/Math/`.

MatML (Materials Property Data Markup Language) An XML-BASED MARKUP LANGUAGE for the exchange of information about material and its properties (for example, aluminum alloy data). More details about MatML are available at `http://www.matml.org/`.

maxLength facet In an XML SCHEMA, a FACET that restricts the maximal number of units of length of a SIMPLE TYPE, such as the number of characters or the number of items in a list.

maxOccurs attribute In an XML SCHEMA, a special ATTRIBUTE that is used as an INDICATOR that specifies the maximum number of times the declared ELEMENT can occur. In the example shown in Figure M.3, the "CatalogItem" element can occur in an

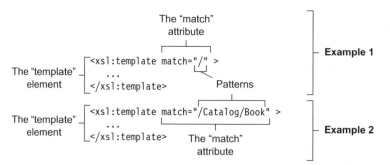

Figure M.2 Examples of XSLT "match" attributes.

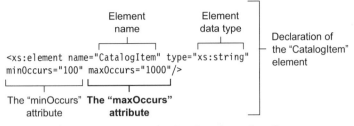

Figure M.3 An example of an "maxOccurs" attribute.

XML DOCUMENT a maximum of 1000 times. *See also* MINOCCURS ATTRIBUTE.

maxOccurs indicator *See* INDICATOR.

MCF (Meta Content Framework Using XML) An XML-based data model for representing a wide range of information (metadata) about content. Details of MCF are available at http://www.textuality.com/sgml-erb/w3c-mcf.html.

MDDL (Market Data Definition Language) An XML-BASED MARKUP LANGUAGE for describing financial instruments, corporate events affecting value and tradability, and market-related information. More details about MDDL can be obtained from http://www.mddl.org/.

MDL (Meaning Definition Language) An XML-BASED MARKUP LANGUAGE that is intended to define what XML documents mean (in terms of a UML class model), and how that meaning is encoded in the nodes of the document. More details of MDL may be obtained from http://www.charteris.com/XMLToolkit/Downloads/MDL206.pdf.

Meaning Generally, the thing or idea that a word, expression, or symbol represents. In XML, the meaning of data is represented using METADATA MARKUP. In the examples shown in Figure M.4, the word "Miss" has two different meanings: (1) the title of a book; (2) the title of a girl. XML uses TAGS containing METADATA to specify the meaning of the words "Miss" and "Title". Note that the "Book" and "Person" tags of the metadata markup define

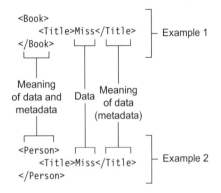

Figure M.4 Marking up meanings in XML.

the meaning of the word "Miss" not directly but by specifying the meaning of the word "Title" that is used as metadata markup. Thus, there is a hierarchy of meanings expressed by different levels of metadata (metadata, meta-metadata, and so forth).

Meaning Definition Language *See* MDL.

Message component In the WSDL COMPONENT MODEL, a component that describes the abstract format of a particular message that a WEB SERVICE sends and receives. The XML representation of the message component is the wsdl:message ELEMENT, as shown in Figure M.5.

Message exchange pattern *See* SOAP MESSAGE.

Message Markup Language *See* MESSAGEML.

93

**The place of the message component
in the WSDL component model**

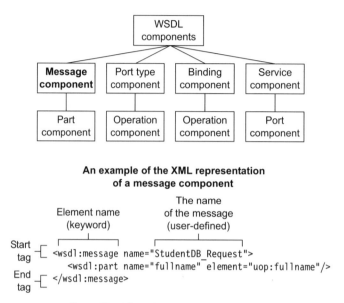

**An example of the XML representation
of a message component**

Figure M.5 The WSDL message component.

MessageML (Message Markup Language) An XML-BASED MARKUP LANGUAGE for sending and processing messages based on the meaning of their content. See http://www.messageml.org/ for more details.

Meta- A word prefix derived from a Greek word that denotes something of a higher or more fundamental nature. Examples from computing include: metafile (a file consisting of other files); METALANGUAGE (a language used to build other languages) and METADATA (data used to describe other data). XML and SGML are metalanguages.

Meta Content Framework Using XML *See* MCF.

Metadata There are several similar definitions of metadata: (1) data about data; (2) information about information; (3) the MEANING or semantics of data; (4) a RESOURCE that provides information about another resource; (5) descriptive information about a WEB RESOURCE. Metadata is a fundamental STRUCTURAL CONSTRUCT of the SEMANTIC WEB. Its development is basically a process of adding new and more advanced levels of metadata to the existing ones. Several technologies are used to implement this development, such as XML, RDF, OWL, DUBLIN CORE and TOPIC MAPS.

XML provides developers with basic-level facilities for adding metadata to XML DATA. In XML, for example, the word "Wood" can be described as a person's last name by adding the appropriate metadata tags, as shown in Figure M.6. Even such simple metadata MARKUP can help a program (for instance, a search engine) to understand the meaning of the word in question and to distinguish a person's last name from timber, firewood or forest.

RDF enables a higher level of metadata. In the example shown in Figure M.6, RDF and Dublin Core syntax are used to represent an RDF STATEMENT that can be read as "John Wood is the creator of

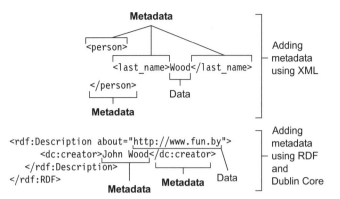

Figure M.6 Adding metadata with XML, RDF, and Dublin Core.

the www.fun.by Web site". *See also* MEANING; METADATA MARKUP.

Metadata Encoding and Transmission Standard *See* METS.

Metadata markup A type of MARKUP that is intended for specifying explicitly the logical structure of a document and the MEANING of the document data, by adding special TAGS containing METADATA. Also called STRUCTURAL MARKUP. *Contrast* PRESENTATIONAL MARKUP.

Meta-information Information about information. A term that is sometimes used to refer to METADATA.

Metalanguage A language (such as XML or SGML) for creating or describing other languages. XML is a metalanguage that allows the creation of markup languages for arbitrary specialized domains and purposes. Note that although it is quite common to use the phrase "a document written in XML", it is, strictly speaking, impossible to write even one single document in XML because XML is not a language. It has no tags for describing any specific content and therefore can be used only as a language-definition tool. It means that one has first to develop a specialized XML-BASED MARKUP LANGUAGE (for example, "MyML")

and only after this to obtain the possibility of creating documents that are written not in XML but in MyML using XML SYNTAX.

MetaLex An XML-based language for the markup of legal documents. More details are available at http://www.metalex.nl/.

Meta-markup language *See* METALANGUAGE.

META tag The special TAG of HTML that is intended to put METADATA into WEB PAGES. It provides META-INFORMATION for search engines about who created the page, what the page is about, and which keywords represent the page's content. See Figure M.7.

METS (Metadata Encoding and Transmission Standard) An XML-based metadata framework for encoding descriptive, administrative and structural metadata for digital library objects. A METS document has four structural components:

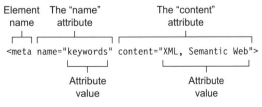

Figure M.7 An example of a META tag.

descriptive metadata, administrative metadata, file inventory, and structural map. For more details, see the information at http://www.loc.gov/standards/mets/.

MFDX (Multi-Family Data Exchange) An XML-BASED MARKUP LANGUAGE for the exchange of apartment data. More details about MFDX may be obtained from http://www.mfdx.com/.

Microarray Gene Expression Markup Language *See* MAGE-ML.

MIME (Multipurpose Internet Mail Extension) A protocol and file format for sending a variety of multimedia data through electronic mail. The particular format of the data is identified by an assigned "MIME type". Five MIME types for XML are specified in RFC 3023 ("XML Media Types"): (1) text/xml; (2) application/xml; (3) text/xml-external-parsed-entity; (4) application/xml-external-parsed-entity; (5) application/xml-dtd. XML Media Types is one of the NON-NORMATIVE REFERENCES of the XML 1.0 RECOMMENDATION. More information is available at http://www.ietf.org/rfc/rfc3023.txt.

minLength facet In an XML SCHEMA, a FACET that restricts the minimal number of units of length of a SIMPLE TYPE, such as the number of characters or the number of items in a list.

minOccurs attribute In an XML SCHEMA, a special ATTRIBUTE that is used as an INDICATOR that specifies the minimum number of times the declared

ELEMENT can occur. In example shown in Figure M.8, the "CatalogItem" element can occur in an XML DOCUMENT a minimum of 100 times. If no minOccurs attribute is specified an element by default can occur a minimum of once. *See also* MAXOCCURS ATTRIBUTE.

minOccurs indicator *See* INDICATOR.

Mixed content In a DTD, a CONTENT MODEL for an ELEMENT that combines both elements and CHARACTER DATA.

MML (Music Markup Language) An XML-BASED MARKUP LANGUAGE for describing music objects and events. More details about MML are available at http://www.musicmarkup.info/.

Mobile SVG Profiles Subsets of SVG designed for use on cell phones (SVG Tiny) and PDAS (SVG Basic). For more information about these, see http://www.w3.org/TR/SVGMobile/.

Model element *See* XFORMS MODEL.

MPML (Multimodal Presentation Markup Language) An XML-BASED MARKUP LANGUAGE that is intended for the description of multimodal presentation using character agents. Details of MPML can be found at http://www.miv.t.u-tokyo.ac.jp/MPML/en/.

MRML (Multimedia Retrieval Markup Language) An XML-based communication protocol that provides standardized access to multimedia

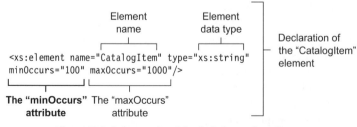

Figure M.8 An example of the "minOccurs" attribute.

retrieval software. More details about MRML are available at http://www.mrml.net/specification/.

MTML (Marine Trading Markup Language) An XML-BASED MARKUP LANGUAGE for electronic exchange of purchasing information in the marine industry. More information about MTML is available at http://www.meca.org.uk/standards.asp?standardsID=6.

Multidirectional link In XLINK, a LINK that has two ARCS that specify the same pair of RESOURCES but switch places as starting and ending resources. *See also* TRAVERSAL.

Multi-Family Data Exchange *See* MFDX.

Multimedia Retrieval Markup Language *See* MRML.

Multimodal Presentation Markup Language *See* MPML.

Multipurpose Internet Mail Extension *See* MIME.

Music Extensible Markup Language *See* MUSICXML.

Music Markup Language *See* MML.

MusicXML (Music Extensible Markup Language) An XML-BASED MARKUP LANGUAGE that is designed for representing sheet music and music notation. For more details, see the information at http://www.musicxml.org/xml.html.

NACS XML Data Interchange *See* NAXML.

Named data type In an XML SCHEMA, a DATA TYPE that has a name and therefore can be reused in the XML schema. *Contrast* ANONYMOUS DATA TYPE.

Named namespace *See* PREFIXED NAMESPACE.

Named type *See* NAMED DATA TYPE.

Namespace An abstract space that is a conceptual collection of related unique names identified by a NAMESPACE NAME. Although a URL is usually used for defining a namespace name, it is not intended to point to a DTD, XML SCHEMA or any other actual file. Generally, a namespace is not an Internet location where physical resources (such as a DTD or an XML schema) reside. This is just a method of creating globally unique names intended to avoid collisions between ELEMENT NAMES that use the same words, phrase or symbol but with different meanings. In the example shown in Figure N.1, the word "Title" is used once as the title of a person ("Sir Arthur Conan Doyle") and again as

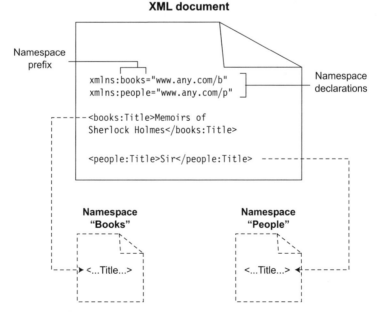

Figure N.1 An example of the use of XML namespaces.

99

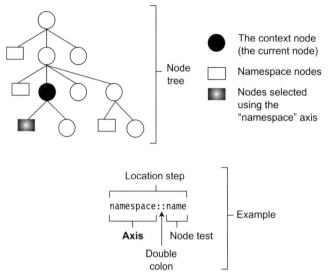

Figure N.2 The "namespace" axis.

the title of one of his books. The name collision is avoided by assigning these two meanings of the word "Title" to two different namespaces ("People" and "Books" respectively). As a result, this word is being used not as a complete element name but just as a LOCAL PART of the two QUALIFIED NAMES "books: Title" and "people: Title". For more details, see http://www.w3.org/TR/REC-xml-names/. *See also* DEFAULT NAMESPACE; NAMESPACE DECLARATION; NAMESPACE PREFIX; PREFIXED NAMESPACE; UNPREFIXED NAMESPACE; XMLNS ATTRIBUTE.

namespace axis In XPATH, an AXIS that selects the NAMESPACE NODES of the CONTEXT NODE. See Figure N.2.

Namespace declaration A method of declaring a NAMESPACE using the reserved XMLNS ATTRIBUTE, as shown in Figure N.3. There are two types of namespace declaration: (1) the declaration of a PREFIXED NAMESPACE, which uses the "xmlns" keyword and a NAMESPACE PREFIX as the ATTRIBUTE NAME of the XMLNS attribute; and (2) the declaration of an UNPREFIXED NAMESPACE (also known as DEFAULT NAMESPACE), which

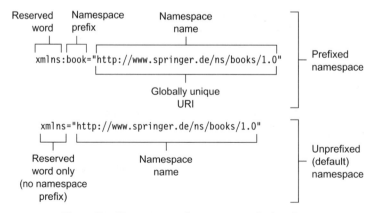

Figure N.3 The anatomy of a namespace declaration.

Figure N.4 The "namespace" information item and its properties.

uses the single "xmlns" keyword and no namespace prefix as the attribute name of the XMLNS attribute.

Namespace Identifier *See* NID.

Namespace information item One of the 11 types of INFORMATION ITEM in the INFORMATION SET. Like all of them, it is an abstract description of a STRUCTURAL CONSTRUCT of an XML DOCUMENT. This description is intended for use in other XML-related specifications, which need to conform to the information set. There is one namespace information item in the information set for each NAMESPACE DECLARATION in the XML document. This information item has two properties, as shown in Figure N.4. For more details, see http://www.w3.org/TR/xml-infoset/.

Namespace name The name of a NAMESPACE in the form of a URI (i.e. a URL or URN) that is (1) unique; (2) persistent (in other words, permanent); and (3) consistent (if numerous namespaces are created). It is common practice, to use URLs (i.e. Web addresses) for defining namespace names because the use a domain name (the address of a specific Web site) can ensure that the names are unique. Notice that a URL used for defining a namespace name is not intended to point to a DTD, XML SCHEMA

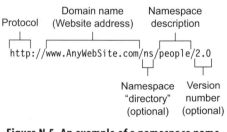

Figure N.5 An example of a namespace name in the form of a URL.

or any other actual file at all. In fact, it is better to use a URL of a "location" that does not exist and therefore will not ever be changed. See Figure N.5. *See also* NAMESPACE DECLARATION; XMLNS ATTRIBUTE.

Namespace node One of seven NODE TYPE of an XPATH DATA MODEL that represents a NAMESPACE.

Namespace prefix A special shortcut that can be declared for a NAMESPACE in order to make it a PREFIXED NAMESPACE. The prefix can then be used as part of a QUALIFIED NAME to indicate that a specific individual ELEMENT belongs to the namespace. A prefix may not begin with the character string "xml" (in any combination of upper and lower cases). Notice that the prefix is an integral part of the qualified name of an element and therefore must be used in both the START TAG and the END TAG. See Figure N.6. *See also* DEFAULT NAMESPACE; NAMESPACE DECLARATION; NAMESPACE NAME; OVERRIDING NAMESPACES; UNPREFIXED NAMESPACE; XMLNS ATTRIBUTE.

Namespace scope The part of an XML DOCUMENT to which a specific NAMESPACE is applied. An UNPREFIXED NAMESPACE declared for the ROOT ELEMENT or any other specific ELEMENT is applied by default to all the document's elements or to all the elements contained in the specified element. A DEFAULT NAMESPACE can be overridden by specifying a PREFIXED NAMESPACE and then using a QUALIFIED NAME for an individual element. *See also* NAMESPACE DECLARATION; OVERRIDING NAMESPACES; XMLNS ATTRIBUTE.

Namespace Specific String *See* NSS.

Namespaces in XML The title of the W3C RECOMMENDATION that specifies the syntax and use of NAMESPACES. This RECOMMENDATION is available at http://www.w3.org/TR/REC-xml-names/.

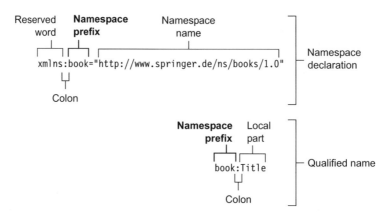

Figure N.6 The use of a namespace prefix in a namespace declaration and a qualified name.

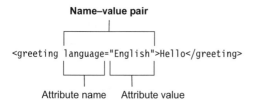

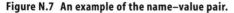

Figure N.7 An example of the name–value pair.

Name–value pair A term used to refer to an ATTRIBUTE in order to put emphasis on its STRUCTURAL CONSTRUCTS. Any ATTRIBUTE is actually a name–value pair that is made up of an ATTRIBUTE NAME, an equals sign and an ATTRIBUTE VALUE, as shown in Figure N.7.

Nano Markup Language *See* NANOML.

NanoML (Nano Markup Language) An XML-BASED MARKUP LANGUAGE for describing and interchanging data about designs of different devices and systems based on nanotechnology. The term "nanotechnology" refers to the manipulation of atoms and molecules to create atomically precise devices. Details of NanoML can be found at http://www.nanotitan.com/.

Natural Language Semantics Markup Language *See* NLSML.

Navigation Markup Language *See* NVML.

NAXML (NACS XML Data Interchange) A set of XML-based data formats for supporting e-business document exchange within the convenience store industry, developed by the National Association of Convenience Stores (NACS). More information about NAXML is available at http://www.naxml.org/.

NCName (Non-Colonized Name) A VALID XML NAME that does not include a colon (:) in it. Since the colon is reserved for connecting a NAMESPACE PREFIX to a LOCAL PART, both of these parts of a QUALIFIED NAME must be NCNames.

Nested A term used to refer to ELEMENTS or other structural constructs of a document that are enclosed one within another. XML ELEMENTS must be nested properly, without overlapping; CSS COMMENTS and XML COMMENTS cannot be nested. *See also* NESTING ELEMENTS; OVERLAPPING ELEMENTS; RUSSIAN DOLL APPROACH.

Nested elements *See* NESTED; NESTING ELEMENTS.

Nesting A term used to describe how XML elements are contained within other elements. *See* NESTING ELEMENTS.

Nesting elements One of general principles underlying the structure of an XML DOCUMENT. The XML elements must be entirely enclosed within

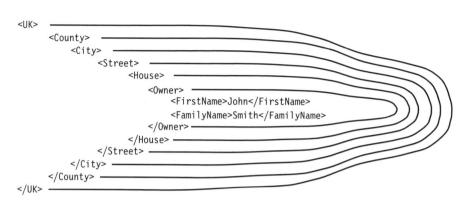

Figure N.8 Nesting XML elements (Russian doll approach).

one another without overlapping, as shown in Figure N.8. Sometimes this principle is also called RUSSIAN DOLL APPROACH.

.NET Framework Microsoft's environment for building, deploying, and running XML-BASED WEB SERVICES and other applications. It consists of three main parts: (1) the common language runtime; (2) The Framework classes; (3) ASP.NET. XML is a key enabling technology for Microsoft .NET. For more details, see the information at http://msdn.microsoft.com/netframework/.

News Industry Text Format *See* NITF.

News Markup Language *See* NEWSML.

NewsML (News Markup Language) An XML-BASED MARKUP LANGUAGE for representing and managing news throughout its life cycle (including creation, interchange and delivery). See http://www.newsml.org/ for more details.

NID (Namespace Identifier) The second part of a URN.

NITF (News Industry Text Format) An XML-BASED MARKUP LANGUAGE that is intended for the delivery of news content in a variety of ways, including print, wireless devices and the Web. More information is available at http://www.nitf.org/.

NLSML (Natural Language Semantics Markup Language) An XML-BASED MARKUP LANGUAGE for representing the meaning of a natural language utterance. It can be used as a standard data interchange format between voice browser components. More details about NLSML can be obtained from http://www.w3.org/TR/nl-spec/.

Node In XPATH, the main STRUCTURAL CONSTRUCT of a NODE TREE that represent a STRUCTURAL CONSTRUCT of an XML DOCUMENT, such as an ELEMENT or ATTRIBUTE. *See also* NODE TYPE; XPATH DATA MODEL.

Node set In XPATH, an unordered collection of NODES (without duplicates) selected by a LOCATION PATH. *See also* NODE TREE.

Node test In XPATH, the second part of the LOCATION STEP. It filters the NODES selected by the AXIS (which is the first part of a LOCATION STEP) on the basis of their NODE TYPES or node name EXPANDED NAMES. In the example shown in Figure N.9, the node test selects all "book" ELEMENTS that are children of the CONTEXT NODE.

Node tree In XPATH, a NODE SET represented in the form of an abstract HIERARCHICAL TREE STRUCTURE, as shown in Figure N.10. The node tree has one and only one ROOT NODE. *See also* XPATH DATA MODEL.

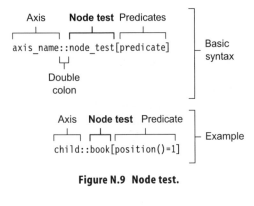

Figure N.9 Node test.

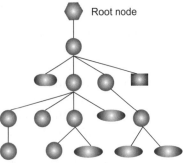

Figure N.10 An example of a node tree.

Node type A STRUCTURAL CONSTRUCT of the XPATH DATA MODEL. There are seven types of NODE: (1) ROOT NODES; (2) ELEMENT NODES; (3) TEXT NODES; (5) ATTRIBUTE NODES; (6) NAMESPACE NODES; (7) PROCESSING INSTRUCTION NODES; (7) COMMENT NODES.

Node value In XPATH, a value assigned to an ELEMENT NODE or ATTRIBUTE NODE. The value of an ELEMENT NODE is the concatenation of all TEXT NODE DESCENDANTS with the exception of ATTRIBUTE VALUES, as shown in Figure N.11.

Nodeset *See* NODE SET.

Non-Colonized Name *See* NCNAME.

Non-linear way of thinking *See* HIERARCHICAL WAY OF THINKING.

Non-normative References References to other standards and specifications in the XML 1.0 RECOMMENDATION that are either used to specify some ATTRIBUTE VALUES in XML, or related to the design of XML. The major Non-normative References include: (1) UTF-8; (2) UTF-16; (3) URI; (4) URL; (5) URN; (6) MIME types for XML; (7) SGML; (8) Web SGML; (9) LANGUAGE CODES; (10) COUNTRY CODES; (11) HYTIME. More details are available at http://www.w3.org/TR/REC-xml/. *Contrast* NORMATIVE REFERENCES.

Non-text data In XML DOCUMENTS, any data that are not in a PLAIN TEXT format, such as images, sound and other binary data. An XML document cannot embed these data within the text and therefore uses references to external files that contain non-text data.

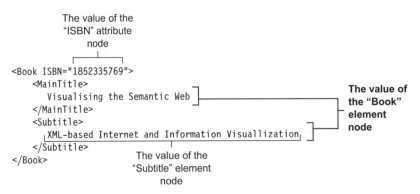

Figure N.11 Examples of node values.

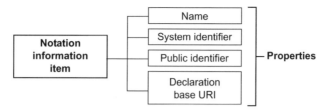

Figure N.12 The notation information item and its properties.

Non-validating parser An XML PARSER that does not check an XML document against any DTD or XML SCHEMA. It checks only whether the document is well formed. *See also* VALIDATING PARSER; VALID XML DOCUMENT; WELL-FORMED XML DOCUMENT.

Non-well-formed XML document An XML DOCUMENT that is not a WELL-FORMED XML DOCUMENT.

Non-XML syntax Any SYNTAX other than XML SYNTAX used by a member of the XML FAMILY OF TECHNOLOGIES, such as CSS, XPATH, XPOINTER and XQUERY. *See also* NON-XML-BASED LANGUAGES.

Non-XML-based languages The members of the XML FAMILY OF TECHNOLOGIES that do not use the XML SYNTAX, such as CSS, XPATH, XPOINTER and XQUERY. *See also* NON-XML SYNTAX.

Normative References References to non-W3C standards and specifications in the XML 1.0 RECOMMENDATION that are crucial for understanding both the RECOMMENDATION and its implementation. The Normative References include: (1) UCS (2) UNICODE; (5) IETF LANGUAGE TAGS; (6) IANA CHARACTER SET NAMES. For more details, see http://www.w3.org/TR/REC-xml/. *Contrast* NON-NORMATIVE REFERENCES.

Notation information item One of the 11 types of INFORMATION ITEM in the INFORMATION SET. Like all of them, it is an abstract description of a STRUCTURAL CONSTRUCT of an XML DOCUMENT. This description is intended for use in other XML-related specifications, which need to conform to the information set. There is one notation information item in the information set for each notation declared in the DTD. This information item has four properties, as shown in Figure N.12. For more details, see http://www.w3.org/TR/xml-infoset/.

NOTATION keyword A keyword used in a DTD DECLARATION to declare external NON-TEXT DATA.

Note *See* W3C NOTE.

Nothing class In OWL, a predefined empty CLASS. *See also* THING CLASS.

NSS (Namespace Specific String) The third part of a URN.

NVML (Navigation Markup Language) An XML-BASED MARKUP LANGUAGE for describing navigation information for a variety of mobile devices, such as smart phones, PDAs (Personal Digital Assistants) equipped with GPS (Global Positioning System), and car navigation systems. More details are available at http://www.w3.org/TR/NVML/.

OAGIS (Open Applications Group Integration Specification) A set of XML-based Business Object Documents (BODs) and integration scenarios for horizontal industry provided by the Open Application Group, Inc (OAGI). OAGI is a non-profit consortium that focuses on best practices and process-based XML content for e-business and application integration. For more details, see http://www.openapplications.org/.

OASIS (Organization for the Advancement of Structured Information Standards) A non-profit, international consortium that is devoted to accelerating the adoption of product-independent formats based upon public standards, including XML, SGML and HTML. OASIS is intended to encourage interoperability between vertical and horizontal industries that use XML. It hosts the XML INDUSTRY PORTAL (http://www.xml.org/) that is a repository for an increasing number of XML SPECIFICATIONS, SCHEMAS and VOCABULARIES. More details of OASIS may be obtained from http://www.oasis-open.org/.

OBI (Open Buying on the Internet) An XML-based standard for business-to-business purchasing on the Internet, focused especially on high-volume, low-cost-per-item transactions. It is provided by the OBI Consortium – a non-profit organization dedicated to developing standards for business-to-business Internet commerce. For more details, see http://www.openbuy.org/.

Object Management Group *See* OMG.

Object property A type of OWL property that is used to relate a RESOURCE to another resource. An object property can be defined using the owl:ObjectProperty ELEMENT, as shown in Figure O.1. *Contrast* DATATYPE PROPERTY. *See also* OWL VOCABULARY.

Object resource In RDF and RDF SCHEMA, a RESOURCE that describes another resource (called a SUBJECT RESOURCE) using a PROPERTY (which specifies the relationship between these two resources). In the example shown in Figure O.2, the object resource is the wood.com/~john WEB SITE, which identifies a person (probably called "John") who is the creator of the index.html WEB PAGE. Note that in the name of the dc:Creator property (which is used to specify the relationship between the resources), the "dc" prefix is the DUBLIN CORE NAMESPACE prefix. A subject resource, an object resource and a property make up a TRIPLE.

Occurrence indicator *See* INDICATOR.

OCS (Open Content Syndication) An XML-BASED MARKUP LANGUAGE that enables channel listings to be constructed for use by portal Web sites and other applications. It allows public channels of a Web site to be easily shared with portals from other organizations. More details about OCS are available at http://internetalchemy.org/ocs/.

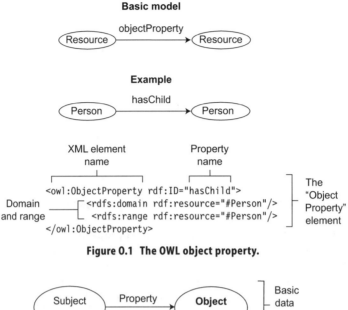

Basic model

Example

Figure 0.1 The OWL object property.

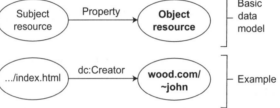

Figure 0.2 The object resource.

ODRL (Open Digital Rights Language) An XML-BASED MARKUP LANGUAGE for rights management expressions related to digital assets, including permissions, constraints, obligations, conditions, and offers and agreements with rights holders. More details are available at http://www.w3.org/TR/odrl/ and http://odrl.net/.

odrXML (Online Dispute Resolution XML) An XML-BASED MARKUP LANGUAGE for the interchange of ODR (Online Dispute Resolution) cases between ODR systems. For more details, see http://econfidence.jrc.it/default/page.gx?_app.page=entity.html&_app.action=entity&_entity.object=EC_FORUM00000000000 00118C&_entity.name=odr001-2001-09-07.html.

OFX (Open Financial Exchange) An XML-based specification for exchanging financial data between institutions, business and consumers via the Internet. More information is available at http://www.ofx.net/.

OIL (Ontology Inference Layer) A standard for specifying and exchanging ONTOLOGIES. OIL is compatible with RDF SCHEMAS and presents a layered approach to an ontology language with the formal semantics and reasoning services provided by description logics. OIL has been merged with DAML to form DAML+OIL. More information about OIL is available at http://www.ontoknowledge.org/oil/.

OMG (Object Management Group) An open membership, not-for-profit consortium that is intended to create a component-based software marketplace by accelerating the introduction of standardized object software. It produces and maintains computer industry specifications for several object-oriented systems and languages. See http://www.omg.org/ for more details.

Online Dispute Resolution XML *See* ODRXML.

Ontology 1. An explicit representation of the MEANING of terms in a VOCABULARY, and their interrelationships. In an ontology definition language (such as OWL or RDF), an ontology is the collection of STATEMENTS or other semantic definitions for a DOMAIN. Ontologies are one of the STRUCTURAL CONSTRUCTS of the SEMANTIC WEB ARCHITECTURE. Several SEMANTIC WEB TECHNOLOGIES can be used for building ontologies with different levels of expressiveness. Note that originally the term "ontology" was used in philosophy to refer to the study of the kinds of entities in the world and how they are related.

2. An ONTOLOGY DOCUMENT. For examples of ontologies, see the DAML Ontology Library at http://www.daml.org/ontologies/.

Ontology document A Web document that contains an ontology, such as an OWL ONTOLOGY. *See also* OWL DOCUMENT; OWL VOCABULARY.

Ontology element An XML ELEMENT of the Web Ontology Language (OWL) that is intended to contain METADATA for an OWL DOCUMENT, and that is used as the "ontology header". It is actually used to indicate that a document is an ONTOLOGY DOCUMENT. Figure O.3 shows some CHILDREN of the owl:Ontology ELEMENT: (1) the rdfs:comment element, which can be used to annotate an ONTOLOGY (*see also* COMMENT PROPERTY); (2) the

owl:priorVersion element, which contains information about the previous version of an ontology; (3) the rdfs:label element, which is used to provide a human-readable version of the name of an ontology (*see also* LABEL PROPERTY). *See also* OWL VOCABULARY.

Ontology header *See* ONTOLOGY ELEMENT.

Ontology Inference Layer *See* OIL.

Ontology Interchange Language *See* OIL.

Open Applications Group Integration Specification *See* OAGIS.

Open Buying on the Internet *See* OBI.

Open Content Syndication *See* OCS.

Open Digital Rights Language *See* ODRL.

Open Financial Exchange *See* OFX.

Opening angle bracket *See* ANGLE BRACKETS.

Opening tag *See* START TAG.

OpenMath An XML-BASED MARKUP LANGUAGE for describing and communicating mathematical objects with their semantics. OpenMath deals with the meaning (or content) of mathematical objects, while MATHML mostly focuses on their presentation. For more details, see the information at http://www.openmath.org/.

Open Scriptural Information Standard *See* OSIS.

```
Start tag   ┤<owl:Ontology rdf:about="">
  Comment   ──┤<rdfs:comment>An example OWL ontology</rdfs:comment>
                ┌ <owl:priorVersion
Prior version ──┤
                └ rdf:resource="http://www.springer.de/book-303.owl"/>
    Label   ──┤<rdfs:label>Book Ontology</rdfs:label>
  End tag   ┤</owl:Ontology>
```

Figure O.3 An example of an OWL ontology element.

Open Software Description Format *See* OSD.

Open source software *See* OSS.

Open standard *See* OSS.

Open tag *See* START TAG.

OPML (Outline Processor Markup Language)
An XML-BASED MARKUP LANGUAGE that allows exchange of outline-structured information between applications running on different operating systems and environments. More details of OPML may be obtained from http://www.opml.org/.

Optional attribute In an XML SCHEMA, an ATTRIBUTE that is explicitly specified as optional using the optional value of the USE ATTRIBUTE. Note that by default all attributes are optional. See Figure O.4. *See also* PROHIBITED ATTRIBUTE; REQUIRED ATTRIBUTE.

Order indicator *See* INDICATOR.

Organization for the Advancement of Structured Information Standards *See* OASIS.

OSD (Open Software Description Format) An XML-BASED MARKUP LANGUAGE for describing software packages and their interdependencies for heterogeneous clients. More details about OSD can be obtained from http://www.w3.org/TR/NOTE-OSD.html/.

OSIS (Open Scriptural Information Standard)
An XML-BASED MARKUP LANGUAGE for describing the text of the Bible. Details of OSIS can be found at http://www.bibletechnologies.net/.

OSS (Open source software) Software whose source code is freely distributed.

Outbound arc In XLINK, an ARC that has a LOCAL STARTING RESOURCE and a REMOTE ENDING RESOURCE. Note that LINKS of this type are similar to HTML links. *Compare* INBOUND ARC; THIRD-PARTY ARC.

Outbound link In XLINK, a LINK that is based on an OUTBOUND ARC.

Outline Processor Markup Language *See* OPML.

Overlapping elements In XML and XHTML, elements that are not NESTED correctly and do not follow the RUSSIAN DOLL APPROACH. XML and XHTML documents that contain one or more overlapping elements are not WELL FORMED. Note that in HTML overlapping is allowed, as shown in Figure O.5. *See also* NESTING ELEMENTS.

Overriding namespaces A method of assigning a NAMESPACE, other than the DEFAULT NAMESPACE, to a specified ELEMENT. To achieve this, a PREFIXED NAMESPACE has to be declared and then a QUALIFIED NAME for an individual element should be used, as shown in Figure O.6. *See also* NAMESPACE; NAMESPACE DECLARATION; NAMESPACE NAME; UNPREFIXED NAMESPACE.

Overriding properties *See* INHERITING AND OVERRIDING PROPERTIES.

OWL (Web Ontology Language) An XML-BASED MARKUP LANGUAGE for defining and instantiating Web ONTOLOGIES to enable machine-processable SEMANTICS. It can be used to explicitly represent the meaning of terms in a VOCABULARY and the relationships of

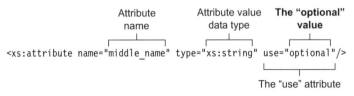

Figure O.4 The XML Schema declaration of an optional attribute.

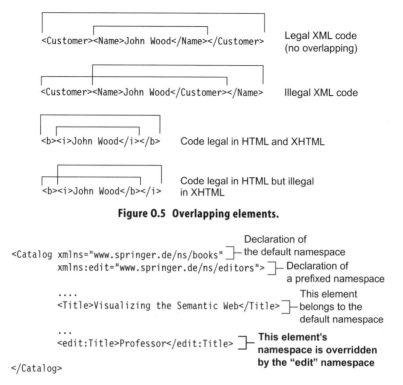

Figure 0.5 Overlapping elements.

Figure 0.6 Overriding a default namespace.

those terms. OWL is divided into three increasingly expressive OWL SUBLANGUAGES: (1) OWL Lite; (2) OWL DL; and (3) OWL Full.

OWL relationships to other XML technologies are shown in Figure 0.7. OWL is a revision of the DAML+OIL Web ontology language. It is based on XML, RDF and RDF SCHEMAS but goes beyond these languages by providing more facilities for expressing the semantics of Web data. OWL extends RDF Schemas with a richer OWL VOCABULARY that provides advanced inferencing capabilities. At present, OWL is one of the main SEMANTIC WEB TECHNOLOGIES. More details of OWL, including OWL-related W3C SPECIFICATIONS are available at http://www.w3.org/2001/sw/WebOnt/. *See also* ONTOLOGY ELEMENT; OWL DOCUMENT; OWL NAMESPACE; OWL VOCABULARY.

owl:AllDifferent element *See* ALL DIFFERENT STATEMENT.

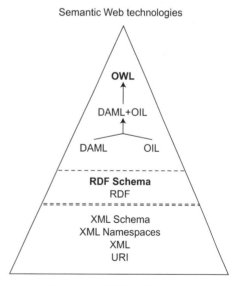

Figure 0.7 The genesis of OWL and its relationships to other XML technologies.

owl:DatatypeProperty element *See* DATATYPE PROPERTY.

owl:differentFrom element *See* DIFFERENT FROM STATEMENT.

owl:disjointWith element *See* DISJOINT CLASSES.

owl:equivalentClass element *See* EQUIVALENT CLASS.

owl:FunctionalProperty element *See* FUNCTIONAL PROPERTY.

owl:InverseFunctionalProperty element *See* INVERSE FUNCTIONAL PROPERTY.

owl:inverseOf element *See* INVERSE PROPERTY.

owl:Nothing class *See* NOTHING CLASS.

owl:ObjectProperty element *See* OBJECT PROPERTY.

owl:Ontology element *See* ONTOLOGY ELEMENT.

owl:priorVersion element *See* ONTOLOGY ELEMENT.

owl:sameAs element *See* SAME AS STATEMENT.

owl:SymmetricProperty element *See* SYMMETRIC PROPERTY.

owl:Thing class *See* THING CLASS.

owl:TransitiveProperty element *See* TRANSITIVE PROPERTY.

OWL All Different statement *See* ALL DIFFERENT STATEMENT.

OWL class class *See* CLASS CLASS.

OWL Datatype Property *See* DATATYPE PROPERTY.

OWL Different From statement *See* DIFFERENT FROM STATEMENT.

OWL disjoint classes *See* DISJOINT CLASSES.

OWL DL (Web Ontology Language Description Logics) An OWL SUBLANGUAGE.

OWL document An XML DOCUMENT written in OWL that describes an OWL ONTOLOGY. An OWL document has the structure shown in Figure O.8. Like any XML document, it begins with an optional XML DECLARATION. An RDF ELEMENT serves as the

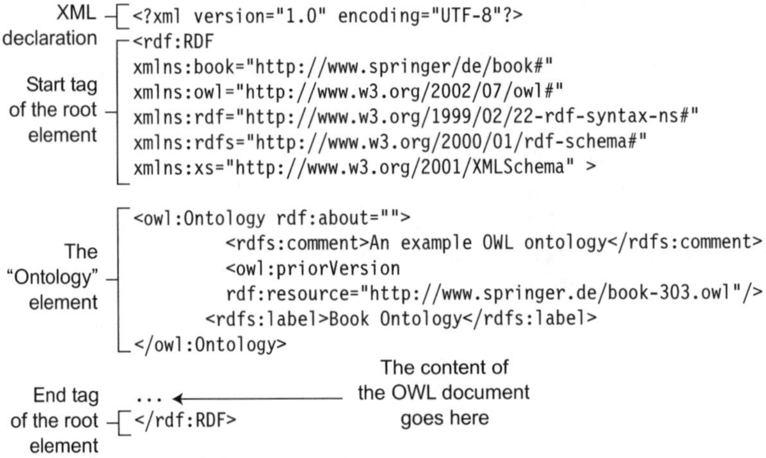

```
XML ─┌ <?xml version="1.0" encoding="UTF-8"?>
declaration  ┌ <rdf:RDF
                xmlns:book="http://www.springer/de/book#"
Start tag     xmlns:owl="http://www.w3.org/2002/07/owl#"
of the root ─  xmlns:rdf="http://www.w3.org/1999/02/22-rdf-syntax-ns#"
element       xmlns:rdfs="http://www.w3.org/2000/01/rdf-schema#"
              xmlns:xs="http://www.w3.org/2001/XMLSchema" >

            ┌ <owl:Ontology rdf:about="">
The              <rdfs:comment>An example OWL ontology</rdfs:comment>
"Ontology" ─     <owl:priorVersion
element          rdf:resource="http://www.springer.de/book-303.owl"/>
               <rdfs:label>Book Ontology</rdfs:label>
            └ </owl:Ontology>
                                        The content of
End tag    ...  ◄────────────── the OWL document
of the root ─┌ </rdf:RDF>               goes here
element
```

Figure O.8 The structure of an OWL document.

ROOT ELEMENT of every OWL document. The first CHILD of the RDF element is a special ONTOLOGY ELEMENT that indicates that the document is an ONTOLOGY DOCUMENT. *See also* OWL NAMESPACE; OWL VOCABULARY.

OWL Equivalent Class *See* EQUIVALENT CLASS.

OWL Full (Web Ontology Language Full) An OWL SUBLANGUAGE.

OWL Functional Property *See* FUNCTIONAL PROPERTY.

OWL Individual *See* INDIVIDUAL.

OWL Inverse Functional Property *See* INVERSE FUNCTIONAL PROPERTY.

OWL Inverse Property *See* INVERSE PROPERTY.

OWL Lite (Web Ontology Language Light) An OWL SUBLANGUAGE.

OWL namespace The NAMESPACE of the OWL language that is declared using a NAMESPACE

DECLARATION. The NAMESPACE PREFIX is "owl" by convention. The OWL namespace declaration is an ATTRIBUTE of the RDF ELEMENT that is the ROOT ELEMENT of every OWL DOCUMENT. The ATTRIBUTE NAME is "xmlns:owl". Other namespaces, used in an OWL ONTOLOGY, can also be declared within the START TAG of the RDF element, primary RDF NAMESPACE, RDF SCHEMA NAMESPACE and DEFAULT NAMESPACE. See Figure O.9. *See also* OWL VOCABULARY.

OWL Nothing class *See* NOTHING CLASS.

OWL Object Property *See* OBJECT PROPERTY.

OWL ontology An ONTOLOGY expressed in OWL. It includes a description of classes, properties and their instances and interrelationships. *See also* ONTOLOGY DOCUMENT; OWL DOCUMENT; OWL VOCABULARY.

OWL ontology header *See* ONTOLOGY ELEMENT.

OWL sublanguage One of the three increasingly expressive languages into which OWL is divided: (1) "OWL Lite", which supports only simple

The start tag of the "rdf:RDF" element
(the root element of every OWL document)

```
                        <rdf:RDF
Default
namespace  ------>   xmlns    ="http://www.springer/de/book#"
OWL namespace ----> xmlns:owl="http://www.w3.org/2002/07/owl#"
RDF namespace -----> xmlns:rdf="http://www.w3.org/1999/02/22-rdf-syntax-ns#"
RDFS namespace ----> xmlns:rdfs="http://www.w3.org/2000/01/rdf-schema#"
XML schema  ------> xmlns:xs="http://www.w3.org/2001/XMLSchema" >
namespace
```

Figure O.9 Declaring namespaces in an OWL document.

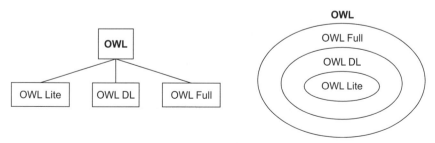

Figure O.10 Three sublanguages of OWL and their relationships.

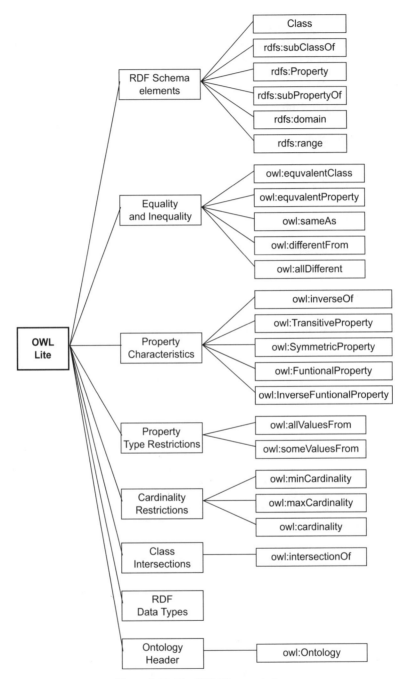

Figure 0.11 The OWL Lite vocabulary.

constraints and, because of this, allows users to build basic ONTOLOGIES quickly and easily; (2) "OWL DL", which includes all OWL constructs, though with several restrictions, and allows users to create more advanced ontologies ("DL" stands for "Description Logics"); and (3) "OWL Full", which has maximum expressiveness for building Web ontologies, but is rather complicated. Figure O.10 shows the relationships between these three sublanguages of OWL. *See also* OWL VOCABULARY.

OWL Symmetric Property *See* SYMMETRIC PROPERTY.

OWL Thing class *See* THING CLASS.

OWL Transitive Property *See* TRANSITIVE PROPERTY.

OWL version A term that is sometimes used to refer to an OWL SUBLANGUAGE.

OWL vocabulary The XML-based VOCABULARY of OWL that extends an RDF SCHEMA and hence enables developers to build much more sophisticated ONTOLOGIES for the Web. The OWL vocabulary is a set of XML ELEMENTS. A hierarchical tree representation of the OWL LITE vocabulary is shown in Figure O.11. *See also* ALL DIFFERENT STATEMENT; CLASS; CLASS CLASS; DIFFERENT FROM STATEMENT; DOMAIN PROPERTY; EQUIVALENT CLASS; FUNCTIONAL PROPERTY; INVERSE FUNCTIONAL PROPERTY; INVERSE PROPERTY; ONTOLOGY ELEMENT; RANGE PROPERTY; SAME AS STATEMENT; SYMMETRIC PROPERTY; TRANSITIVE PROPERTY.

P

P&C XML (Property & Casualty Extensible Markup Language) An XML-BASED MARKUP LANGUAGE for exchanging data between producers, insurers, rating bureaus, service providers etc. More information is available at http://www.acord.org/Standards/propertyxml.aspx.

P3P (Platform for Privacy Preferences) An XML/RDF-based data format and a protocol that enables WEB SITES to express their privacy practices in a standard way that can be retrieved automatically. It provides a standard XML data format (known as a "P3P policy") for a Web site to encode its data collection practices in machine-readable form. Details of P3P can be found at http://www.w3.org/TR/P3P/.

P3P policy *See* P3P.

Parameter entity An ENTITY that is exclusively used within a DTD. Parameter entities are always PARSED ENTITIES. *Contrast* GENERAL ENTITY.

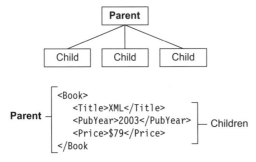

Figure P.1 Parent.

Parent An ELEMENT, a NODE or another STRUCTURAL CONSTRUCT of a HIERARCHICAL TREE STRUCTURE that includes one or more sub-elements, sub-nodes, or other sub-constructs (called CHILDREN). The concept of parent is based on the PARENT–CHILD METAPHOR. See Figure P.1.

parent axis In XPATH, an AXIS that selects the PARENT of the CONTEXT NODE. See Figure P.2.

Parent–child *See* PARENT–CHILD METAPHOR.

Parent–child metaphor A metaphor that is often used to express vertical relationships in a HIERARCHICAL TREE STRUCTURE of ELEMENTS, NODES and the

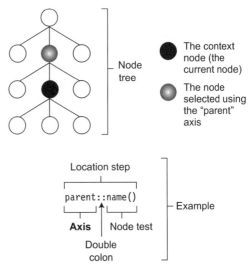

Figure P.2 The "parent" axis.

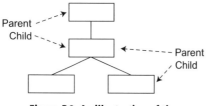

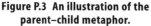

Figure P.3 An illustration of the parent–child metaphor.

like. Note that, like most other metaphorical expressions, this metaphor does not imply a perfect analogy between a genealogical tree and a hierarchical tree structure of an XML DOCUMENT or a DATA MODEL. For example, every human being has two parents, but every CHILD in a hierarchical tree structure has one and only one PARENT. See Figure P.3.

Parent element An ELEMENT that has one or more elements nested within it. Elements nested within a parent element are called CHILD ELEMENTS. *See* NESTING ELEMENTS.

parentref attribute *See* FRAGMENT CONTEXT SPECIFICATION.

Parliamentary Language Markup Language *See* PARLML.

ParlML (Parliamentary Language Markup Language) An XML-BASED MARKUP LANGUAGE for describing parliamentary texts and information. More information about ParlML is available at http://www.europarl.eu.int/docman/ParlML/.

Parsed character data *See* PCDATA.

Parsed entity An ENTITY that is analyzed by an XML PARSER. *Contrast* UNPARSED ENTITY. *See also* INTERNAL GENERAL ENTITY.

Parser *See* XML PARSER.

Parser implementation A term that is sometimes used to refer to one of two possible

implementations of an XML PARSER as (1) EVENT-DRIVEN PARSER or (2) TREE-BASED PARSER.

Part component In the WSDL COMPONENT MODEL, a component that describes a portion of a particular message that a WEB SERVICE sends and receives. The part component is a subcomponent of the MESSAGE COMPONENT. The XML representation of the part component is the wsdl:part ELEMENT that is a CHILD of the wsdl:message element. See Figure P.4.

Participating resource In XLINK, any RESOURCE that is part of a LINK. Although all RESOURCES can potentially be part of a link, a resource becomes a participating resource only when a LOCATOR is used to include it as part of a link.

Path expression *See* EXPRESSION.

Pattern A term that is often used to refer to the ATTRIBUTE VALUE of the MATCH ATTRIBUTE.

pattern facet In an XML SCHEMA, a FACET that restricts a SIMPLE TYPE in terms of matching the pattern of a regular expression, such as a zip code or telephone area code.

PCDATA (Parsed character data) 1. In an XML DOCUMENT, CHARACTER DATA that are intended to be parsed by an XML PARSER. They may also include CHARACTER REFERENCES that will be expanded by a VALIDATING PARSER.
2. Generally, any part of an XML document that will be parsed by an XML parser. Any TAGS inside the part will be treated as MARKUP, in contrast, for example, to the text of a CDATA SECTION, which will not be parsed by a parser.

PDA (Personal Digital Assistant) A handheld computing device with a small screen used to track personal data such as calendars, contacts and email.

PDML (Product Data Markup Language) An XML-BASED MARKUP LANGUAGE for support the

**The place of the part component
in the WSDL component model**

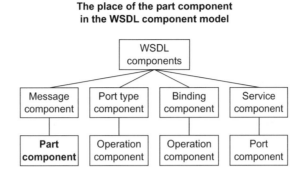

**An example of the XML representation
of a part component**

```
The       <wsdl:message name="StudentDB_Request">
"wsdl:part" ⌐ <wsdl:part name="fullname" element="uop:fullname"/>
element   </wsdl:message>
                              The value
                            of the "name"
                              attribute
```

Figure P.4 The WSDL part component.

interchange of product information among commercial or governmental systems. More details about PDML can be obtained from http://www.pdit.com/pdml/pdmlintro.html.

PDX (Product Definition Exchange) An XML-BASED MARKUP LANGUAGE for describing and communicating product content information between original equipment manufacturers (OEM), electronic manufacturing service (EMS) providers, and component suppliers. Details of PDX can be found at http://www.pdxstandard.org/pdx/.

PE An acronym for PARAMETER ENTITY.

Persistent Uniform Resource Locator See PURL.

Personal Digital Assistant See PDA.

Personal external DTD A term sometimes used to refer to an EXTERNAL DTD that is associated with an XML DOCUMENT using a DOCTYPE DECLARATION with the SYSTEM keyword. This term is intended to emphasize that this DTD is not a standardized,

corporate one (like the PUBLIC keyword – see DOCTYPE DECLARATION) but a "personal" DTD that may be written by everyone.

Personalized Print Markup Language See PPML.

Petri Net Markup Language See PNML.

Petroleum Extensible Markup Language See PETROXML.

PetroXML (Petroleum Extensible Markup Language) An XML-BASED MARKUP LANGUAGE that enable data interchange between the disparate accounting and EDI systems of petroleum vendors and other oil and gas industry companies. Details of PetroXML can be found at http://www.petroxml.org/.

PGML (Precision Graphics Markup Language) An XML-BASED MARKUP LANGUAGE for describing 2D scalable graphics that is suitable for both precision graphics created by graphics artists and simple vector graphics produced by casual users.

119

Details of PGML are available at `http://www.w3.org/TR/1998/NOTE-PGML`.

Physical Markup Language *See* PML.

PI An acronym for PROCESSING INSTRUCTION.

PICS (Platform for Internet Content Selection)
A system for associating METADATA (PICS "labels") with Web content that provides a mechanism that enables independent groups to develop metadata vocabularies without naming conflict. Originally, PICS was designed to help parents and teachers control what children access on the Internet, but now it is also used as a platform on which other rating services and filtering software can be built. More details about PICS are available at `http://www.w3.org/PICS/`.

Plain text A document format that contains nothing but text. This means that it includes no invisible formatting information such as font size or bold style. All XML DOCUMENTS are in plain text format and can be opened and edited using a simple text editor, such as Microsoft Notepad.

Plain text format *See* PLAIN TEXT.

Platform for Internet Content Selection *See* PICS.

Platform for Privacy Preferences *See* P3P.

PML (Physical Markup Language) An XML-BASED MARKUP LANGUAGE for describing complex physical objects, as well as industrial and commercial processes. Details of PML can be found at `http://web.mit.edu/mecheng/pml/`.

PMML (Predictive Model Markup Language)
An XML-BASED MARKUP LANGUAGE for describing statistical and data mining models. More details of PMML may be obtained from `http://www.dmg.org/`.

PMXML (Project Management XML Schema)
An XML-BASED MARKUP LANGUAGE for describing project data (such as project status and resource assignments) and for exchanging information between project management tools. More details are available at `http://www.pacificedge.com/xml/`.

PNML (Petri Net Markup Language) An XML-based standardized interchange format for Petri nets. (Petri nets are formal graphical notations for modeling complex systems). Details of PNML can be found at `http://www.informatik.hu-berlin.de/top/pnml/`.

Point Of Interest Exchange Language *See* POIX.

POIX (Point Of Interest Exchange Language)
An XML-BASED MARKUP LANGUAGE for describing and exchanging location-related information over the Internet. It can be used by location-related service providers and mobile device and also server software developers. More information is available at `http://www.w3.org/TR/poix/`.

Portable Site Information *See* PSI.

Port component In the WSDL COMPONENT MODEL, a component that describes a target address at which a given service is available. A collection of ports is a service (*see* SERVICE COMPONENT). The XML representation of the port component is the `wsdl:port` ELEMENT, as shown in Figure P.5.

Port type component In the WSDL COMPONENT MODEL, a component that describes a set of messages that a WEB SERVICE sends and receives. The XML representation of the message component is the `wsdl:port` ELEMENT that is used to group related input and output messages into operations. Essentially, a port type is a set of operations. See Figure P.6.

Port type operation component In the WSDL COMPONENT MODEL, a component that describes an operation that a given PORT TYPE COMPONENT

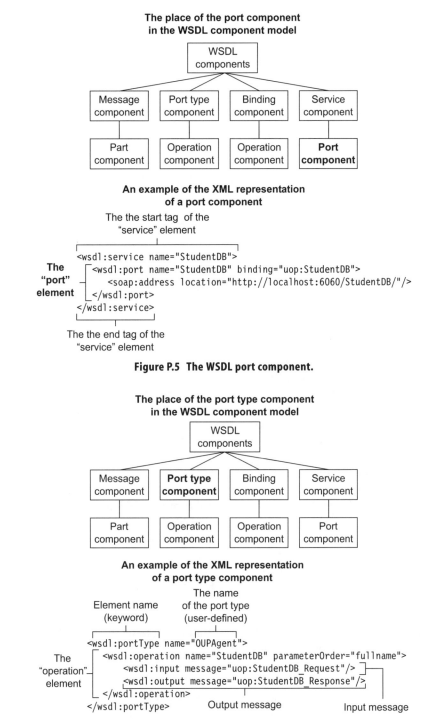

**The place of the port component
in the WSDL component model**

**An example of the XML representation
of a port component**

Figure P.5 The WSDL port component.

**The place of the port type component
in the WSDL component model**

**An example of the XML representation
of a port type component**

Figure P.6 The WSDL port type component.

121

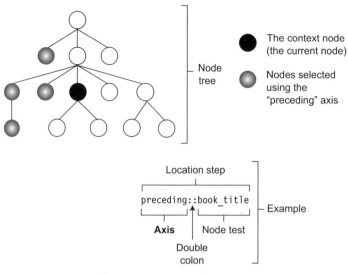

The context node
(the current node)

Nodes selected
using the
"preceding" axis

Node
tree

Location step

preceding::book_title

Axis | Node test

Double
colon

Example

Figure P.7 The "preceding" axis.

supports. An operation is a set of input and output messages. The XML representation of the port type operation component is the `wsdl:operation` ELEMENT that is used to group related input and output messages. For more details, see PORT TYPE COMPONENT and Figure P.6.

PPML (Personalized Print Markup Language)
An XML-BASED MARKUP LANGUAGE for describing personalized print applications with reusable content. See `http://www.ppml.info/` for more details.

PR (Proposed Recommendations) *See* W3C PROPOSED RECOMMENDATION.

Pragmatics In linguistics, the study of how words and phrases in a language are chosen and used with special meanings in particular situations. *Compare* SEMANTICS; SYNTAX.

preceding axis In XPATH, an AXIS that selects all NODES that are before the CONTEXT NODE. See Figure P.7.

preceding-sibling axis In XPATH, an AXIS that selects sibling NODES of the CONTEXT NODE that are before the context node. See Figure P.8.

Precision Graphics Markup Language *See* PGML.

Predefined internal entity *See* PREDEFINED INTERNAL ENTITY.

Predefined XML entity One of the five XML ENTITYIES that are used for an alternative representation of five corresponding SPECIAL SYMBOLS in an XML DOCUMENT. They are also sometimes called "predefined internal entities". See SPECIAL SYMBOLS for more details.

Predicate In XPATH, the third (optional) part of a LOCATION STEP that is used to refine or filter the NODE SET selected by the first two parts (the AXIS and the NODE TEST). A predicate is enclosed within a pair of square brackets ("[ ]"). In the example shown in Figure P.9, the predicate is used to select the *first* "book" ELEMENT that is a CHILD of the current node.

Predictive Model Markup Language *See* PMML.

Prefix *See* NAMESPACE PREFIX.

Prefixed name A term sometimes used to refer to a QUALIFIED NAME.

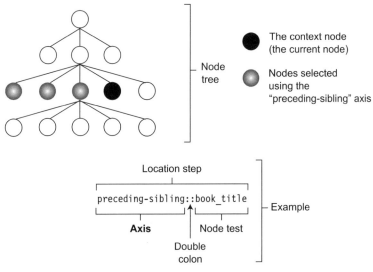

Node tree

The context node
(the current node)

Nodes selected
using the
"preceding-sibling" axis

Location step

```
preceding-sibling::book_title
```

Example

Axis Node test

Double
colon

Figure P.8 The "preceding-sibling" axis.

Axis Node test **Predicates**

```
axis_name::node_test[predicate]
```

Double
colon **Square brackets**

Basic
syntax

Axis Node test **Predicate**

```
child::book[position()=1]
```

Square brackets

Example

Figure P.9 The predicate.

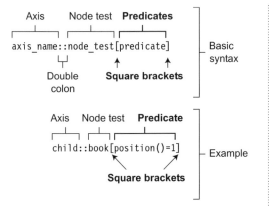

Prefixed namespace A NAMESPACE that is declared using a NAMESPACE PREFIX. This allows applying this namespace to any individual elements within the NAMESPACE SCOPE. See Figure P.10. *Contrast* UNPREFIXED NAMESPACE. *See also* NAMESPACE DECLARATION; NAMESPACE NAME; OVERRIDING NAMESPACES; XMLNS ATTRIBUTE.

Presentational markup A term that sometimes refers to MARKUP that defines the visual formatting of the text such as font size or color. HTML is a well known example of presentational markup. See Figure P.11. *Contrast* STRUCTURAL MARKUP.

Reserved
word **Namespace
prefix** Namespace
name

```
xmlns:book="http://www.springer.de/ns/books/1.0"
```

**Prefixed
namespace**

```
xmlns="http://www.springer.de/ns/books/1.0"
```

Reserved
word only
(no namespace
prefix) Namespace
name

Unprefixed
namespace

Figure P.10 A comparison of a prefixed namespace with an unprefixed namespace.

123

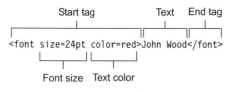

Figure P.11 An example of presentational markup with HTML.

Primary component *See* XML SCHEMA COMPONENT.

Primitive data type In an XML SCHEMA, a BUILT-IN DATA TYPE that cannot be defined using other DATA TYPES.

Primitive type *See* PRIMITIVE DATA TYPE.

Printing Industry Markup Language *See* PRINTML.

PrintML (Printing Industry Markup Language) An XML-BASED MARKUP LANGUAGE for the use in the graphic art industry. More details are available at `http://printml.org/`.

Prior version *See* ONTOLOGY ELEMENT.

PRISM (Publishing Requirements for Industry Standard Metadata) A set of METADATA vocabularies for the automation of publishing production processes and content exchange. In particular, PRISM augments the DUBLIN CORE METADATA ELEMENT SET to allow more detailed

descriptions. For instance, the DC:DATE ELEMENT is extended by several elements with the "prism" NAMESPACE, such as `prism:publicationTime` or `prism:releaseTime`. For more details, see the information at `http://www.prismstandard.org/`.

Processing instruction (PI) A STRUCTURAL CONSTRUCT of an XML DOCUMENT that allows the document to contain instructions for applications. A processing instruction uses a special TAG that begins with the (<?) DELIMITER, ends with the (?>) delimiter, and has no END TAG. Processing instructions can be placed in any location in an XML document. They are mostly used for declaring the XML version in the XML DECLARATION and for ASSOCIATING STYLE SHEETS WITH XML DOCUMENTS. Generally, however, they can be used to identify an application to which the instruction needs to be directed. In the basic syntax of processing instructions shown in Figure P.12. The compulsory "target" portion is to include a VALID XML NAME that identifies the application to which instruction are being passed, while the optional "instruction" portion can include the commands to be sent to the application. In an XML SCHEMA, information for applications (known as "application information") can be inserted using an APPINFO ELEMENT and used similarly to a processing instruction.

Processing instruction information item One of the 11 types of INFORMATION ITEM in the INFORMATION SET. Like all of them, it is an abstract description

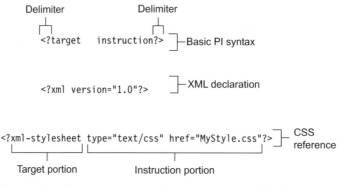

Figure P.12 The anatomy and main types of the processing instruction.

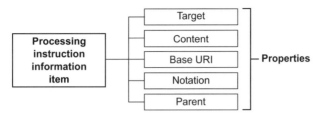

Figure P.13 The processing instruction information item and its properties.

of a STRUCTURAL CONSTRUCT of an XML DOCUMENT. This description is intended for use in other XML-related specifications, which need to conform to the information set. There is one processing instruction information item in the INFORMATION SET for each PROCESSING INSTRUCTION in the document. The Processing instruction information item has five properties, as shown in Figure P.13. For more details, see http://www.w3.org/TR/xml-infoset/.

Processing instruction node One of seven NODE TYPES of XPATH DATA MODEL that represents a PROCESSING INSTRUCTION.

Processor *See* XML PROCESSOR.

Process Specification Language *See* PSL.

Product Data Markup Language *See* PDML.

Product Definition Exchange *See* PDX.

Prohibited attribute In an XML SCHEMA, an ATTRIBUTE that is specified as forbidden using the prohibited value of the USE ATTRIBUTE. This attribute must not be presented in an XML

DOCUMENT; otherwise that document will not be a VALID XML DOCUMENT. See Figure P.14. *See also* OPTIONAL ATTRIBUTE; REQUIRED ATTRIBUTE.

Project Management XML Schema *See* PMXML.

Prolog 1. One of three XML DOCUMENT SECTIONS that may consist of (1) an XML DECLARATION; (2) PROCESSING INSTRUCTIONS; (3) a Document Type Declaration (DTD); (4) XML COMMENTS; and (5) WHITE SPACE. A prolog is an optional part of an XML DOCUMENT. See Figure P.15. *See also* BODY; EPILOG.

2. (Short for **Prog**ramming in **Log**ic). A high-level programming language that uses logical operations for artificial intelligence, especially for expert systems and natural language processing applications.

Properly nested elements ELEMENTS that are NESTED without overlapping, in accordance with the RUSSIAN DOLL APPROACH – one of the main concepts underlying the HIERARCHICAL TREE STRUCTURE of XML DOCUMENTS. *Contrast* IMPROPERLY NESTED ELEMENTS. *See also* NESTING ELEMENTS; OVERLAPPING ELEMENTS.

Property In RDF, the part of a STATEMENT that specifies the relationship between a RESOURCE and a

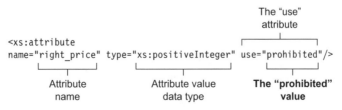

Figure P.14 The XML Schema declaration of a prohibited attribute.

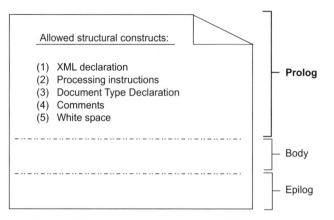

Figure P.15 The prolog as a section of an XML document.

value. For example, properties of a book are: author, title, publisher, publication date, page count and length. An RDF SCHEMA uses a more generic concept of property as a relationship between SUBJECT RESOURCES and OBJECT RESOURCES. In the example shown in Figure P.16, the dc:Creator property specifies the relationship between the index.html WEB PAGE and a person who is probably called "John" and who is identified via his personal WEB SITE. Note that the "dc" prefix is the DUBLIN CORE NAMESPACE prefix. A subject resource, an object resource and a property make up a TRIPLE.

Property & Casualty Extensible Markup Language *See* P&C XML.

Property class In an RDF SCHEMA, the CLASS of RDF PROPERTIES. The rdf:Property class is an INSTANCE of the CLASS CLASS. In the example shown in Figure P.17, the "age" PROPERTY of the "dog" class is defined.

Property–value pair *See* CSS STYLE.

Proposed recommendation *See* W3C PROPOSED RECOMMENDATION.

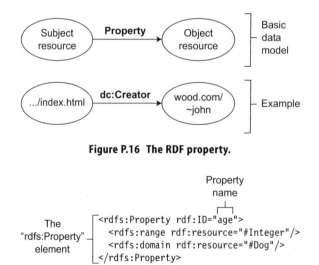

Figure P.16 The RDF property.

```
                                         Property
                                          name
                                          ┌─┐
   The        ┌ <rdfs:Property rdf:ID="age">
"rdfs:Property" ─    <rdfs:range rdf:resource="#Integer"/>
  element       │    <rdfs:domain rdf:resource="#Dog"/>
              └ </rdfs:Property>
```

Figure P.17 An example of defining an RDF property.

126

Protein Extensible Markup Language *See* PROXIML.

Protocol A method, language or formal set of rules and conventions that allows computers to communicate to each other over the Internet in a well-defined way. *See also* HTTP.

PROXIML (Protein Extensible Markup Language) An XML-BASED MARKUP LANGUAGE for describing and exchanging protein-related data. For more details, see http://www.cse.ucsc.edu/~douglas/proximl/.

Proxy resource *See* RESOURCE.

PSI (Portable Site Information) An XML-BASED MARKUP LANGUAGE for interchanging storage structure and data between different web content platforms. More information about PSI is available at http://psilib.sourceforge.net/.

PSL (Process Specification Language) An XML-BASED MARKUP LANGUAGE for describing manufacturing processes and exchanging process information automatically among a wide variety of manufacturing applications. More information

about PSL is available at http://ats.nist.gov/psl/.

PUBLIC keyword *See* DOCTYPE DECLARATION.

Published subject A mechanism for creating URIS identifying resources or subjects that are not electronic. For more information, see http://www.ontopia.net/tmp/pubsubj-gentle-intro.htm.

Publisher element One of the 15 ELEMENTS of the DUBLIN CORE METADATA ELEMENT SET. The <dc:publisher> element specifies the person or organization responsible for making the RESOURCE available. Note that "dc" is the NAMESPACE PREFIX of the DUBLIN CORE NAMESPACE.

Publishing Requirements for Industry Standard Metadata *See* PRISM.

PURL (Persistent Uniform Resource Locator) A special type of URL that does not point directly to the Internet location of a resource. Instead of this, it points to an intermediate resolution service that associates the PURL with the actual URL.

qbXML (QuickBooks Extensible Markup Language) An XML-BASED MARKUP LANGUAGE that enables data integration between QuickBooks and third-party programs. (QuickBooks is popular small business accounting software). Details of qbXML can be found at http://developer.intuit.com/library/quickbooks/qbxml_overview.pdf.

QML (Quest Markup Language) An XML-BASED MARKUP LANGUAGE for defining interactive text-based adventures that can include images, sound, random events etc. Details of QML are available at http://questml.com/.

QName An abbreviation for QUALIFIED NAME.

Qualified name A qualified name (also known as QName) is an ELEMENT NAME or an ATTRIBUTE NAME that consists of two parts separated by a colon: (1) the NAMESPACE PREFIX and (2) the LOCAL PART. The use of qualified names prevents name collisions while combining XML DOCUMENTS that contain ELEMENTS with the same element names that have different meanings. Qualified names may have the same LOCAL PARTS, but the use of a namespace prefix makes them unique. In the example shown in Figure Q.1, the word "Title" is used as a local part of several qualified names but all of them are

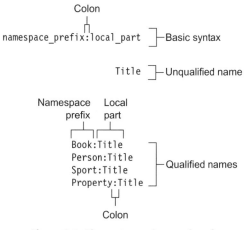
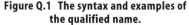

Figure Q.1 The syntax and examples of the qualified name.

unique and therefore different element names. *Contrast* UNQUALIFIED NAME. *See also* NAMESPACE DECLARATION; NAMESPACE NAME; OVERRIDING NAMESPACES; PREFIXED NAMESPACE; UNPREFIXED NAMESPACE.

Quest Markup Language *See* QML.

QuickBooks Extensible Markup Language *See* QBXML.

R

Range property In RDF SCHEMA, the `rdfs:range` PROPERTY is a property that is used to state that the values of a property are INSTANCES of one or more CLASSES. In the example shown in Figure R.1, the range of the "age" property of the "dog" class is specified as an integer.

RDDL (Resource Directory Description Language) An extension of XHTML BASIC with a new element named "rddl:resource" that serves as an XLink to the referenced resource. See `http://www.rddl.org/` for more details.

rdf The FILENAME EXTENSION of RDF documents. For example, "Catalog.rdf".

RDF (Resource Description Framework) An XML-BASED MARKUP LANGUAGE for describing RESOURCES on the Web using METADATA. RDF provides a generic metadata architecture. It includes: (1) RDF DATA MODEL; (2) RDF SYNTAX; (3) RDF SCHEMA. RDF-based structural, machine-understandable metadata provide additional meaning to the content of XML DOCUMENTS. At present, RDF is said to be one of the main SEMANTIC WEB TECHNOLOGIES. More information about RDF and also W3C SPECIFICATIONS related to RDF are available at `http://www.w3.org/RDF/`.

rdf:about attribute An ATTRIBUTE of the RDF:DESCRIPTION ELEMENT that identifies the subject of the STATEMENT.

rdf:Alt class *See* ALT CLASS.

rdf:Alt element *See* ALTERNATIVE CONTAINER.

rdf:Bag class *See* BAG CLASS.

rdf:Bag element *See* BAG CONTAINER.

rdf:Description element In RDF, an ELEMENT that is used to represent STATEMENTS. A collection of statements about a RESOURCE forms a "description". See Figure R.2.

rdf:Property class *See* PROPERTY CLASS.

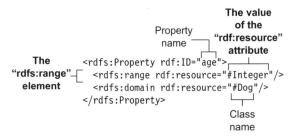

Figure R.1 An example of the Range property.

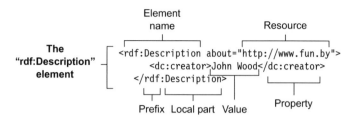

Figure R.2 An example of the "rdf:Description" element.

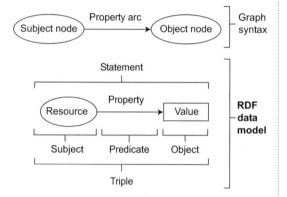

Figure R.3 The RDF data model.

rdf:RDF element *See* RDF ELEMENT.

rdf:Seq class *See* SEQ CLASS.

rdf:Seq element *See* SEQUENCE CONTAINER.

rdf:value property *See* VALUE PROPERTY.

RDF container *See* CONTAINER.

RDF data model A DATA MODEL underlying RDF and, in particular, any RDF STATEMENT. The RDF data model is graph-based and therefore independent of any specific serialization syntax. It uses so-called "graph syntax": directed labeled graphs that consist of nodes and labeled directed arcs that link pairs of nodes. See Figure R.3. An oval represents a RESOURCE, an arrow represents a PROPERTY, and a box represents a literal value. An RDF statement represented using this formal semantics is sometimes called a TRIPLE or an RDF graph. For more information about the RDF data model, see http://www.w3.org/RDF/. See also RDF SYNTAX.

RDF description *See* DESCRIPTION.

RDF element The ROOT ELEMENT of every RDF or RDF SCHEMA document. The ELEMENT NAME is comprised of the NAMESPACE PREFIX "rdf" and the LOCAL PART "RDF". The rdf:RDF element can also have one or more attributes, such as an RDF NAMESPACE declaration and an RDF SCHEMA NAMESPACE declaration. See Figure R.4.

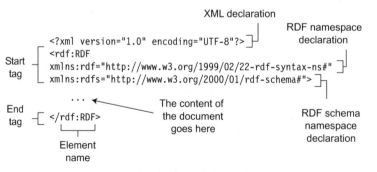

Figure R.4 The RDF element.

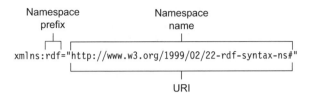

Figure R.5 Declaring the RDF namespace.

RDF graph *See* RDF DATA MODEL.

RDF metadata model *See* RDF DATA MODEL.

RDF namespace The NAMESPACE of the RDF language that is declared using a NAMESPACE DECLARATION, shown in Figure R.5. Note that the NAMESPACE PREFIX is "rdf" by convention.

RDF property *See* PROPERTY.

RDF root element *See* RDF ELEMENT.

rdfs:Class class See CLASS CLASS.

rdfs:comment property *See* COMMENT PROPERTY.

rdfs:Container class *See* CONTAINER CLASS.

rdfs:domain property *See* DOMAIN PROPERTY.

rdfs:isDefinedBy property *See* ISDEFINEDBY PROPERTY.

rdfs:label property *See* LABEL PROPERTY.

rdfs:Literal *See* LITERAL CLASS.

rdfs:range property *See* RANGE PROPERTY.

rdfs:Resource class *See* RESOURCE CLASS.

rdfs:seeAlso property *See* SEEALSO PROPERTY.

rdfs:subClassOf property *See* SUBCLASSOF PROPERTY.

rdfs:type property *See* TYPE PROPERTY.

rdfs:XMLLiteral *See* XMLLITERAL CLASS.

RDFS (RDF Schema) *See* RDF SCHEMA.

RDF-S (RDF Schema) *See* RDF SCHEMA.

RDF Schema Also known as RDF Vocabulary Description Language (an official name) or RDFS (an acronym). Part of RDF that is an extension of RDF that provides mechanisms for describing CLASSES of related RESOURCES and their PROPERTIES in a form that is machine-processable. In other words, an RDF Schema provides an XML VOCABULARY to express classes and their relationships (SUPERCLASS–SUBCLASS), and also to define properties and associate them with classes.

RDF Schema documents are written in RDF using the XML SYNTAX. This means that every RDF Schema document is also a VALID XML DOCUMENT and an RDF document. It starts with an XML DECLARATION followed by an RDF ELEMENT as a ROOT ELEMENT. Figure R.6 shows a simple RDF Schema document that defines the class of dogs (as a subclass of the class of pets) and also defines its "age" property. For more information about RDF Schemas, visit http://www.w3.org/RDF/.

RDF Schema class *See* CLASS.

RDF Schema namespace The NAMESPACE of the RDF SCHEMA language that is declared using a NAMESPACE DECLARATION, shown in Figure R.7. Note that the NAMESPACE PREFIX is "rdfs" by convention.

RDF Schema root element *See* RDF ELEMENT.

RDF Site Summary *See* RSS.

133

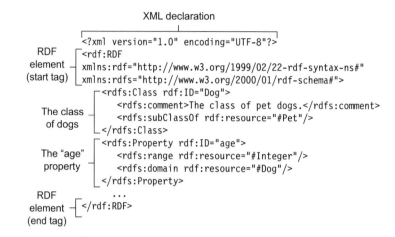

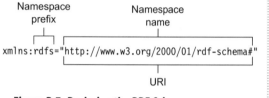

Figure R.6 An example of an RDF Schema document.

Figure R.7 Declaring the RDF Schema namespace.

RDFS namespace *See* RDF SCHEMA NAMESPACE.

RDF statement *See* STATEMENT.

RDF syntax A normative syntax for serialization of the RDF DATA MODEL that is based on XML. This DATA MODEL is graph-based and can therefore be serialized using other syntaxes, but the XML SYNTAX is the only syntax recommended by W3C. This means that an RDF document or RDF SCHEMA should be a VALID XML DOCUMENT. See Figure R.8. RDF syntax is defined at `http://www.w3.org/TR/REC-rdf-syntax/`.

RDF triple *See* TRIPLE.

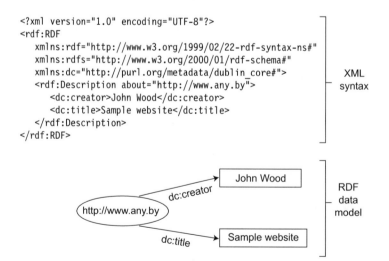

Figure R.8 An example of XML-based RDF syntax and its underlying data model.

RDF vCard Document *See* VCARD RDF/XML SPECIFICATION.

RDF vCard Specification *See* VCARD RDF/XML SPECIFICATION.

RDF Vocabulary Description Language The official name of RDF SCHEMA.

Readability *See* MACHINE AND HUMAN READABILITY.

Real Estate Extensible Markup Language *See* REXML.

Real resource *See* RESOURCE.

Really Simple Syndication *See* RSS.

REC (Recommendation) *See* W3C RECOMMENDATION.

Recipe Markup Language *See* RECIPEML.

RecipeML (Recipe Markup Language) An XML-BASED MARKUP LANGUAGE for describing recipes. Details of RecipeML are available at http://www.formatdata.com/recipeml/.

Recommendation *See* W3C RECOMMENDATION.

Recommendation track technical reports *See* W3C RECOMMENDATION TRACK TECHNICAL REPORTS.

Regular Language Description for XML *See* RELAX.

Regular Language Description for XML – New Generation *See* RELAX NG.

Relational-Functional Markup Language *See* RFML.

Relation element One of the 15 ELEMENTS of the DUBLIN CORE METADATA ELEMENT SET. The <dc:relation> element specifies another RESOURCE and its relationship to this one. Examples include chapters in

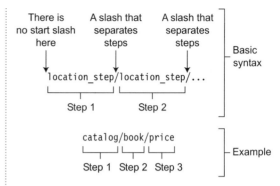

Figure R.9 Relative location path.

a book or images in a document. Note that "dc" is the NAMESPACE PREFIX of the DUBLIN CORE NAMESPACE.

Relative expression *See* RELATIVE LOCATION PATH.

Relative location path In XPATH, a LOCATION PATH that does not start at the ROOT NODE of a NODE TREE and therefore its syntax does not begin with a forward slash (which would indicate the root node). A relative location path is a sequence of LOCATION STEPS, each separated by a forward slash. In the example shown in Figure R.9, the absolute location path selects all the "price" elements of all the "book" elements of all the "catalog" elements that are children of the CONTEXT NODE. *Contrast* ABSOLUTE LOCATION PATH. *See also* ABBREVIATED SYNTAX.

RELAX (Regular Language Description for XML) A SCHEMA language for XML that may be seen as a less complex alternative to an XML SCHEMA. It is written in XML SYNTAX and based on regular expressions. RELAX has been merged with TREX to create RELAX NG. More information about RELAX is available at http://www.xml.gr.jp/relax/. *See also* DSD; SCHEMATRON.

RELAX NG (Regular Language Description for XML – New Generation) A simple SCHEMA language for XML that is the unification of TREX and RELAX. A RELAX NG schema uses XML syntax to specify a pattern for the structure and content of an XML DOCUMENT. RELAX NG may be seen as a less complex complementary alternative to an XML SCHEMA that is not intended to replace the W3C XML SCHEMA. RELAX NG is a specification by OASIS, available at `http://www.oasis-open.org/com-mittees/relax-ng/`. *See also* DSD; SCHEMATRON.

Remote ending resource In XLINK, a REMOTE RESOURCE from with TRAVERSAL begins.

Remote resource In XLINK, a RESOURCE or its portion that is specified in a LINK using a URI reference. *Contrast* LOCAL RESOURCE.

Remote starting resource In XLINK, a REMOTE RESOURCE that is the destination of TRAVERSAL.

Rendering XML documents Presenting an XML DOCUMENT in a visual, aural, multimedia or other form. An XML document contains only data and METADATA and nothing else that would specify how the data should be rendered. This principle of constructing XML documents is known as SEPARATION OF FORM FROM CONTENT. Technically, an XML document can be rendered in any desired form by using XSL for styling it or for transforming it into another presentation format, such as SMIL, SVG, VOICEXML, WML, X3D or XHTML.

A simple but very limited way of presenting XML as an HTML document is provided by CSS, which uses NON-XML SYNTAX. If no STYLE SHEET is associated with an XML document, a WEB BROWSER usually renders the document using its default STYLE SHEET, as in the example shown in Figure R.10. For the source code of this document, see XML DOCUMENT. Note that the browser displays the document in a very basic form. It differs from the PLAIN TEXT source code only in two aspects: (1) it formats

Figure R.10 An XML document rendered with Internet Explorer.

and colors the MARKUP; (2) it presents PARENT and CHILD ELEMENTS similar to a hierarchical file system, where the child elements can be hidden and shown just by clicking on a plus (+) or minus (–) sign.

Repeating elements *See* REUSING REPEATING ELEMENTS.

Request for Comments *See* RFC.

Required attribute In an XML SCHEMA, an ATTRIBUTE that is specified as mandatory using the `required` value of the USE ATTRIBUTE. This attribute must be presented in an XML DOCUMENT; otherwise that document will not be a VALID XML DOCUMENT. Note that by

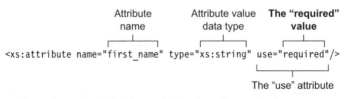

Figure R.11 The XML Schema declaration of a required attribute.

default all attributes are optional. See Figure R.11. *See also* OPTIONAL ATTRIBUTE; PROHIBITED ATTRIBUTE.

Research Information Exchange Markup Language *See* RIXML.

Resource A particular object of information provided on the Internet, such as a WEB PAGE, a picture, or anything else that has a unique URI. Essentially, a resource can be anything that has identity. Some distinguish two kinds of Web resource: (1) real resources (anything that has a URL and can really be accessed using a WEB BROWSER or other application); (2) proxy resources (URI-based representations of real-world objects that are not retrievable from the Web, such as persons or books).

Resource class In an RDF SCHEMA, a CLASS of all RESOURCES. Since everything described by an RDF SCHEMA is a resource, all other CLASSES are SUBCLASSES of the `rdfs:Resource` class. Note that this class is an INSTANCE of the CLASS CLASS.

Resource Description Framework *See* RDF.

Resource Directory Description Language *See* RDDL.

Resource-type element In XLINK, the ELEMENT of an XML DOCUMENT that has a TYPE ATTRIBUTE with the "resource" ATTRIBUTE VALUE and therefore can be used to supply LOCAL RESOURCES participating in the LINK.

restriction element A special ELEMENT of an XML SCHEMA that is used for specifying facets. For more details, see FACET.

Result document *See* TRANSFORMATION.

Result tree *See* TRANSFORMATION.

RETML (Real Estate Transaction Markup Language) An XML-BASED MARKUP LANGUAGE for exchanging real estate transaction information.

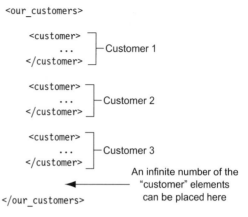

Figure R.12 Reusing repeating elements to define a list of customers.

Details of RETML are available at `http://www.rets-wg.org/`.

Reusing repeating elements One of the general principles underlying the structure of an XML DOCUMENT, in accordance with which multiple instances of the same type of ELEMENT can be created just by reusing the ELEMENT NAME and the names and structural relationships of elements NESTED within it. Reusing repeating elements is a special case of NESTING ELEMENTS. It makes an XML document similar to a self-describing database and makes it possible to define lists, as shown in Figure R.12.

reXML (Real Estate Extensible Markup Language) An XML-BASED MARKUP LANGUAGE for commercial real estate industry. More details are available at `http://www.therealm.com/reXML.html`.

RFC (Request for Comments) A special document that describes a protocol or other Internet-related information and often serves as a standard. RFCs are available from `http://www.ietf.org/rfc.html`.

RFC 3066 (Request for Comment 3066) *See* IETF LANGUAGE TAGS.

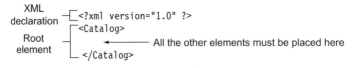

Figure R.13 Root element.

RFML (Relational-Functional Markup Language) An XML-BASED MARKUP LANGUAGE for RELFUN-style declarative programming and knowledge representation. RELFUN (the Relational-Functional Language) is a logic programming language. More details about RFML are available at http://www.relfun.org/rfml/.

Rich Site Summary *See* RSS.

Rights element One of the 15 ELEMENTS of the DUBLIN CORE METADATA ELEMENT SET. The <dc:rights> element specifies the intellectual property rights adhering to the RESOURCE, or a pointer to them. Note that "dc" is the NAMESPACE PREFIX of the DUBLIN CORE NAMESPACE.

RIXML (Research Information Exchange Markup Language) An XML-BASED MARKUP LANGUAGE for the investment banking market that is intended to facilitate the deployment of and searching for market research information. Details of RIXML can be found at http://www.rixml.org/.

RoboML (Robotic Markup Language) An XML-BASED MARKUP LANGUAGE for standardized representation and interchange of robotics-related data. More details about RoboML are available at http://www.roboml.org/.

Robotic Markup Language *See* ROBOML.

Root A term used to refer to either the ROOT ELEMENT or the DOCUMENT ROOT. The use of this term can sometimes be confusing.

Root element A term commonly used to refer to the ELEMENT that contains all of the other elements in the XML DOCUMENT, as shown in Figure R.13. A VALID XML DOCUMENT has exactly one root element. Only PROCESSING INSTRUCTIONS (including the XML DECLARATION) and COMMENTS may precede the START TAG of the root element. Note that the official term for "root element" is "DOCUMENT ELEMENT". *See also* DOCUMENT ROOT.

Root node One of seven NODE TYPES of the XPATH DATA MODEL. A root node is the root of the NODE TREE and does not occur except as the root of the tree. Each XML DOCUMENT has one and only one root note that is actually represent the DOCUMENT ROOT. The ELEMENT NODE for the ROOT ELEMENT is a special CHILD of the root node. The root node can also have as children PROCESSING INSTRUCTION NODES and COMMENT NODES.

RosettaNet A non-profit consortium dedicated to creating, implementing and promoting open e-business standards that form a common e-business language. More information is available at http://www.rosettanet.org/.

RPC (Remote Procedure Calls) *See* XML-RPC.

RPC over XML *See* XML-RPC.

RSS (RDF Site Summary) Also known as "Rich Site Summary" and "Really Simple Syndication". An XML-BASED MARKUP LANGUAGE used for describing and distributing news and other Web content. Special directories of RSS files make this content available to Web users who can access it using a normal WEB BROWSER or a special program that can read RSS-distributed content. More details of RSS are available at http://groups.yahoo.com/group/rss-dev/files/namespace.html.

Rule Markup Language *See* RULEML.

RuleML (Rule Markup Language) An XML-BASED
MARKUP LANGUAGE that makes possible Web-based
rule storage, interchange, retrieval and application. It can be used for many purposes, including
specifying queries and inferences in Web
ONTOLOGIES, as well as mappings between them.
Details of RuleML are available at `http://`
`www.dfki.uni-kl.de/ruleml/`.

Russian doll approach A term that is sometimes
used to refer to the principle of NESTING ELEMENTS.
XML elements must be enclosed one within
another without overlapping, like hollow Russian
dolls of different sizes. This approach is illustrated in Figure R.14.

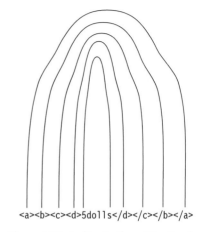

`<a><b><c><d>5dolls</d></c></b></a>`

**Figure R.14 An illustration of the Russian
doll approach.**

SALT (Speech Application Language Tags) An XML-BASED MARKUP LANGUAGE that enables multimodal and telephony-enabled access to information, applications, and Web services from PCs, telephones, tablet PCs, and wireless personal digital assistants (PDAs). More details about SALT are available at `http://www.saltforum.org/`.

sameAs element *See* SAME AS STATEMENT.

Same As statement In OWL, a statement that indicates that two INSTANCES are the same. It allows the author to describe or define a number of different names that refer to the same INDIVIDUAL. In the example shown in Figure S.1, a person known as "Marilyn Monroe" is stated to be the same individual as "Norma Jean Mortenson". *See also* ALL DIFFERENT STATEMENT; DIFFERENT FROM STATEMENT; OWL VOCABULARY.

SAML (Security Assertion Markup Language) An XML-based framework for exchanging authentication and authorization information between systems within an organization or between organizations in a transaction. More information about SAML is available at `http://www.oasis-open.org/committees/security/`.

SAX (Simple API for XML) An industry-standard API for the EVENT-DRIVEN PARSING of XML DOCUMENTS. More details of SAX may be obtained from `http://www.saxproject.org/`. *Compare* DOM.

SBM (Semantic Business Model) An open effort to develop OWL-based semantic models of both businesses in general and vertical industries in particular. See `http://www.semanticworld.org/` for more details.

SBML (Systems Biology Markup Language) An XML-BASED MARKUP LANGUAGE for representing and exchanging biochemical network models. More details about SBML can be obtained from `http://www.cds.caltech.edu/erato/sbml/`.

Scalable Vector Graphics *See* SVG.

Scene graph The logical structure of an X3D or VRML file that represents the relationships of objects especially as they are seen in the resulting

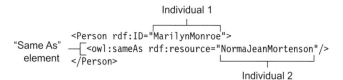

Figure S.1 Stating that two individuals are the same.

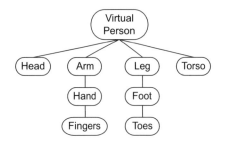

Figure S.2 An example of a simple scene graph.

visible scene. Scene graphs are often used to orga-
nize and manage 3D scenes. A scene graph is a
HIERARCHICAL TREE STRUCTURE known as a NODE TREE. This
similarity with the structural organization of an
XML DOCUMENT is beneficial for X3D, which is the
latest version of VRML written in XML. See
Figure S.2.

Schema A generic term for a document (either
external or embedded) that describes the
VOCABULARY and structural organization of an XML-
BASED MARKUP LANGUAGE. The best-known examples of
schemas are DTDS and XML SCHEMAS.

Schema component *See* XML SCHEMA COMPONENT.

schema element The ROOT ELEMENT of every XML
SCHEMA. The ELEMENT NAME is comprised of a
NAMESPACE PREFIX (other xs or xsd) and the LOCAL PART
(schema). Note that both element names
(xs:schema and xsd:schema) are legal. The element can also have one or more attributes, as
shown in Figure S.3. *See also* XML SCHEMA DOCUMENT.

Schema for Object-Oriented XML *See* SOX.

Schema of Schemas A term that is sometimes
used to refer to the URI of the W3C XML SCHEMA that is
used in the SCHEMA ELEMENT of every specific XML
SCHEMA as the NAMESPACE NAME for the W3C XML
schema NAMESPACE DECLARATION. The NAMESPACE PREFIX
for the Schema of Schemas can be either "xs" or
"xsd". See Figure S.4.

Schematron A structural SCHEMA language for
XML that is based on matching combinations of
XPATH EXPRESSIONS. It uses standard XSL syntax, and
may be seen as a useful supplement to an XML
SCHEMA. Schematron is also suitable for annotating
XML documents by automatically generating
external MARKUP, such as RDFS, XLINKS, and TOPIC MAPS.
For more details, see http://www.ascc.net/xml/

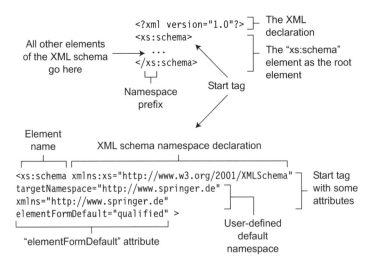

Figure S.3 The XML Schema root element and its attributes.

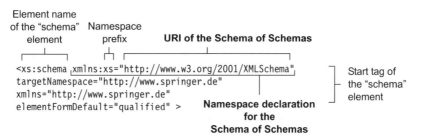

Figure S.4 The Schema of Schemas.

resource/schematron/. *See also* DSD; RELAX; RELAX NG; TREX.

Schools Interoperability Framework *See* SIF.

SDML (Signed Document Markup Language)
An XML-BASED MARKUP LANGUAGE that defines a generic method for digitally signing a document (a Web page, an email message or any other text-based document), a section of a document, or multiple documents. For more details, see http://www.w3.org/TR/NOTE-SDML/.

Secondary component *See* XML SCHEMA COMPONENT.

Second-Generation Web A term that is sometimes used to refer to the SEMANTIC WEB as an extension of the existing FIRST-GENERATION WEB.

Security Assertion Markup Language *See* SAML.

seeAlso property In RDF SCHEMA, the rdfs:seeAlso PROPERTY is a property that is used to indicate a RESOURCE that can provide additional information about the SUBJECT RESOURCE.

Select attribute In XSLT, an ATTRIBUTE of a VALUE-OF ELEMENT, FOR-EACH ELEMENT etc. used to select specified NODES of an XML DOCUMENT.

Selector The part of a CSS STYLE that is located before the opening brace. It specifies one or more XML ELEMENTS to which the CSS style should be applied by referencing their names. See Figure S.5.

Figure S.5 The CSS selector.

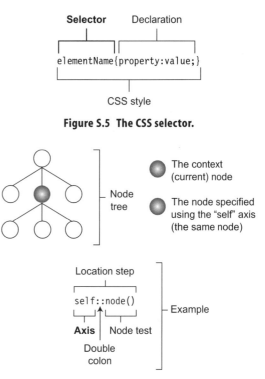

Figure S.6 The "self" axis.

See also CSS STYLE SHEET; GROUPING SELECTORS; HIDING ELEMENTS.

self axis In XPATH, an AXIS that specifies that the CONTEXT NODE itself is to be selected as the next context node. See Figure S.6.

Self-describing data A term used to refer to ability of a MARKUP LANGUAGE not only to represent

143

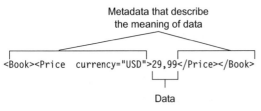

Metadata that describe
the meaning of data

```
<Book><Price  currency="USD">29,99</Price></Book>
```

Data

**Figure S.7 An example showing XML as
self-describing data.**

data but also to describe the meaning of the data
using METADATA. Any document written in any XML-
BASED MARKUP LANGUAGE contains self-describing data.
This makes it a self-contained source of information that can be read and understand by humans
and computers at any time. For example, it is easy
to comprehend that in an XML code snippet,
shown in Figure S.7, the number "29, 99" is actually the price of a book in US dollars.

Self-describing language *See* SELF-DESCRIBING DATA.

Self-documenting language *See* SELF-DESCRIBING
DATA.

Self-referential language *See* SELF-DESCRIBING DATA.

Semantic Relating to meaning, especially
meaning in language. *See also* MEANING; SEMANTICS.

Semantic Business Model *See* SBM.

Semantics 1. The meaning of words, phrases or
symbols.

2. In linguistics, the science or study of
meaning in language forms. *Compare* PRAGMATICS;
SYNTAX.

3. In computing, the meaning of words or symbols used in programs or relationships between
them and their intended meanings. In XML and the
SEMANTIC WEB, this term is usually used to refer to
the MEANING of data. *Compare* MARKUP; METADATA.

Semantic Web The emerging Second-Generation
Web that is an extension of the current,

FIRST-GENERATION WEB. The concept of the Semantic
Web was produced by Tim BERNERS-LEE, who has
also coined the term. The main idea of the
Semantic Web is to delegate many current human-
specific Web activities to computers. This will be
possible if Web data are expressed in a machine-
readable format suitable for completely automate
transactions. It can be achieved by adding several
hierarchical levels of METADATA to Web data and
using specialist technologies that can make use of
these metadata. More details about the Semantic
Web can be obtained from `http://www.w3.org/`
`2001/sw/`. *See also* SEMANTIC WEB ARCHITECTURE;
SEMANTIC WEB TECHNOLOGIES.

Semantic Web architecture A high-level plan of
the SEMANTIC WEB that originates in the "Semantic
Web Road Map" introduced by Tim BERNERS-LEE in
1998 and available at `http://www.w3.org/`
`DesignIssues/Semantic.html`. Most graphical
representations of the architecture of the
Semantic Web are based on the famous "layer
cake" diagram, presented by Berners-Lee at the
"XML 2000" conference and available at `http://`
`www.w3.org/2000/Talks/1206-xml2k-tbl/`
`slide10-0.html`. According to him, the Semantic
Web will be built by adding more layers on top of
existing ones and may take around ten years to
complete.

Figure S.8 shows several architectural relationships within the Semantic Web. Its highest layers
are yet to be fully developed. The logic layer will
contain logical rules that allow computers to make
inferences and deductions in order to derive new
knowledge. The proof layer will implement languages and mechanisms for distinguishing between
Web RESOURCES with different levels of trustworthi-
ness. The logic and proof, together with the XML
SIGNATURE and XML ENCRYPTION, will enable developers
to construct the "Web of Trust", where autonomous software agents will be able and allowed to
undertake important tasks such as finding and
buying expensive goods without any human inter-
vention. It is an open question at this moment
how many extra layers will be needed in the

Semantic Web
content

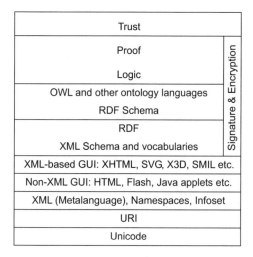

Semantic Web
technologies

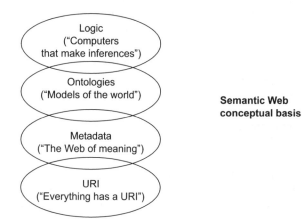

Semantic Web
conceptual basis

Figure S.8 Architectural structures of the Semantic Web.

future and what kind of new technologies should be implemented. *See also* INFORMATION SET; NAMESPACE; OWL; RDF; RDF SCHEMA; SEMANTIC WEB TECHNOLOGIES; SMIL; SVG; UNICODE; URI; X3D; XHTML; XML FAMILY OF TECHNOLOGIES. For more information, see http://www.w3.org/2001/sw/.

```
            <rdf:Description about="http://www.springer.de">
              <SPC_Bestseller>
             ⎡<rdf:Seq>
                  <rdf:li resource="http://www.springer.de/spc/book1"/>
The "rdf:Seq" ⎥   <rdf:li resource="http://www.springer.de/spc/book2"/>
  element      ⎥   <rdf:li resource="http://www.springer.de/spc/book3"/>
             ⎣</rdf:Seq>
              </SPC_Bestseller>
            </rdf:Description>
```

Figure S.9 An example of an RDF "Sequence" container.

Semantic Web language *See* SEMANTIC WEB TECHNOLOGIES.

Semantic Web technologies A group of technologies that are specially intended for developing the SEMANTIC WEB ARCHITECTURE and other essential features of the emerging Second-Generation Web. Most of these technologies are XML-BASED MARKUP LANGUAGES developed by the W3C and also members of the XML FAMILY OF TECHNOLOGIES. These technologies are based on several fundamental concepts of the SEMANTIC WEB, such as URI, METADATA, ONTOLOGIES and logic. At present, the major Semantic Web technologies include XML, RDF, RDF SCHEMA, DAML+OIL, OWL, TOPIC MAPS, and some other XML-based languages. In the future, new and more powerful technologies are expected to be developed. For the latest information about Semantic Web technologies, see http://www.w3.org/2001/sw/.

Separation of data from presentation *See* SEPARATION OF FORM FROM CONTENT.

Separation of form from content One of the general principles underlying XML, in accordance with which the content of an XML DOCUMENT is separated from its presentation rules. As a result, the same content or any of its fragments can be presented in many different forms on a variety of devices, such as computers, mobile phones, PDAS or printers.

Separation of semantics and presentation *See* SEPARATION OF FORM FROM CONTENT.

Seq (Sequence) *See* SEQUENCE CONTAINER.

Seq class In an RDF SCHEMA, the rdf:Seq CLASS is the class of SEQUENCE CONTAINERS. It is a SUBCLASS of the CONTAINER CLASS.

Seq element *See* SEQUENCE CONTAINER.

Sequence container In RDF, the rdf:Seq Sequence container is a CONTAINER that is an ordered collection of RESOURCES or LITERALS, as shown in Figure S.9. Note that in the rdf:li ELEMENT, the "li" LOCAL PART means "a list item".

sequence element In an XML SCHEMA, a special ELEMENT that is used as an INDICATOR that specifies that the declared CHILD ELEMENTS must appear in an XML DOCUMENT in a particular order. The QUALIFIED NAME of the "sequence" element can be either "xs:sequence" or "xsd:sequence", depending on whether the XS NAMESPACE PREFIX or XSD NAMESPACE PREFIX is being used. See Figure S.10.

sequence indicator *See* INDICATOR.

Server *See* WEB SERVER.

Service component In the WSDL COMPONENT MODEL, a component that describes the set of port types (*see* PORT TYPE COMPONENT) that a service provides and the ports (*see* PORT COMPONENT) that they are provided over. The XML representation of the service component is the wsdl:service ELEMENT , as shown in Figure S.11. Essentially, a service is a collection of ports.

Service Provisioning Markup Language *See* SPML.

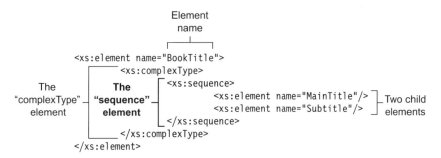

Figure S.10 The use of the "sequence" element.

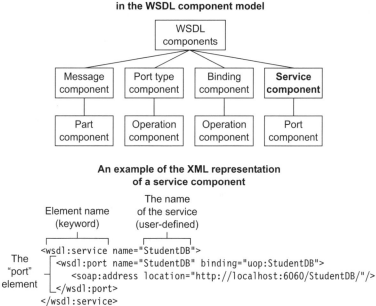

Figure S.11 The WSDL "service" component.

SGF (Structured Graph Format) An XML-BASED MARKUP LANGUAGE for describing the structure of a Web site using structured graphs. More details are available at http://decweb.ethz.ch/WWW7/1850/com1850.htm.

SGML (Standard Generalized Markup Language) A METALANGUAGE for marking the structure of an arbitrary set of data. GML (Generalized Markup Language) was invented in 1969 by Ed Mosher, Ray Lorie and Charles F. Goldfarb of IBM Research. Later, it was adopted as the ISO 8879:1986 standard named "Information Processing – Text and Office Systems – Standard Generalized Markup Language (SGML)". HTML is an SGML-based MARKUP LANGUAGE. XML is a METALANGUAGE that is a subset of SGML. See Figure S.12. SGML is one of the NON-NORMATIVE REFERENCES of the XML 1.0 RECOMMENDATION. More information about SGML is available at http://www.w3.org/MarkUp/SGML/.

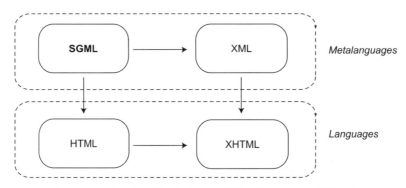

Figure S.12 Relationships between SGML, XML, HTML and XHTML.

SHOE (Simple HTML Ontology Extensions) An HTML-based language for embedding METADATA and simple ONTOLOGIES into WEB PAGES. SHOE has been superseded by DAML+OIL and OWL, which are in part based on SHOE. Details of SHOE are available at http://www.cs.umd.edu/projects/plus/SHOE/.

Show attribute In XLINK, an ATTRIBUTE used to specify the desired presentation of the ENDING RESOURCE on TRAVERSAL from the STARTING RESOURCE. Its main ATTRIBUTE VALUES are: (1) "new" – the ending resource is to be loaded in a new window, frame, pane, or similar (see Figure S.13); (2) "replace" – the ending resource should be loaded in the same window, frame, pane etc. in with the starting resource was loaded; (3) "embed" – the ending resource will be embedded in the source document in place of the LINK representation.

SIDES (Staffing Industry Data Exchange Standards) A set of XML-based standards (languages) for exchanging data between staffing customers, staffing suppliers, and other stakeholders in the staffing supply chain. Details of SIDES can be found at http://www.hr-xml.org/sides/.

SIF (Schools Interoperability Framework) An industry initiative to develop an XML-BASED LANGUAGE that enables effective integration of K-12 instructional and administrative software applications. This language is provided in form of the SIF Implementation Specification. More details of SIF may be obtained from http://www.sifinfo.org/.

Signature *See* XML SIGNATURE.

Signed Document Markup Language *See* SDML.

Simple API for XML *See* SAX.

Simple element A term that is sometimes used to refer to an ELEMENT that is a SIMPLE TYPE. *Contrast* COMPLEX ELEMENT. *See also* ELEMENT DECLARATION; SIMPLE TYPE DEFINITION.

Simple HTML Ontology Extensions *See* SHOE.

Simple link In XLINK, a type of LINK that is an OUTBOUND LINK with exactly two PARTICIPATING RESOURCES. Simple links provide shorthand syntax for a common kind of link to which all HTML links belong. To use an XML ELEMENT as a container for a

```
            <catalog xmlns:xlink="http://www.w3.org/1999/xlink"
XLink ─┌─xlink:type="simple"
 type   └─xlink:href="Catalog.xml"─┤─ Ending resource
"show" ─┌─xlink:show="new"
attribute  xlink:actuate="onRequest"/>
```

Figure S.13 An example of a XLink "show" attribute.

```
            <catalog xmlns="http://www.springer.de/spc"
                     xmlns:xlink="http://www.w3.org/1999/xlink"
  XLink  ⌐ xlink:type="simple"
  type   └ xlink:href="Catalog.xml" ⌐ Resource
            xlink:show="new"
            xlink:actuate="onRequest">
  Linked ⌐ See our Book Catalog!
  text   └ </catalog>
```

Figure S.14 An example of a simple link in XLink.

simple link, the XLINK NAMESPACE must be declared and the ATTRIBUTE VALUE of the TYPE ATTRIBUTE must be specified as "simple". See Figure S.14. *Contrast* EXTENDED LINK.

Simple Object Access Protocol *See* SOAP.

Simple text *See* PLAIN TEXT.

Simple type A term used to refer to the ELEMENTS of the XML SCHEMA that can contain only CHARACTER DATA, but no other ELEMENTS or ATTRIBUTES. Since attributes cannot contain any data other that character data within their ATTRIBUTE VALUES, all attributes are considered to be of simple type. *Contrast* COMPLEX TYPE.

Simple type definition An XML SCHEMA COMPONENT that defines ELEMENTS of the SIMPLE TYPE using a special XML SCHEMA element called "simpleType". Its QUALIFIED NAME can be either "xs:simpleType" or "xsd:simpleType", depending on whether the XS NAMESPACE PREFIX or XSD NAMESPACE PREFIX is being used. In the example shown in Figure S.15, the "Password" element is defined as of simple type. Its

ELEMENT CONTENT is restricted to a CHARACTER STRING that may be up to eight characters long. *Contrast* COMPLEX TYPE DEFINITION.

simpleType element A special ELEMENT of the XML SCHEMA language that is used in simple type definitions for defining SIMPLE TYPES. For more information, see SIMPLE TYPE DEFINITION.

smil The FILENAME EXTENSION for SMIL files. For example, "Catalog.smil".

SMIL (Synchronized Multimedia Integration Language) SMIL (pronounced "smile") is an XML-BASED MARKUP LANGUAGE for describing synchronized multimedia presentations. It enables simple authoring of interactive audiovisual presentations that integrate streaming audio and video with images, text or any other media type. In the example shown in Figure S.16, a simple SMIL presentation includes an image, text and sound. Note that the image, text and sound files are external to the SMIL file. SMIL just defines where to present these multimedia components, for how long etc. Details of SMIL can be found at http://www.w3.org/AudioVideo/.

SML (Spacecraft Markup Language) An XML-BASED MARKUP LANGUAGE that provides a standardized data representation for the space domain, and allows the definition of spacecraft and other support data objects. More details of SML may be obtained from http://www.interfacecontrol.com/sml/.

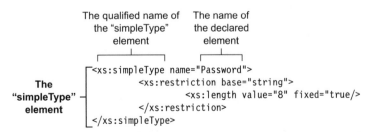

```
                    The qualified name of    The name of
                     the "simpleType"        the declared
                         element              element
                            ↓                    ↓
                  ⌐ <xs:simpleType name="Password">
      The              <xs:restriction base="string">
  "simpleType" ─           <xs:length value="8" fixed="true/>
    element            </xs:restriction>
                  └ </xs:simpleType>
```

Figure S.15 An example of a simple type definition.

Start tag
of "smil"
element

```
                        Presentation
<smil>                    layout        The size of
   <head>                               presentation window
     ┌<layout>
        <root-layout width="300" height="200" background-color="white"/>
        <region id="r1" left="75" top="40" width="100" height="100"/>
        <region id="r2" left="170" top="60" width="150" height="150"/>
     └</layout>
   </head>        Region 2       Region 1
   <body>        (for image)     (for text)
     <par>
        <audio src="hello.wav" type="audio/wav" repeat="2" />  ─ Sound
        <text src="Hello.txt" region="r1"/>─ Text
        <img src="smile.gif" region="r2" dur="2s" repeat="4"/> ─ Image
     </par>
   </body>
</smil>
```

End tag
of "smil"
element

Figure S.16 An example SMIL file and its view in the RealOne Player.

SOAP (Simple Object Access Protocol) An XML-based COMMUNICATION PROTOCOL for exchanging XML-encoded information (known as SOAP MESSAGES) in a decentralized distributed environment and especially for accessing a WEB SERVICE. Details of SOAP can be found at http://www.w3.org/TR/SOAP/. *See also* SOAP INTERMEDIARY; SOAP MESSAGE STRUCTURE.

SOAP active intermediary *See* SOAP INTERMEDIARY.

SOAP Body *See* BODY.

SOAP Envelope *See* ENVELOPE.

SOAP Fault element *See* FAULT ELEMENT.

SOAP forwarding intermediary *See* SOAP INTERMEDIARY.

SOAP Header *See* HEADER.

Figure S.17 The use of SOAP intermediaries.

SOAP intermediary A SOAP processing NODE on a SOAP MESSAGE path from an initial SOAP sender to an ultimate SOAP receiver. Essentially, SOAP intermediaries are intended to provide value-added services by changing the HEADER of a SOAP message. There are two types of SOAP interme-diary: (1) forwarding intermediaries, which are used just to forward a SOAP message to another SOAP node; and (2) active intermediaries, which include some additional information into the header before forwarding the SOAP message to another SOAP node. See Figure S.17.

SOAP message An XML DOCUMENT that is written using SOAP syntax. The use of the ENVELOPE ele-ment as the ROOT ELEMENT identifies the XML docu-ment as a SOAP message. Basically, a SOAP message is one-way transmission between a SOAP sender and a SOAP receiver. More complex inter-action pattern can include request/response or multiple message exchange, as shown in Figure S.18. Moreover, the transmission of a SOAP mes-sage can involve the participation of not only a SOAP sender and a SOAP receiver but also of other SOAP nodes known as SOAP INTERMEDIARIES. *See also* SOAP MESSAGE STRUCTURE.

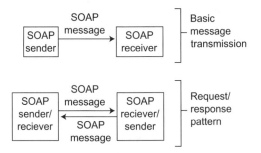

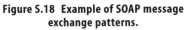

Figure S.18 Example of SOAP message exchange patterns.

SOAP message path *See* SOAP INTERMEDIARY.

SOAP message structure The construction of a SOAP MESSAGE that includes four parts: (1) a required ENVELOPE; (2) an optional HEADER; (3) a required BODY ELEMENT; and (4) an optional FAULT ELEMENT. See Figure S.19.

SOAP namespace *See* ENVELOPE.

SOAP receiver *See* SOAP MESSAGE.

SOAP root element *See* ENVELOPE.

SOAP sender *See* SOAP MESSAGE.

Software agent *See* INTELLIGENT AGENT.

sort element An ELEMENT of an XSLT STYLE SHEET that is used in a TEMPLATE to sort the output. In the example shown in Figure S.20, the xsl:sort ele-ment sorts the ELEMENT CONTENT of the "Title" elements.

Source document *See* TRANSFORMATION.

Source element One of the 15 ELEMENTS of the DUBLIN CORE METADATA ELEMENT SET. The <dc:source> element specifies another RESOURCE that this resource is derived from (if applicable). Note that "dc" is the NAMESPACE PREFIX of the DUBLIN CORE NAMESPACE.

Source tree *See* TRANSFORMATION.

SOX (Schema for Object-Oriented XML) One of the early SCHEMA language proposals that led to the current XML SCHEMA language. More details about

151

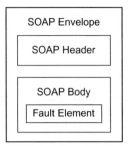

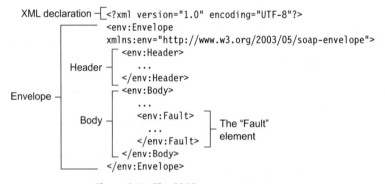

Figure S.19 The SOAP message structure.

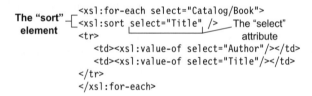

Figure S.20 An example of an XSLT "sort" element.

SOX are available at http://www.w3.org/TR/ NOTE-SOX/. *See also* DDML; DT4DTD; XML-DATA.

Spacecraft Markup Language *See* SML.

Special attributes *See* XML RESERVED ATTRIBUTES.

Special markup characters *See* SPECIAL SYMBOLS.

Special-purpose markup A term sometimes used to refer to additional STRUCTURAL CONSTRUCTS of an XML DOCUMENT, such as (1) PROCESSING INSTRUCTIONS; (2) COMMENTS; and (3) CDATA SECTIONS.

Special symbols In XML, five characters that have special meaning in XML MARKUP because they are used as DELIMITERS for markup and text strings. To avoid the situation in which an XML PARSER could confuse a displayable text character (such as <) with an identical markup symbol (that is, <), XML provides a default mechanism for the alternative representation of special symbols. Each of the special symbols has its corresponding ENTITY REFERENCE, which can replace it. See Figure S.21. In the example shown in this figure, XML code contains all the five special symbols that are displayed

SPECIAL SYMBOLS	ENTITY REFERENCES
< (Left angle bracket, or Less-than sign)	&lt;
> (Right angle bracket, or Greater-than sign)	&gt;
& (Ampersand)	&amp;
' (Apostrophe, or Single quotation mark)	&apos;
" (Quotation mark, or Double quotation mark)	&quot;

Example: XML code and its browser view

```
<discussion>James wrote: &quot;In John&apos;s opinion,
the use of the &lt;first_name&gt; &amp; &lt;family_name&gt;
           tags is the best choice&quot;</discussion>
```

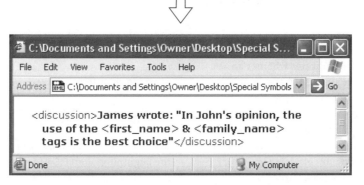

Figure S.21 Special symbols and corresponding entity references.

in a WEB BROWSER as regular text characters and not as XML markup.

Specification In Web technologies, a document that is a detailed official description of a Web standard or other normative or non-normative rules and guidelines. The term "specification" is used to refer to both a W3C RECOMMENDATION and a W3C TECHNICAL REPORT of a lower level of maturity, such as a W3C CANDIDATE RECOMMENDATION or a W3C PROPOSED RECOMMENDATION.

Speech Application Language Tags *See* SALT.

Speech Synthesis Markup Language *See* SSML.

SPML (Service Provisioning Markup Language) An XML-based framework and markup language that is intended to automate, centralize, and manage the process of provisioning user access to corporate systems and data. More details about SPML can be obtained from http://www.oasis-open.org/committees/provision/.

Sports Markup Language *See* SPORTSML.

SportsML (Sports Markup Language) An XML-based language for the interchange of sports data such as scores, schedules and statistics. More information about SportsML is available at http://www.sportsml.com/.

153

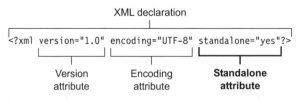

Figure S.22 The "standalone" attribute of the XML declaration.

SSML (Speech Synthesis Markup Language)
An XML-BASED MARKUP LANGUAGE that provides a standardized annotation for instructing speech synthesizers on how to convert written language
input into synthetic speech output, including
voice, pitch, rate, volume, pronunciation and other
characteristics. More information is available at
http://www.w3.org/TR/speech-synthesis/.

Staffing Industry Data Exchange Standards *See*
SIDES.

Standalone attribute An optional property of
an XML DECLARATION that indicates whether an XML
DOCUMENT depends on other XML files (such as a
DTD or a SCHEMA) in order to be VALID. The
standalone attribute must take either a "yes" or
"no" value. The default value is "yes", which
means that the XML document does not depend
on any other XML documents. See Figure S.22. *See
also* ENCODING ATTRIBUTE; VERSION ATTRIBUTE.

Standalone metadata A type of METADATA that is
stored and maintained independently of the
object it describes. *Contrast* EMBEDDED METADATA.

**Standard for the Exchange of Product Model
Data Markup Language** *See* STEPML.

Standard Generalized Markup Language *See*
SGML.

Standards for Technology in Automotive Retail
See STAR.

**STAR (Standards for Technology in Automotive
Retail)** A set of XML-based standards (languages)
for the retail automotive industry developed by

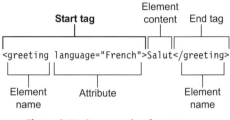

Figure S.23 An example of a start tag.

the STAR Group. For more details, see the information at http://www.starstandard.org/.

Starting resource *See* TRAVERSAL.

Starting tag *See* START TAG.

Start tag A TAG that is used as a DELIMITER to show
the beginning of an ELEMENT and the ELEMENT CONTENT.
It consists of an ELEMENT NAME followed by none or
more ATTRIBUTES, enclosed within ANGLE BRACKETS, as
shown in Figure S.23. In XML, each start tag
(except the EMPTY-ELEMENT TAG) must have a
matching END TAG with the same element name. The
start tag is also called the opening tag, open tag,
beginning tag or starting-tag. *Contrast* END TAG.

Statement The main STRUCTURAL CONSTRUCT of RDF
that is intended to specify the PROPERTIES and values
of Web RESOURCES. An RDF statement consists of a
subject (what the statement is about), a predicate
(property or characteristic of the subject), and an
object (part that identifies the value of the property). This three-part construct is also called a
TRIPLE. A collection of statements about a resource
forms a DESCRIPTION that is represented through a
RDF:DESCRIPTION ELEMENT. The statement, shown in

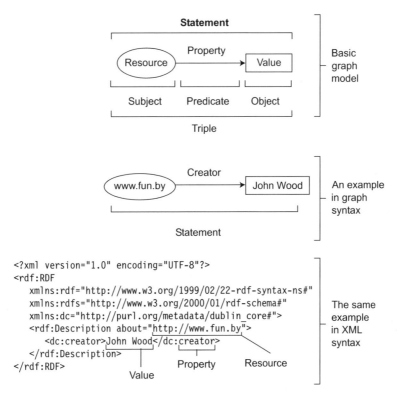

Figure S.24 The anatomy and an example of the RDF statement.

Figure S.24, can be read as "John Wood is the creator of the www.fun.by Web site".

STEPML (Standard for the Exchange of Product Model Data Markup Language) A set of XML-BASED MARKUP LANGUAGES for product data based on the content models from the STEP (STandard for the Exchange of Product Model Data) standard. See http://www.stepml.org/ for more details.

STPML (Straight Through Processing Markup Language) An XML message specification that enables straight-through processing for the financial securities trading industry by supporting most industry standards for data exchange. More information about STPML is available at http://www.stpml.org/.

Straight Through Processing Markup Language See STPML.

String See CHARACTER STRING.

String data type In XML SCHEMA, a DATA TYPE that is used for specifying a value that is a CHARACTER STRING.

String literal In programming, a constant that consists of a sequence of characters. In XML, string literals are used for ATTRIBUTE VALUES, INTERNAL ENTITIES and EXTERNAL ENTITIES. All string literals must be in single (') or double (") quotes, with the closing DELIMITER matching the opening delimiter. *See also* LITERAL; LITERAL STRING; CHARACTER STRING.

Structural construct A generic term used to refer to a building block of an XML DOCUMENT, a DATA MODEL, a NODE TREE or other HIERARCHICAL TREE STRUCTURES. For example, the main structural constructs of an XML document include: (1) ELEMENTS; (2) ATTRIBUTES; (3) ATTRIBUTE VALUES. Additional

Figure S.25 An example of structural markup with XML.

structural constructs (also sometimes called SPECIAL-PURPOSE MARKUP) include: (1) PROCESSING INSTRUCTIONS; (2) COMMENTS; (3) CDATA SECTIONS. In general, INFORMATION ITEMS can be considered as structural constructs of an XML-BASED MARKUP LANGUAGE. Note that the term "structural construct" is, in principle, synonymous to "element", "component", "part" and the like, but its use is sometimes preferable since many of the other terms have special meanings in XML-related technologies (as, for example "element").

Structural markup A term that sometimes refers to MARKUP that makes explicit certain structural and semantic features of text, such as logical divisions or meanings (METADATA). XML and SGML are examples of structural markup languages. See Figure S.25. *Contrast* PRESENTATIONAL MARKUP.

Structured Graph Format *See* SGF.

Structured value In RDF, a complex property value that is part of a STATEMENT, as shown in Figure S.26.

Style A STRUCTURAL CONSTRUCT of a CSS STYLE SHEET that is used to define how a particular fragment of an

XML or HTML document will be presented in a WEB BROWSER in terms of font size, color, placement and other details.

Style sheet A generic term that can refer to either a CSS STYLE SHEET or an XSLT STYLE SHEET. In both cases, a style sheet is a formatting document used to define the appearance of an XML DOCUMENT or other types of documents. A style sheet is specified at the beginning of a document as either an embedded style sheet or an external (linked) style sheet. *See also* ASSOCIATING STYLE SHEETS WITH XML DOCUMENTS; RENDERING XML DOCUMENTS.

Stylesheet *See* STYLE SHEET.

Style sheet declaration A term that is sometimes used to refer to the use of an XSLT ROOT ELEMENT that declares an XML DOCUMENT to be an XSLT STYLE SHEET.

Style sheet element One of the two synonymous ELEMENTS that can be used as the ROOT ELEMENT of an XSLT STYLE SHEET. Its ATTRIBUTES are used to declare the XSLT namespace and to specify the version of the XSLT language. See Figure S.27. *Compare* TRANSFORM ELEMENT.

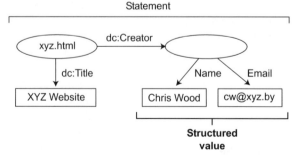

Figure S.26 An example of a structured value.

156

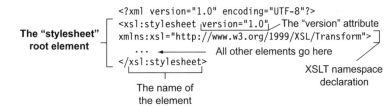

The "stylesheet" root element

The "version" attribute

All other elements go here

XSLT namespace declaration

The name of the element

Figure S.27 The "style sheet" element.

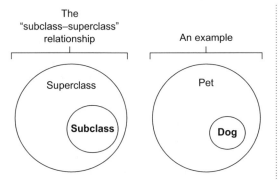

Figure S.28 An illustration of the "subclass" concept in RDF Schema.

Styling XML documents A term that refers to applying a CSS or XSL style sheet to an XML DOCUMENT in order to specify how it will be displayed. *See also* STYLE SHEET; CSS STYLE SHEET; XSLT STYLE SHEET.

Subclass In RDF SCHEMA, a CLASS that is part of another class known as a SUPERCLASS. Note that all classes are subclasses of themselves. See Figure S.28. *See also* SUBCLASSOF PROPERTY.

subClassOf property In an RDF SCHEMA, the `rdfs:subClassOf` PROPERTY that is used to state that all the INSTANCES of one CLASS are instances of another. *See also* SUBCLASS.

Subelement A term sometimes used to refer to a CHILD of an ELEMENT.

Subject element One of the 15 ELEMENTS of the DUBLIN CORE METADATA ELEMENT SET. The `<dc:subject>` element specifies what the RESOURCE is about. Note that "dc" is the NAMESPACE PREFIX of the DUBLIN CORE NAMESPACE.

Subject resource In RDF and RDF SCHEMAS, a RESOURCE that is being described by another resource (called an OBJECT RESOURCE) and a PROPERTY (which specifies a relationship between these two resources). In the example shown in Figure S.29, the `index.html` WEB PAGE is the subject resource that is being described as created by a person (who is probably called "John" and who is identified via his personal WEB SITE). The `dc:Creator` property specifies the relationship between the two resources. Note that the "dc" prefix is the DUBLIN CORE NAMESPACE prefix. A subject resource, an object resource and a property make up a TRIPLE. *See also* CREATOR ELEMENT.

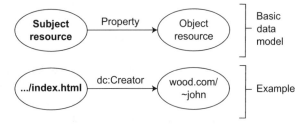

Figure S.29 The subject resource.

Figure S.30 An example of a property hierarchy.

Submit element *See* FORM CONTROLS.

Subproperty In RDF SCHEMA, a PROPERTY that is derived from another property. In the example shown in Figure S.30, the "retailPrice" and "salePrice" are subproperties of the "price" property.

Suffix Another term for FILENAME EXTENSION.

Superclass In an RDF SCHEMA, a CLASS that includes another class known as a SUBCLASS. See Figure S.31. *See also* SUBCLASSOF PROPERTY.

svg The FILENAME EXTENSION of SVG files. For example, "Catalog.svg".

SVG (Scalable Vector Graphics) An XML-BASED MARKUP LANGUAGE for describing two-dimensional graphics. It supports three types of graphic

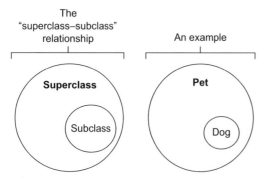

Figure S.31 An illustration of the "superclass" concept in an RDF Schema.

object: (1) vector graphic shapes; (2) bit-mapped images; and (3) text. Six predefined vector shapes include: (1) rectangle <rect>; (2) circle <circle>; (3) ellipse <ellipse>; (4) polyline <polyline>; (5) polygon <polygon>; and (6) path <path>. SVG benefits from its tight integration with other members of the XML FAMILY OF TECHNOLOGIES, such as XSL, RDF, SMIL, XLINK and XPOINTER. Details of SVG can be found at http://www.w3.org/TR/SVG/.

In the SVG file shown in Figure S.32, a rectangle, an ellipse and text are defined. The <svg> tag tells a browser or standalone viewer that this file is an SVG document and also includes the attributes width and height that define the canvas of the SVG document. All the SVG content is placed between the <svg> and </svg> tags. The <rect/> tag is the code that defines a rectangle and declares its properties, such as the width and height. The <ellipse/> tag defines an ellipse by the coordinates of its center and by its radius in a horizontal (rx) and vertical (ry) direction. The <text> tag contains text as character data and defines its font size and position on the screen (using the x and y attributes).

Symmetric property In OWL, a property that describes the following relationships between two RESOURCES: "If resource A has a property P linking it to resource B, then resource B also has a property P linking it to resource A". For example, "if John is a friend of Chris, Chris is a friend of John". A symmetric property can be defined using the owl:SymmetricProperty ELEMENT, as shown in Figure S.33. *See also* OWL VOCABULARY.

Synchronization Markup Language *See* SYNCML.

Synchronized Multimedia Integration Language *See* SMIL.

SyncML (Synchronization Markup Language) An XML-BASED MARKUP LANGUAGE for synchronizing all types of devices and applications over any network. More information about SyncML is available at http://www.openmobilealliance.org/syncml/.

XML declaration ——→ `<?xml version="1.0"?>`
The "svg" start tag ——→ `<svg width="17cm" height="14cm">`
The "rectangle" ————→ `<rect x="4cm" y="1.5cm" width="3cm" height="3cm"/>`
The "ellipse" element ——→ `<ellipse cx="8cm" cy="9cm" rx="4cm" ry="2cm" />`
⌐ `<text style="font-size:24pt;" x="3cm" y="6cm">`
The "text" element ——— `    Hello, the SVG World!`
⌐ `</text>`
The "svg" end tag ——→ `</svg>`

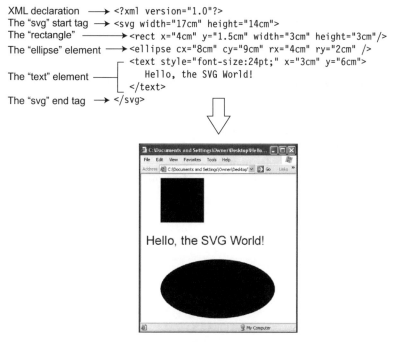

Figure S.32 A simple SVG file and its view in a browser.

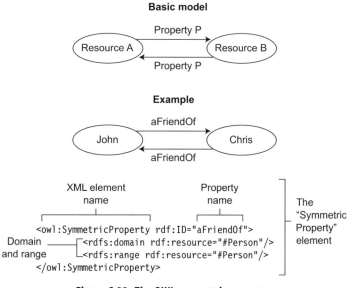

Figure S.33 The OWL symmetric property.

Syntax 1. In linguistics, the rules about how words are arranged and connected to form sentences and phrases. Also, the study of these rules. *Compare* PRAGMATICS; SEMANTICS.

2. In computing, the rules governing construction of a programming or MARKUP LANGUAGE.

Syntax highlighting A feature of an XML EDITOR. The program recognizes the syntax of XML and applies color coding accordingly, in order to make it easier to identify TAGS and separate them from the content.

Synthetic Infoset (Synthetic Information Set) A type of INFORMATION SET that does not result from parsing an XML DOCUMENT but is constructed by other means, such as the use of DOM or transformations of existing information sets. More details are available at `http://www.w3.org/TR/xml-infoset/`.

SYSTEM keyword *See* DOCTYPE DECLARATION.

Systems Biology Markup Language *See* SBML.

Tag The main STRUCTURAL CONSTRUCT of a MARKUP LANGUAGE, such as XML, HTML and SGML. A simple tag consists of a STRING (i.e. text) called a tag name or an ELEMENT NAME that is enclosed in ANGLE BRACKETS. In XML, there are three main types of tag: (1) START TAG; (2) END TAG; (3) EMPTY-ELEMENT TAG. A start tag and a matching end tag form an ELEMENT. A start tag can include not only an element name but also one or more ATTRIBUTES. See Figure T.1.

Tags are used to mark up the content of a document, i.e. to delimit and label logical and structural parts of the document. The term "tag" is sometimes used to refer to other types of MARKUP that use angle brackets as DELIMITERS, such as PROCESSING INSTRUCTIONS or XML COMMENTS. Tags are also called "markup tags".

Tag name *See* TAG.

Tag-valid In SGML, a concept that is equivalent to the WELL-FORMED concept in XML. *See also* TYPE-VALID.

Talk Markup Language *See* TALKML.

TalkML (Talk Markup Language) An experimental XML-BASED MARKUP LANGUAGE for voice browsers that describes spoken dialogs, in particular prompts, speech grammars and production rules for acting on responses. It is intended to test out ideas for using context-free grammars for more flexible voice interaction dialogs. See http://www.w3.org/Voice/TalkML/ for more details.

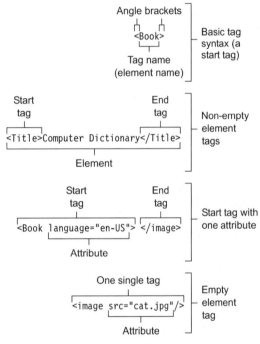

Figure T.1 Types of tags in XML.

Target The main part of a PROCESSING INSTRUCTION that specifies the application to which the processing instruction is directed. *See also* ASSOCIATING STYLE SHEETS WITH XML DOCUMENTS; XML DECLARATION.

Technical Report *See* W3C TECHNICAL REPORT.

TEI (Text Encoding Initiative) An international research effort intended to produce an XML/

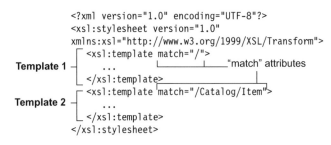

Figure T.2 Examples of XSLT templates.

SGML-based standard for encoding and interchange of literary and linguistic texts in electronic form. See http://www.tei-c.org/ for more details.

Telecommunications Interchange Markup *See* TIM.

Template The main STRUCTURAL CONSTRUCT of an XSLT STYLE SHEET. The xsl:template ELEMENT contains rules to apply when a specified NODE is matched. The MATCH ATTRIBUTE of the element is used to associate the template with an element. The XSLT style sheet, shown in Figure T.2, consists of two templates. Note that the ATTRIBUTE VALUE of the MATCH ATTRIBUTE is an XPATH LOCATION PATH. Template 1 matches the ROOT NODE of the XPATH NODE TREE. Note that the root node represents not the ROOT ELEMENT but the DOCUMENT ROOT. Template 2 matches the "Item" elements, which are CHILD ELEMENTS of the "Catalog" element. The "Catalog" element is the root element of the XML DOCUMENT and should not be confused with the root node (i.e. with the document root) represented by the starting forward slash. A template is also sometimes called "a template rule" or "a construction rule".

Template rule A term that is sometimes used to refer to a TEMPLATE.

Text encoding *See* MARKUP.

Text Encoding Initiative *See* TEI.

Text entity An ENTITY that associates CHARACTER DATA with an entity name.

Text node One of seven NODE TYPES of XPATH DATA MODEL that represents CHARACTER DATA.

Text properties In CSS, text properties are the collection of properties and values that control textual features of ELEMENT CONTENT. The most common text properties and values include: (1) the font-family property, which can specify a family-name (a font family name, like Arial or Courier), a generic-family (five possible values: serif, sans-serif, cursive, fantasy, monospace) or both. (2) the font-style property that can take one of the three values: normal, italic and oblique. (3) The font-weight property, which possible values include four relative values (normal, lighter, bold, bolder) and nine range values (100, 200, 300, 400, 500, 600, 700, 800, 900). (4) the COLOR PROPERTY.

Theological Markup Language *See* THML.

Thing class A predefined OWL class that is the CLASS of all INDIVIDUALS and hence a SUPERCLASS of all OWL classes. Every individual in OWL is a member of the "owl:Thing" class. In the example shown in Figure T.3 an individual "Teddy" is defined as an instance of the "Thing" class and also of the "Dog" class. It can be read as: "Teddy is a Thing. Specifically, it is a Dog Thing". *See also* OWL VOCABULARY.

The "Thing" class as a superclass of all OWL classes

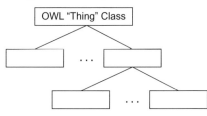

The "Thing" class as the class of all individials

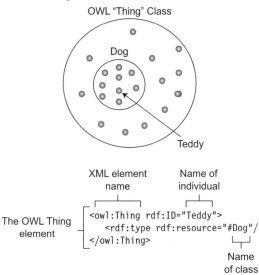

Figure T.3 The OWL "Thing" class.

Third-party arc In XLINK, an ARC in which neither the STARTING RESOURCE nor the ENDING RESOURCE is a LOCAL RESOURCE. *Compare* INBOUND ARC; OUTBOUND ARC.

Third-party link In XLINK, a LINK that is based on a THIRD-PARTY ARC.

ThML (Theological Markup Language) An XML-BASED MARKUP LANGUAGE for marking up theological texts, especially the Christian Classics Ethereal Library (CCEL). For more details, see `http://www.ccel.org/ThML/`.

TIM (Telecommunications Interchange Markup) An XML/SGML-based markup language for describing the structure of

telecommunications and other technical documents. More details about TIM can be obtained from `http://www.atis.org/atis/tcif/ipi/dl_tim.htm`.

Title element One of the 15 ELEMENTS of the DUBLIN CORE METADATA ELEMENT SET. The `<dc:title>` element specifies the name given to the RESOURCE. Note that "dc" is the NAMESPACE PREFIX of the DUBLIN CORE NAMESPACE.

Title-type element In XLINK, the ELEMENT of an XML DOCUMENT that has a TYPE ATTRIBUTE with the "title" ATTRIBUTE VALUE and therefore can be used to provide a human-readable label for the LINK.

TM An acronym used to refer both to TOPIC MAPS as a technology and to a specific topic map.

TMCL (Topic Map Constraint Language) A formal language for defining schemas and constraints for TOPIC MAPS. It is intended to perform the same role for topic maps that DTDS or XML SCHEMAS do for XML. For more details about TMCL, see `http://www.isotopicmaps.org/tmcl/`.

TMML (Turing Machine Markup Language) An XML-BASED MARKUP LANGUAGE that can be used for the description of Turing machines. For more details, see the information at `http://www.unidex.com/turing/`.

TMQL (Topic Map Query Language) A language for accessing data stored in TOPIC MAPS. More information about TMQL is available at `http://www.isotopicmaps.org/tmql/`.

Topic Map Constraint Language *See* TMCL.

Topic Map Query Language *See* TMQL.

Topic maps The ISO 13250:2003 standard. Like RDF and RDFS, it can be used to annotate WEB RESOURCES in order to make them processable by computers. The topic maps technology allows

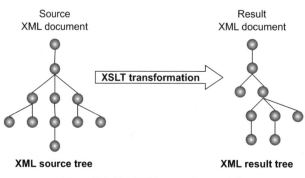

Figure T.4 The XSLT processing model.

users to build a semantic network above information RESOURCES, and thus to dramatically enhance navigation in very complex data sets. A topic map is based on the following fundamental concepts: (1) topics, (2) associations and (3) occurrences. Similar to an entry in an encyclopedia, a topic can represent any subject and therefore almost everything in a topic map is a topic. Topics are connected by associations, and point to resources through occurrences. An association expresses a relationship between several topics. A topic can be linked to one or more occurrences – information resources that are somehow related to this topic. For example, "the Web" and "the Internet" are topics that have an association "is part of" and several occurrences (places where they are mentioned, including not only text but also images) in this dictionary. Topic maps may be used to model RDF and vice versa.

Top-level element *See* ROOT ELEMENT.

TR (Technical Report) *See* W3C TECHNICAL REPORT.

Transaction Authority Markup Language *See* XAML.

Transformation In XSLT, the process of applying TEMPLATE rules specified in an XSLT STYLE SHEET to a source XML DOCUMENT. Note that the XSLT processing model describes the transformation process as transforming the NODE TREE of the source document (called "an XML source tree") into the node tree of the result document (called "an XML result tree"), as shown in Figure T.4.

Transformation template *See* TEMPLATE.

Transform element One of the two synonymous ELEMENTS that can be used as the ROOT ELEMENT of an XSLT STYLE SHEET. Its ATTRIBUTES are used to declare the XSLT NAMESPACE and to specify the version of the XSL language. See Figure T.5. *Compare* STYLE SHEET ELEMENT.

Transitive property In OWL, a property that describes the type of relationships between three or more RESOURCES, as shown in Figure T.6. For

```
<?xml version="1.0" encoding="UTF-8"?>
<xsl:transform version="1.0"
xmlns:xsl="http://www.w3.org/1999/XSL/Transform">
  ...
</xsl:transform>
```

XML declaration

The "transform" root element

The "version" attribute

All other elements go here

XSLT namespace declaration

The name of the element

Figure T.5 The "transform" element.

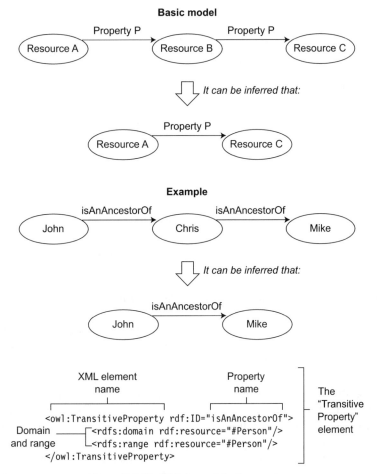

Basic model

Example

XML element name

Property name

The "Transitive Property" element

```
<owl:TransitiveProperty rdf:ID="isAnAncestorOf">
    <rdfs:domain rdf:resource="#Person"/>
    <rdfs:range rdf:resource="#Person"/>
</owl:TransitiveProperty>
```

Domain and range

Figure T.6 The OWL "transitive" property.

example, if "isAnAncestorOf" is defined to be a transitive property, from the statement "John is an ancestor of Chris, Chris is an ancestor of Mike" it can be inferred that "John is an ancestor of Mike". A transitive property can be defined using the owl:TransitiveProperty ELEMENT. *See also* OWL VOCABULARY.

Transportation Extensible Markup Language *See* TXML.

TranXML (XML for Transportation-Related Transactions) An XML-based messaging system that allows carrier and shipper legacy systems to exchange data for transportation and logistics. Details of TranXML can be found at http://www.tranxml.org/.

Traversal In XLINK, using or following a LINK for any purpose. Traversal always involves a pair of RESOURCES: the starting resource and the ending resource. Note that in this context the term "resources" can refer not only to whole resources but also to resource portions.

Tree-based parser An XML PARSER that processes XML DOCUMENTS in such a way that the entire document structure is represented in the computer

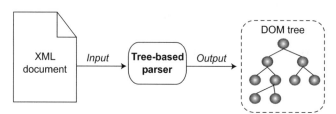

Figure T.7 Tree-based parser.

memory as an XML DOM tree, and is available all at once. This method is useful for assessing, manipulating and transforming XML documents, but is memory-intensive and requires major computing power for processing large documents. See Figure T.7. Note that a tree-based parser can be either a VALIDATING PARSER or a NON-VALIDATING PARSER. *Contrast* EVENT-DRIVEN PARSER.

Tree-based parsing A document-centric method of parsing XML DOCUMENTS that is employed in TREE-BASED PARSERS.

Tree Regular Expressions for XML *See* TREX.

TREX (Tree Regular Expressions for XML) A SCHEMA language for XML that may be seen as a less complex alternative to an XML SCHEMA. It is written in XML SYNTAX. TREX has been merged with RELAX to create RELAX NG. Details of TREX can be found at http://www.thaiopensource.com/trex/. *See also* DSD; SCHEMATRON.

Triple A STRUCTURAL CONSTRUCT of the RDF DATA MODEL. It consists of three parts: (1) a subject (a RESOURCE); (2) a predicate (a resource); and (3) an object (a resource or a LITERAL). Together they form a STATEMENT. There are number of ways to represent triples, such as lists, directed labeled graphs or XML syntax. The triple, shown in Figure T.8, can be read as "John Wood is the creator of www.fun.by".

Triple-s (Triple-s Survey Interchange Standard) An XML-BASED MARKUP LANGUAGE for describing survey metadata such as question and response texts, or valid ranges for responses. The meaning of the word "triple-s" comes from a KISSS (Keep It Simple Standard Stupid) approach to the design of Triple-s. For more details, see the information at http://www.triple-s.org/.

Triple-s Survey Interchange Standard *See* TRIPLE-S.

Turing Machine Markup Language *See* TMML.

tXML (Transportation Extensible Markup Language) An XML-BASED MARKUP LANGUAGE that enables standard application integration among all members of a logistics chain as well as intra-enterprise requirements between legacy and new systems. For more details, see http://www.logistics.com/products/architecture/tXML.asp.

Type attribute In XLINK, an ATTRIBUTE that is used to specify the use of the ELEMENT in terms of the XLINK language functionality. The main possible ATTRIBUTE VALUES of the xlink:type attribute are: (1) "simple" – defines a SIMPLE LINK; (2) "extended" – defines an EXTENDED LINK; (3) "locator" (*see* LOCATOR); (4) "resources" (*see* RESOURCE-TYPE ELEMENT); (5) "arc" (*see* ARC; ARC-TYPE ELEMENT); (6) "title" (*see* TITLE-TYPE ELEMENT). See Figure T.9.

Type definition *See* TYPE DEFINITION COMPONENT.

Type definition component A generic term for a primary SCHEMA COMPONENT that is either a SIMPLE TYPE DEFINITION or a COMPLEX TYPE DEFINITION. Also known as "Type definition".

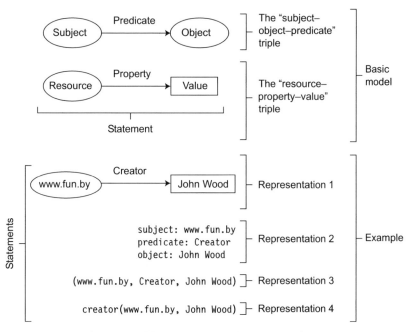

Figure T.8 Different representations of RDF triples.

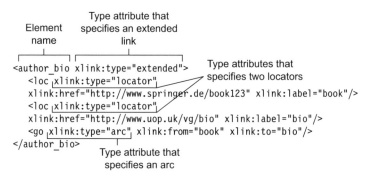

Figure T.9 Example of XLink type attributes.

Type element One of the 15 ELEMENTS of the DUBLIN CORE METADATA ELEMENT SET. The <dc:type> element specifies the type of the RESOURCE, such as dictionary, home page, technical report or photograph. Note that "dc" is the NAMESPACE PREFIX of the DUBLIN CORE NAMESPACE.

Type property In an RDF SCHEMA, the rdfs:type PROPERTY, which is used to state that a RESOURCE is an INSTANCE of a CLASS.

Type system components In the WSDL COMPONENT MODEL, a subcomponent of the top-level DEFINITIONS COMPONENT that includes ELEMENT DECLARATIONS and type definitions (*see* TYPE DEFINITION COMPONENT) as defined by an XML SCHEMA.

Type-valid In SGML, a concept that is equivalent to the VALID XML DOCUMENT concept in XML. *See also* TAG-VALID.

UBL (Universal Business Language) An XML-BASED MARKUP LANGUAGE that defines libraries of business documents (such as purchase orders and invoices) exchanged in E-COMMERCE. For more details, see `http://www.oasis-open.org/committees/ubl/`.

UCS (Universal Character Set) A character encoding standard defined in ISO/IEC 10646 or (the latest version) ISO/IEC 10646-1. More details about UCS can be obtained from `http://www.iso.ch/`.

UCS Transformation Format *See* UTF-16.

UDDI (Universal Description, Discover and Integration) A global directory of XML WEB SERVICES, in which businesses offering Web services are registered and can be searched for. UDDI is a platform-independent framework that uses (1) existing Internet standards, such as XML, HTTP and DNS; (2) WSDL to describe interfaces to Web services; and (3) SOAP as a COMMUNICATION PROTOCOL. UDDI makes it possible to discover the right Web service from the millions currently available online. It can be compared to the white, yellow and green pages in a telephone directory. More information about UDDI is available at `http://www.uddi.org/`.

UIML (User Interface Markup Language) An XML language that describes user interface elements such as buttons, menus, lists and other controls. It also defines the design of controls and their event-driven actions. Details of UIML are available at `http://www.uiml.org/`.

ULF (Universal Learning Format) A set of XML-based formats for describing and exchanging various types of e-learning data, such as education catalogs and online course content. Details of ULF can be found at `http://www.saba.com/standards/ulf/`.

Ultimate SOAP receiver *See* SOAP INTERMEDIARY.

UML (Unified Modeling Language) An object-oriented language that is intended for specifying, developing, and documenting software, business models, and other complex systems. The main modeling concepts include object classes, associations and interfaces. UML can be effectively used for modeling XML, RDF and RDFS data.

UML Exchange Format *See* UXF.

Unabbreviated syntax In XPATH, full SYNTAX for a LOCATION STEP in the form shown in Figure U.1. *Contrast* ABBREVIATED SYNTAX.

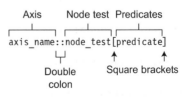

Figure U.1 Unabbreviated syntax for a location step.

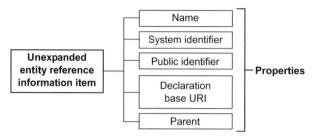

Figure U.2 The unexpanded entity reference information item and its properties.

Unexpanded entity reference information item
One of the 11 types of INFORMATION ITEM in the
INFORMATION SET. Like all of them, it is an abstract
description of a STRUCTURAL CONSTRUCT of an XML
DOCUMENT. This description is intended for use in
other XML-related specifications, which need to
conform to the information set. The unexpanded
entity reference information item is a placeholder
that can be used by a NON-VALIDATING PARSER to indicate that it does not read and expand EXTERNAL
ENTITIES. This information item has five properties,
as shown in Figure U.2. For more details, see
`http://www.w3.org/TR/xml-infoset/`.

Unicode (Universal Character Code) A universal character set that is intended to provide an
unambiguous encoding of the content of PLAIN TEXT,
covering all of the world's languages, alphabets
and scripts. The latest version is Unicode 3.0, on
which the Second Edition of the XML 1.0
RECOMMENDATION is based. *See also* NON-NORMATIVE
REFERENCES; NORMATIVE REFERENCES; XML 1.0 REFERENCES.
Details of Unicode can be found at `http://`
`www.unicode.org/`.

Unicode Transformation Format *See* UTF-16.

Unicode Transformation Format 8 *See* UTF-8.

Unified Modeling Language *See* UML.

Uniform Resource Identifier *See* URI.

Uniform Resource Locator *See* URL.

Uniform Resource Name *See* URN.

Union data type In an XML SCHEMA, a DATA TYPE that
is a union of different ATOMIC DATA TYPES and LIST DATA
TYPES.

Universal Business Language *See* UBL.

Universal Character Set *See* UCS.

**Universal Description, Discover and
Integration** *See* UDDI.

Universal Learning Format *See* ULF.

Universal Resource Identifier *See* URI.

Universal Resource Locator *See* URL.

Unnamed namespace *See* UNPREFIXED NAMESPACE.

Unparsed entity An ENTITY that is not analyzed by
an XML PARSER, since it usually points to binary NON-
TEXT DATA. *Contrast* PARSED ENTITY.

Unparsed entity information item One of the
11 types of INFORMATION ITEM in the INFORMATION SET.
Like all of them, it is an abstract description of a
STRUCTURAL CONSTRUCT of an XML DOCUMENT. This
description is intended for use in other XML-
related specifications, which need to conform to
the information set. There is one unparsed entity
information item in the information set for each
unparsed general entity declared in the DTD. This

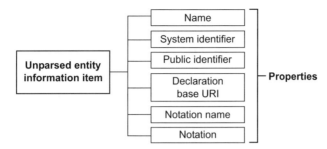

Figure U.3 The unparsed entity information item and its properties.

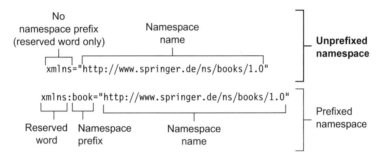

Figure U.4 A comparison of an unprefixed namespace with a prefixed namespace.

information item has six properties, as shown in Figure U.3. For more details, see http://www.w3.org/TR/xml-infoset/.

Unprefixed namespace A NAMESPACE that is declared without using a NAMESPACE PREFIX. Any ELEMENTS within the NAMESPACE SCOPE that have no QUALIFIED NAME (i.e. all unprefixed elements) are by default attached to this namespace. See Figure U.4. *Contrast* PREFIXED NAMESPACE. *See also* DEFAULT NAMESPACE; NAMESPACE DECLARATION; NAMESPACE NAME; OVERRIDING NAMESPACES; XMLNS ATTRIBUTE.

Unqualified name An ELEMENT NAME or an ATTRIBUTE NAME that is not a QUALIFIED NAME, because it does not include a NAMESPACE PREFIX and in fact consists of only a LOCAL PART. The use of identical unqualified names with different meanings in the same document causes a name collision, and makes this document meaningless. Figure U.5 shows the use of unqualified and qualified names in four different contexts. *Contrast* QUALIFIED NAME. *See also*

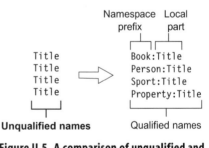
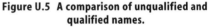

Figure U.5 A comparison of unqualified and qualified names.

NAMESPACE DECLARATION; NAMESPACE NAME; OVERRIDING NAMESPACES; PREFIXED NAMESPACE; UNPREFIXED NAMESPACE.

URI (Uniform Resource Identifier) Also known as Universal Resource Identifier. A generic identifier used to distinguish concrete, abstract, or both concrete and abstract resources on the Internet. There are two main types of URI: (1) URL (for concrete resources); (2) URN (for abstract resources). A URI is comprised of two parts separated by a colon, as shown in Figure U.6. The major URI

171

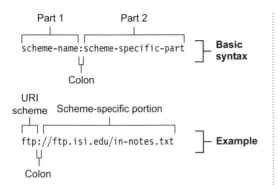

Figure U.6 The syntax and an example of URI.

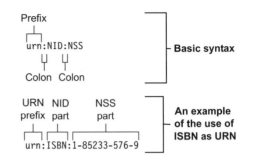

Figure U.7 The syntax and an example of a URN.

schemes are: (1) http (for HTTP); (2) ftp (for File Transfer Protocol); (3) mailto (for an email address); (4) file (for system-specific file names); and (5) news (for a newsgroup). URI (RFC 2396) is one of the NON-NORMATIVE REFERENCES of the XML 1.0 RECOMMENDATION. URIs serve as one of the foundations of the SEMANTIC WEB. More details about URIs can be obtained from http://www.w3.org/Addressing/. *See also* SEMANTIC WEB ARCHITECTURE.

URL (Uniform Resource Locator) Also known as Universal Resource Locator. A subset of URI that is intended for describing concrete resources, i.e. resources that can be accessed and retrieved from the network location specified by a URL. Like any URI, a URL is comprised of two parts separated by a colon, for example: http://www.springer.de/. URL (RFC 1738) is one of the NON-NORMATIVE REFERENCES of the XML 1.0 RECOMMENDATION. Details of URLs can be found at http://www.w3.org/Addressing/. *See also* URN.

URN (Uniform Resource Name) A subset of URI that is intended for specifying generic abstract resource names that are globally unique, persistent and location-independent. Unlike a URL, a URN can refer to resources that do not exist on the Internet, or which exist in the real world, such as a theory or a dog. It is very important to understand that URN uses names that just look like Web addresses (URLs) for identifying anything –

Internet resources or real-world "resources" (objects), but unlike URLs, URN-specified resources are not intended to be accessed or retrieved using a computer.

A URN consists of three parts separated by colons, as shown in Figure U.7: (1) the URN prefix string "urn"; (2) the Namespace Identifier (NID); and (3) the Namespace Specific String (NSS). Note that a URN is not CASE-SENSITIVE and no embedded WHITE SPACE is allowed. URN (RFC 2141) is one of the NON-NORMATIVE REFERENCES of the XML 1.0 RECOMMENDATION. Details of URNs can be found at http://www.w3.org/Addressing/.

use attribute In an XML SCHEMA, the ATTRIBUTE of an ATTRIBUTE DECLARATION that is used for specifying the DEFAULT VALUE, FIXED VALUE or prohibited value, which the declared ATTRIBUTE takes when it appears in an XML DOCUMENT.

User agent *See* INTELLIGENT AGENT.

User-derived data type A DERIVED DATA TYPE that is defined by individual XML SCHEMA authors.

User interface In XFORMS, one of three XFORMS SECTIONS that are the visual appearance of an XForm as it is rendered in XHTML, SVG or other languages. See Figure U.8. Note that XForms can also be rendered in a different way using a voice browser or other devices.

User Interface Markup Language *See* UIML.

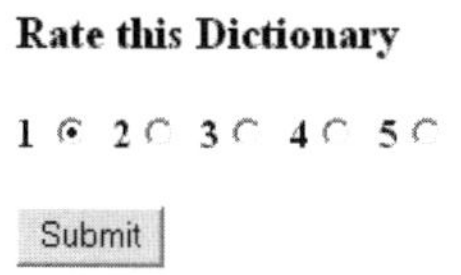

Rate this Dictionary

1 ⦿ 2 ○ 3 ○ 4 ○ 5 ○

[Submit]

Figure U.8 The user interface of an XForm.

UTF (1) In UTF-8, an acronym for "Unicode Trans-
formation Format"; (2) in UTF-16, an acronym for
"UCS Transformation Format". *See also* UCS;
UNICODE.

UTF-16 (UCS Transformation Format) The standard encoding for UNICODE, specified in the ISO
10646 standard. Also called Unicode

Transformation Format. UTF-16 is one of the
NORMATIVE REFERENCES of the XML 1.0 RECOMMENDATION.

UTF-8 (Unicode Transformation Format 8) An
8-bit variable length encoding method for UNICODE
as described in RFC 2279. All Unicode characters
with a value smaller then 128 are transmitted as
is, the rest are encoded. UTF-8 is one of the
NORMATIVE REFERENCES of the XML 1.0 RECOMMENDATION.
For more information, see http://
www.ietf.org/rfc/rfc2279.txt.

UXF (UML Exchange Format) An XML-based
format for describing and interchanging UML
models. More details about UXF are available at
http://www.yy.cs.keio.ac.jp/~suzuki/pro-
ject/uxf/.

Valid *See* VALID XML DOCUMENT.

Valid XML document A WELL-FORMED XML DOCUMENT that adheres to a specific XML SCHEMA or DTD if it has one. Note that an XML DOCUMENT *must be* well-formed and *can be* valid. See Figure V.1.

Valid XML name A sequence of characters that is legal to use for the name of a STRUCTURAL CONSTRUCT of XML, such as an ELEMENT (*see* ELEMENT NAME) or ATTRIBUTE (*see* ATTRIBUTE NAME). A valid XML name must begin with a letter (but not a number), an underscore (_) or a colon (:). They may not begin

with the letters x, m and l in any combination of upper and lower cases, since these are reserved by the W3C for a special use. Here are examples of acceptable element names: firstname, FirstName, _firstName and _2First_name. The following names *are illegal*: 2First_name, xmlFirstName, XMLfirstName and XmL_first_name. No WHITE SPACE is allowed for separating parts of an XML name. Note that it is better to avoid using names that start with a colon (such as :firstName or :2firstName), since colons are used only to separate a NAMESPACE PREFIX from the LOCAL PART of a QUALIFIED NAME.

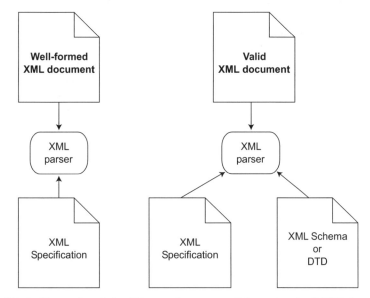

Figure V.1 An illustration of the difference between well-formed and valid XML documents.

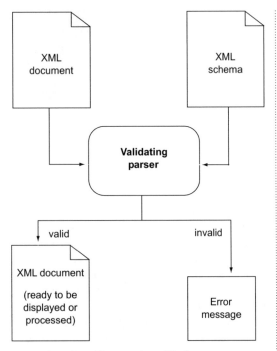

Figure V.2 The use of a validating parser.

Validating parser An XML PARSER that verifies that an XML document conforms to a specific DTD or XML SCHEMA. It checks whether the document is both well-formed and valid. See Figure V.2. *See also* NON-VALIDATING PARSER; VALID XML DOCUMENT; WELL-FORMED XML DOCUMENT.

Validation A check whether a document is the VALID XML DOCUMENT.

Validity *See* VALID XML DOCUMENT.

Validity constraints A term used to refer to rules, specified is a DTD or SCHEMA, that defines the allowable content of an XML DOCUMENT, including its element types and ATTRIBUTE VALUES.

Value Chain Markup Language *See* VCML.

Value property In an RDF SCHEMA, the rdf:value PROPERTY is used to describe STRUCTURED VALUES.

value-of element In XSLT, the ELEMENT of an XSLT STYLE SHEET that is used to select the value of an XML ELEMENT. The ATTRIBUTE VALUE of its "select" ATTRIBUTE is an XPATH LOCATION PATH. Figure V.3 shows two examples of XSLT "value-of" elements. In Example 1, the "select" attribute is used to select the values of all CHILD ELEMENTS of the ROOT NODE of the XPATH NODE TREE (i.e. the entire content of the XML DOCUMENT). In Example 2, the "select" attribute value selects the values of the "Price" element that is the first child element of the "Catalog" element.

Variable In programming, a symbol that represents data that may vary during the execution of a program. *Contrast* LITERAL.

vCard An Internet standard for creating and sharing virtual business cards that enables the common and consistent description of persons. Also known as the Electronic Business Card. *See also* VCARD RDF/XML SPECIFICATION.

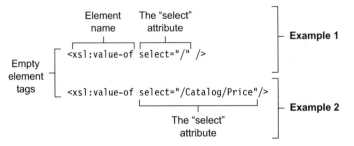

Figure V.3 Examples of XSLT "value-of" elements.

vCard RDF/XML Specification A W3C SPECIFICATION for encoding a VCARD in RDF/XML using the existing semantics of vCard. Documents with the RDF/XML encoding are also known as "RDF vCard" documents. For more details, see the information at http://www.w3.org/TR/vcard-rdf.

VCML (Value Chain Markup Language) A set of XML-based languages for describing standard collaborative business documents such as purchase orders and invoices. It enables value chain collaboration within and across vertical industries using a common VOCABULARY. More details of VCML may be obtained from http://www.vcml.net/.

Vector graphics A method of creating images on a computer using mathematical statements rather than bit-mapped descriptions.

Vector Markup Language *See* VML.

Version attribute A property of an XML DECLARATION that shows the number of the XML SPECIFICATION to which the XML DOCUMENT comforts. This attribute is compulsory if an XML declaration is included. Note that the XML declaration is optional by itself. See Figure V.4. *See also* ENCODING ATTRIBUTE; STANDALONE ATTRIBUTE.

VIML (Virtual Instruments Markup Language) An XML-BASED MARKUP LANGUAGE that describes location, protocol and device information for a network of virtual instrumentation devices and systems. More details are available at http://nacimiento.com/VIML/.

Virtual Instruments Markup Language *See* VIML.

Virtual Observatory Table *See* VOTABLE.

Virtual Reality Modeling Language *See* VRML.

Visa XML Invoice Specification An XML-based message format for managing financial transactions across regions, languages and industry sectors. More details are available at http://international.visa.com/fb/downloads/commprod/visaxmlinvoice/.

VML (Vector Markup Language) An XML-based language which defines a format for encoding of vector information, together with additional markup to describe how that information can be edited and displayed. For more details, see the information at http://www.w3.org/TR/NOTE-VML.

vml/vxml FILENAME EXTENSIONS that indicates that the file is in the VOICEXML format. For example, "Catalog.vml" or "Catalog.vxml".

Vocabulary A set of ELEMENT NAMES and ATTRIBUTE NAMES that are selected or produced in order to create a custom XML-BASED MARKUP LANGUAGE, such as XSLT, SVG or NEWSML. A vocabulary forms the basis of an XML SCHEMA or a DTD that specifies the relationships between ELEMENTS and ATTRIBUTES (still represented by element names and attribute names), the restrictions on ELEMENT CONTENTS and ATTRIBUTE VALUES, allowed DATA TYPES, and so on. The term "vocabulary" is sometimes used to refer to an entire XML-BASED MARKUP LANGUAGE defined in an XML schema or a DTD. Note that, more generally, it means words used in a language.

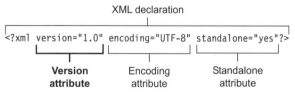

Figure V.4 The version attribute of the XML declaration.

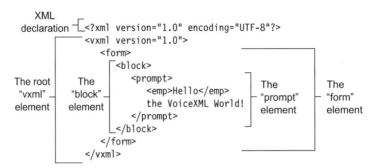

XML declaration

```
<?xml version="1.0" encoding="UTF-8"?>
<vxml version="1.0">
    <form>
        <block>
            <prompt>
                <emp>Hello</emp>
                the VoiceXML World!
            </prompt>
        </block>
    </form>
</vxml>
```

The root "vxml" element

The "block" element

The "prompt" element

The "form" element

Figure V.5 An example of a VoiceXML document.

Voice Extensible Markup Language *See* VOICEXML.

VoiceXML (Voice Extensible Markup Language) An XML-BASED MARKUP LANGUAGE intended for the development of Web-based voice dialog systems. A simple VoiceXML document is shown in Figure V.5. It specifies that the computer is to say "Hello, the VoiceXML World!" The document starts with an XML DECLARATION, followed by the ROOT ELEMENT "vxml". It contains the "prompt" ELEMENT that is NESTED within the "form" element (which is VoiceXML's basic dialog unit) and the "block" element (which is a container for non-interactive code). More details about VoiceXML can be obtained from http://www.voicexml.org/.

VOTable (Virtual Observatory Table) An XML-BASED MARKUP LANGUAGE for describing and exchanging astronomical tables for virtual astronomy. More information is available at http://www.us-vo.org/VOTable/.

VRML (Virtual Reality Modeling Language) A data format for describing three-dimensional objects and environments for graphical display in a standard WEB BROWSER or in a special VR viewer. The latest version of VRML is written in XML and is known as X3D.

W3C (World Wide Web Consortium) A group of member organization founded in 1994 that develops and maintains Web standards known as W3C RECOMMENDATIONS and other types of W3C TECHNICAL REPORTS.

W3C is hosted by three universities: (1) Massachusetts Institute of Technology (MIT) in the USA, (2) the French National Research Institute (INDIA) in Europe and (3) Keio University in Japan. The Director of W3C is Tim BERNERS-LEE the inventor of the World Wide Web. More information about W3C is available on its Web site at http://www.w3.org/.

W3C Candidate Recommendation The maturity level of a W3C RECOMMENDATION TRACK TECHNICAL REPORT that follows the W3C LAST CALL WORKING DRAFT and precedes the W3C PROPOSED RECOMMENDATION, as shown in Figure W.1. The main purpose of this type of W3C TECHNICAL REPORT is to call for implementation experience and feedback. More information is available at http://www.w3.org/Consortium/Process-20010208/tr.html. *See also* W3C SPECIFICATION; W3C TECHNICAL REPORT.

W3C Last Call Working Draft The maturity level of a W3C RECOMMENDATION TRACK TECHNICAL REPORT that follows the W3C WORKING DRAFT and precedes the W3C CANDIDATE RECOMMENDATION, as shown in Figure W.1. It is a special instance of a W3C Working Draft that usually remains at this level of maturity for only three weeks to seek technical review from W3C Working Groups and external parties. For more

details, see Figure W.1 and the information at http://www.w3.org/Consortium/Process-20010208/tr.html. *See also* W3C SPECIFICATION; W3C TECHNICAL REPORT.

W3C Note One of two types of W3C TECHNICAL REPORT. A report of this type is a dated and published record of an idea or a comment. (The other type is a W3C RECOMMENDATION TRACK TECHNICAL REPORT). More information about W3C Note is available at http://www.w3.org/Consortium/Process-20010208/tr.html. *See also* W3C SPECIFICATION.

W3C Proposed Recommendation The maturity level of a W3C RECOMMENDATION TRACK TECHNICAL REPORT that follows the W3C CANDIDATE RECOMMENDATION and precedes the W3C RECOMMENDATION, as shown in Figure W.1. The main purpose of this level of maturity is to adequately address dependencies from the W3C technical community and comments from external reviewers. A W3C TECHNICAL REPORT must remain at this maturity level for at least four weeks before either moving up to the W3C RECOMMENDATION level or moving back to an earlier level. More information is available at http://www.w3.org/Consortium/Process-20010208/tr.html. *See also* W3C CANDIDATE RECOMMENDATION; W3C TECHNICAL REPORT; W3C RECOMMENDATION.

W3C Recommendation The final level of maturity of a W3C RECOMMENDATION TRACK TECHNICAL REPORT that follows the W3C PROPOSED RECOMMENDATION and reflects consensus within the W3C. Also

W3C Recommendation track technical report

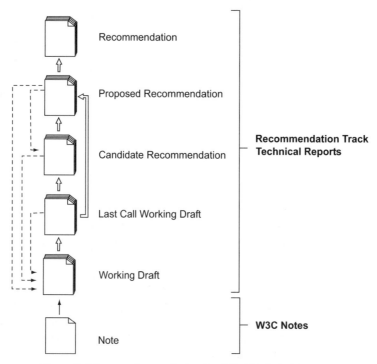

Figure W.1 Types and maturity levels of W3C Technical Reports.

sometimes called "a W3C standard". For more details, see Figure W.1 and the information at http://www.w3.org/Consortium/Process-20010208/tr.html. *See also* W3C TECHNICAL REPORT.

W3C Recommendation track technical report
One of two types of W3C TECHNICAL REPORT. A report of this type can move thought five stages of maturity, until it reaches the final status of a W3C RECOMMENDATION. This process is officially called "the W3C Recommendation track". (W3C NOTE is the other type.) See Figure W.1. More details are available at http://www.w3.org/Consortium/Process-20010208/tr.html. *See also* W3C SPECIFICATION.

W3C Specification A term that is sometimes used to refer to both a W3C RECOMMENDATION or a W3C TECHNICAL REPORT of a lower level of maturity, such as a W3C CANDIDATE RECOMMENDATION or a W3C PROPOSED RECOMMENDATION.

W3C Standard A term used sometimes to refer to a W3C RECOMMENDATION as the final maturity level reached by a W3C TECHNICAL REPORT. Note that a W3C standard is called a recommendation rather that a specification.

W3C Technical Report Main documents developed and published by the W3C. There are two types of Technical Report: (1) W3C RECOMMENDATION TRACK TECHNICAL REPORTS; and (2) W3C NOTES. Generally, a Technical Report begins its life as a W3C Note and then may progress throughout five levels of its maturity to reach the final form and became a W3C RECOMMENDATION. Note that on its way to a W3C Recommendation, a Technical Report can be returned to an earlier level at any time. See Figure W.1. More details are available at http://www.w3.org/Consortium/Process-20010208/tr.html. *See also* W3C CANDIDATE RECOMMENDATION; W3C LAST CALL WORKING DRAFT; W3C NOTE;

W3C PROPOSED RECOMMENDATION; W3C RECOMMENDATION; W3C SPECIFICATION; W3C WORKING DRAFT.

W3C Working Draft The initial level of maturity of a W3C RECOMMENDATION TRACK TECHNICAL REPORT that precedes the W3C LAST CALL WORKING DRAFT. It usually represents work in progress in a particular area of interest and does not assert any consensus about its content and quality. For more details, see Figure W.1 and the information at http:// www.w3.org/Consortium/Process-20010208/ tr.html. *See also* W3C LAST CALL WORKING DRAFT; W3C NOTE; W3C SPECIFICATION; W3C TECHNICAL REPORT.

W3C XML Schema *See* XML SCHEMA.

WAP (Wireless Application Protocol) A set of industry-standard specifications for providing Internet communications and advanced telephony services on wireless devices, such as mobile phones and personal digital assistants (PDAS). It includes WML. More details about WAP are available at http://www.wapforum.org/what/technical.htm.

WD (Working Draft) *See* W3C WORKING DRAFT.

WDDX (Web Distributed Data Exchange) An XML-based technology for exchanging complex data between Web programming languages. Details of WDDX are available at http:// www.openwddx.org/faq/.

Web address An address for a RESOURCE on the Internet, such as http://www.springer.de/. The Web address is more commonly referred to as the URL.

Web agent *See* INTELLIGENT AGENT.

Web bot *See* INTELLIGENT AGENT.

Web browser A program that is used for accessing WEB PAGES and related files. Two well-

known examples include Internet Explorer and Netscape Communicator.

Web Distributed Data Exchange *See* WDDX.

Web metadata *See* METADATA.

WebML (Web Modeling Language) A model-driven approach for specifying complex Web sites on a conceptual level using both a graphical notation and a textual XML syntax. WebML enables the high-level description of a Web site by means of five models: the structural model (the data content of the Web site), the composition model (the pages that compose the Web site), the navigation model (the topology of links between pages), the presentation model (the layout and graphic requirements for page rendering), and the personalization model (the customization features for one-to-one content delivery). See Figure W.2. See http://www.webml.org/ for more details.

Web Modeling Language *See* WEBML.

Web ontology *See* ONTOLOGY.

Web Ontology Language *See* OWL.

Web Ontology Language Description Logics *See* OWL DL.

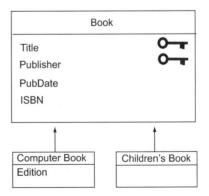

Figure W.2 A sample WebML graphical notation for IS-A hierarchies.

Web Ontology Language Full *See* OWL FULL.

Web Ontology Language Light *See* OWL LITE.

Web page A document or file created with HTML, XML, XHTML or other technologies that is the main STRUCTURAL CONSTRUCT of a WEB SITE and which is usually seen by a Web user as a page of information in a WEB BROWSER.

Web resource *See* RESOURCE.

Web server A computer that stores WEB PAGES and supplies them to other computers when requested via HTTP. The web pages can be viewed using a WEB BROWSER. *Also known* as an HTTP server.

Web services A standardized way of integrating Web-based applications that is based on protocols and technologies for reusable building-block applications which connect to each other via the Internet. This allows developers to integrate disparate applications within and between businesses. Web services use several XML-based technologies, such as: (1) XML as a MARKUP LANGUAGE for the data; (2) SOAP as the communication protocol; (3) WSDL as the interface description language; and (4) UDDI for registering and searching services. Unlike the traditional client–server model, Web services do not provide a GUI and do not require the use of browsers or HTML. Web services are sometimes called "application services". More information is available at http://www.w3.org/2002/ws/.

Web Services Definition Language *See* WSDL.

Web Services Interoperability Organization *See* WS-I.

Web site In the WWW, a collection of related WEB PAGES with the same domain name and usually stored on the same WEB SERVER.

Well-balanced *See* WELL-BALANCED REGION.

Well-balanced region In XFI, a region of an XML DOCUMENT that includes whole INFORMATION ITEMS. For example, if it contains a START TAG it must also contain the corresponding END TAG. A well-balanced region does not need to be a WELL-FORMED subset of an XML DOCUMENT, since it may, for example, include multiple ELEMENTS or text in place of the ROOT ELEMENT.

Well-formed *See* WELL-FORMED XML DOCUMENT.

Well-formed XML document An XML DOCUMENT is well-formed if it adheres to general XML SYNTAX RULES: (1) the document has one and only one ROOT ELEMENT; (2) all ELEMENTS that do not use EMPTY-ELEMENT TAGS have END TAGS; (3) an element has the same ELEMENT NAME in its START TAG and its end tag (note that XML is CASE-SENSITIVE); (4) all elements are NESTED properly without overlap; (5) all ATTRIBUTES are enclosed in quotes (note that either single or double quotes can be used, as long as they match within a single attribute); (6) no element has two or more attributes with the same ATTRIBUTE NAME; (7) SPECIAL SYMBOLS are replaced with their ENTITY REFERENCES; (8) All ENTITIES except PREDEFINED XML ENTITIES are declared before they are used; (9) element names and attribute names begin with a letter (but not a number and not with the letters x, m and l in any combination of upper and lower cases), an underscore (_) or a colon (:).

Any XML document *must* be well formed. Any XML PARSER always checks whether an XML DOCUMENT is well formed. If not, it stops reading and processing the document. The XML code shown in Figure W.3 contains an intentional syntax error and as a result the XML parser generates an error message. This message shows the line and character positions of the XML syntax error and therefore can be used for detecting and correcting the error. *See also* VALID XML DOCUMENT.

Well-formedness *See* WELL-FORMED XML DOCUMENT.

Well Log Markup Language *See* WELLLOGML.

```
<?xml version="1.0"?>
<!-- This document is not well formed -->
<RulesForWritingXML>
    <Rule>XML names are case sensitive.</Rule>
</rulesForWritingXML> ◄——————————— Code that contains a syntax error
```

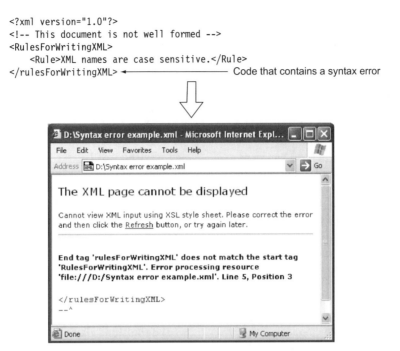

Figure W.3 The code and browser views of an XML document than is not well-formed.

WellLogML (Well Log Markup Language) An XML-BASED MARKUP LANGUAGE for describing all forms of acquired, processed, and interpreted well logs. More information is available at http://www.posc.org/ebiz/WellLogML/.

White space A term used originally to refer to characters that do not put ink on the paper when they are printed. White space can consist of one or more space characters, carriage returns, line feeds or tabs. In XML, it is permissible to add extra white space around the elements by writing them in an indented hierarchical form in order to make the XML code easier to read and edit (*see*

XML DOCUMENT). White space can appear inside an ATTRIBUTE VALUE. No white space is allowed inside a TAG or as part of an ATTRIBUTE NAME. Some examples of valid and invalid XML white space are shown in Figure W.4.

Whitespace *See* WHITE SPACE.

Wireless Application Protocol *See* WAP.

Wireless Markup Language *See* WML.

```
<■Tourist■Destination□□□local■language="British□English"■>□
□□□<City>□Plymouth□</City>□□□□□□□□□□□□□□
</■Tourist■Destination■>□□□□□□□□□□□□□□□□
```

■ Illegal white space
□ Legal white space

Figure W.4 Examples of legal and illegal white space in XML code.

wml A FILENAME EXTENSION indicating the file is a WML (Wireless Markup Language) document. For example, "Catalog.wml".

WML (Wireless Markup Language) An XML-BASED MARKUP LANGUAGE for specifying presentation and user interaction on limited capability devices such as mobile phones and other wireless mobile terminals. A WML document (also known as a deck) consists of one or more cards. In other words, a deck is a transportation container for cards (similar to a Web site) and a card is a unit of navigation and user interface (similar to a web page). Figure W.5 shows a simple WML document consisting of only one card and its appearance in a mobile phone browser. Note that the text "Hello World" is the title of the card (similar to the title of a Web page) and the text "Hello World!" is the actual content of the WML document. Details of WML can be found at http:// www1.wapforum.org/tech/documents/WAP-238-WML-20010911-a.pdf.

Working draft *See* W3C WORKING DRAFT.

World Wide Web *See* WWW.

World Wide Web Consortium *See* W3C.

WSDL (Web Services Description Language) An XML-BASED MARKUP LANGUAGE for describing, locating and accessing XML-BASED WEB SERVICES. It provides a WSDL COMPONENT MODEL and its XML representation for describing both the abstract functionality of a service and its concrete details. A WSDL document is an XML DOCUMENT that contains a set of definitions, such as messages, port types and services. WSDL describes WEB SERVICES using the messages exchanged between the service provider and requestor. An exchange of messages is called an operation. A collection of operations is describes as a port type. More information about WSDL may be obtained from http:// www.w3.org/2002/ws/desc/. For more details, *see* WSDL COMPONENT MODEL.

wsdl:binding element *See* BINDING COMPONENT.

wsdl:definitions element *See* DEFINITIONS ELEMENT.

wsdl:message element *See* MESSAGE COMPONENT.

wsdl:operation element *See* PORT TYPE OPERATION COMPONENT.

wsdl:operation element *See* BINDING OPERATION COMPONENT; PORT TYPE OPERATION COMPONENT.

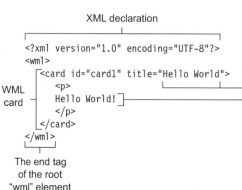

Figure W.5 An example of a WML document.

wsdl:part element *See* PART COMPONENT.

wsdl:portType element *See* MESSAGE COMPONENT.

wsdl:service element *See* SERVICE COMPONENT.

WSDL binding component *See* BINDING COMPONENT.

WSDL binding operation component *See* BINDING OPERATION COMPONENT.

WSDL component model A conceptual DATA MODEL underlying WSDL that is represented as a set of components with properties. The hierarchy of the model components is shown in Figure W.6. It comprises the DEFINITIONS COMPONENT at the top-level and WSDL COMPONENTS and TYPE SYSTEM COMPONENTS at the next level of the hierarchy.

The WSDL components include: (1) the MESSAGE COMPONENT with the PART COMPONENT as its subcomponent; (2) the PORT TYPE COMPONENT with the PORT TYPE OPERATION COMPONENT as its subcomponent; (3) the BINDING COMPONENT with the

The WSDL component model

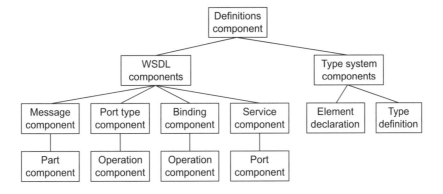

The XML representation of the model

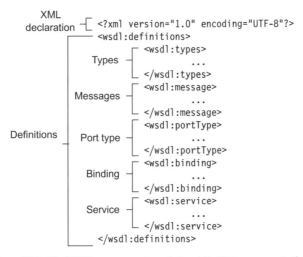

Figure W.6 The WSDL component model and its XML representation.

BINDING OPERATION COMPONENT as its subcomponent; (4) the SERVICE COMPONENT with the port component as its subcomponent. The type system components include: (1) ELEMENT DECLARATIONS; (2) TYPE DEFINITIONS. WSDL provides not only this abstract component model but also its representation (serialization) using XML-based syntax as shown in Figure W.6.

WSDL components In the WSDL COMPONENT MODEL, a subcomponent of the top-level DEFINITIONS COMPONENT that includes: (1) the MESSAGE COMPONENT; (2) the PORT TYPE COMPONENT; (3) the BINDING COMPONENT; and (4) the SERVICE COMPONENT.

WSDL definitions component *See* DEFINITIONS COMPONENT.

WSDL document root element *See* DEFINITIONS ELEMENT.

WSDL message component *See* MESSAGE COMPONENT.

WSDL namespace declaration *See* DEFINITIONS ELEMENT.

WSDL part component *See* PART COMPONENT.

WSDL port component *See* PORT COMPONENT.

WSDL port type component *See* PORT TYPE COMPONENT.

WSDL port type operation component *See* PORT TYPE OPERATION COMPONENT.

WSDL service component *See* SERVICE COMPONENT.

WSDL type system components *See* TYPE SYSTEM COMPONENTS.

WS-I (Web Services Interoperability Organization) An open, industry organization that is intended to promote Web services INTEROPERABILITY across platforms, operating systems, and programming languages. See http://www.ws-i.org/ for more details.

WSIL *See* WS-INSPECTION.

WS-Inspection (Web Services Inspection Language) An XML-BASED MARKUP LANGUAGE for the discovery and aggregation of Web service descriptions in a simple and extensible way. WS-Inspection is a complementary model to UDDI. It is intended to describe services at a functional level, whereas UDDI is at a more business-centric level. WS-Inspection is also known as WSIL. For more details, see http://www-106.ibm.com/developerworks/webservices/library/ws-wsilspec.html.

WWW (World Wide Web) The global set of interlinked WEB SITES that is easily accessible with a WEB BROWSER. Currently, the WWW is evolving from the FIRST-GENERATION WEB to the SECOND-GENERATION WEB, also known as the SEMANTIC WEB.

X3D (Extensible 3D) An XML-BASED MARKUP LANGUAGE for describing three-dimensional objects and environments that can be graphically displayed in a standard WEB BROWSER or in a special VR viewer. Essentially, X3D is the latest version of VRML that is written in XML and that is extending and upgrading the geometry and behavior capability of VRML. The X3D world, shown in Figure X.1, contains two objects: a red sphere and blue text. X3D is also knows as "Extensible 3D Graphics". For more information about X3D, see `http://www.web3d.org/x3d.html`.

XACL (XML Access Control Language) An XML-BASED MARKUP LANGUAGE that provides XML documents with an access control model that enables the initiator to securely update each document element. Details of XACL can be found at `http://www.trl.ibm.com/projects/xml/xacl/`.

XACML (Extensible Access Control Markup Language) An XML-BASED MARKUP LANGUAGE for the expression of authorization policies in XML against objects that are themselves identified in XML. See `http://www.xacml.org/` for more details.

xAL (Extensible Address Language) An XML-BASED MARKUP LANGUAGE for describing customer address data. It is part of XNAL (Extensible Name and Address Language) and is referenced by XCIL. Details of xAL are available at `http://`

`www.oasis-open.org/committees/ciq/`. *See also* XNL.

XAML (Transaction Authority Markup Language) An XML-BASED MARKUP LANGUAGE for coordinating and processing online business transactions. More details are available at `http://www.xaml.org/`.

XBEL (XML Bookmark Exchange Language) An XML-BASED MARKUP LANGUAGE for exchanging Internet "bookmarks". Details of XBEL can be found at `http://www.python.org/topics/xml/xbel/`.

XBRL (Extensible Business Reporting Language) An XML-BASED MARKUP LANGUAGE for describing financial information, such as financial affairs, business management and investment. See `http://www.xbrml.org/` for more details.

XCBF (XML Common Biometric Format) An XML-BASED MARKUP LANGUAGE for describing information that verifies identity based on human characteristics such as DNA, fingerprints, iris scans and hand geometry. More information about XCBF is available at `http://www.oasis-open.org/committees/xcbf/`.

xCBL (XML Common Business Library) A set of XML-based documents and their components developed to facilitate global E-COMMERCE. It is indented to promote INTEROPERABILITY by providing a common language that all participants in

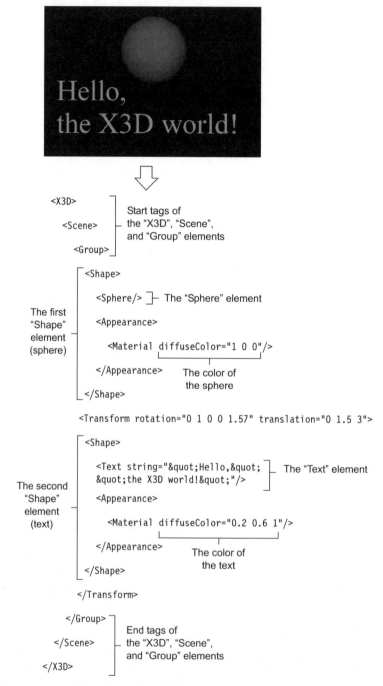

Figure X.1 A simple X3D world and its source code.

e-commerce (buyers, suppliers and providers of business services) can understand and, on this basis, to easily exchange their documents. More information about xCBL is available at http://www.xcbl.org/.

xCIL (Extensible Customer Information Language) An XML-BASED MARKUP LANGUAGE for representing global customer-centric data. It uses XNAL for representing customer name-and-address data. In addition to names and addresses, it allows describing many other customer-related details such as age, gender, marital status, person physical characteristics, and hobbies. XNAL is a sub-language of xCIL. XNL and XAL are referenced by xCIL. Details of xCIL can be found at http://www.oasis-open.org/committees/ciq/.

xCRL (Extensible Customer Relationships Language) An XML-BASED MARKUP LANGUAGE for managing global customer relationship data in order to achieve interoperability between different systems, processes and platforms. It makes it possible to describe the following three categories of customer relationship: Organization to Organization Relationships, Organization to Person Relationships, and Person to Person Relationships. xCRL uses XNAL for representing customer name and address data and XCIL for representing other customer information. For more details, see the information at http://www.oasis-open.org/committees/ciq/.

XDF (Extensible Data Format) An XML-BASED MARKUP LANGUAGE for documents containing most classes of scientific data. It can be used throughout the scientific disciplines. More details about XDF can be obtained from http://xml.gsfc.nasa.gov/XDF/.

xdr The FILENAME EXTENSION of a file that is an XDR (XML Data-Reduced) schema. For example, "Catalog.xsl". *See* XDR SCHEMA.

XDR *See* XDR SCHEMA.

XDR Schema (XML Data-Reduced Schema) One of the early SCHEMA languages that is still used in some of Microsoft's applications. It gets over a number of limitations of DTDS, such as data typing. Details of XDR are available at http://msdn.microsoft.com/library/default.asp?url=/library/en-us/xmlsdk30/htm/xmconintroductiontoschemas.asp. *See also* XML SCHEMA.

XEditor An XML-BASED MARKUP LANGUAGE for specifying an editing list for an XML document. For more details, see http://www.openhealth.org/editor/.

XER (XML encoding rules) A set of rules for encoding values of ASN.1 types using XML. Details of XER can be found at http://www.itu.int/ITU-T/studygroups/com17/languages/X.693_0901.pdf.

XFDL (Extensible Forms Description Language) An XML-BASED MARKUP LANGUAGE for representing complex forms such as those used in government and business.

XFI (XML Fragment Interchange) An XML-BASED MARKUP LANGUAGE for creating and transferring portions of XML DOCUMENTS. It provides mechanisms for specifying contextual information for a FRAGMENT of an XML document that enable the transmission of the fragment without transmitting the entire document. A FRAGMENT INTERCHANGE usually involves two files, as shown in Figure X.2: (1) a file that contains the FRAGMENT BODY; and (2) a FRAGMENT CONTEXT SPECIFICATION file. More details about XFI are available at http://www.w3.org/TR/2001/CR-xml-fragment-20010212/.

XFI context information *See* CONTEXT INFORMATION.

XFI fragment *See* FRAGMENT.

XFI fragment body *See* FRAGMENT BODY.

File 1 – The fragment body file:
```
<Title>Visualizing the Semantic Web</Title>
```

File 2 – The fragment context specification file:

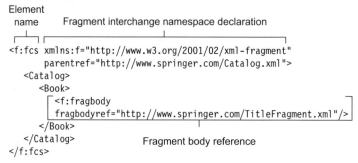

Figure X.2 An example of the use of the XFI language.

XFI namespace *See* FRAGMENT INTERCHANGE NAMESPACE.

XFI root element *See* FCS ELEMENT.

XFML (Exchangeable Faceted Metadata Language) An XML-BASED MARKUP LANGUAGE for exchanging hierarchical faceted metadata between Web sites. Details of XFML are available at http://xfml.org/.

XForms An XML-BASED MARKUP LANGUAGE for describing and creating the next generation forms for the Web. Forms are the primary enabling technology for online interaction, especially in E-COMMERCE.

Compared to traditional HTML forms, XForms have the following main advantages: (1) they are intended for use on the SECOND-GENERATION WEB and can be integrated with other members of the XML FAMILY OF TECHNOLOGIES, especially with XHTML and SVG; (2) they separate user interface from data and logic (*see* SEPARATION OF FORM FROM CONTENT); (3) they are platform- and device-independent. Figure X.3 shows the USER INTERFACE of a simple XForm used in E-COMMERCE. For more information about XForms, visit http://www.w3.org/TR/xforms/. *See also* XFORMS SECTIONS.

xforms:caption element *See* FORM CONTROLS.

Payment Method

Credit Card • Cash ○

Card Number: [   ]

Expiration Date: [   ]

[Submit]

Figure X.3 A simple XForm.

xforms:input element *See* FORM CONTROLS.

xforms:instance element *See* INSTANCE DATA.

xforms:model element *See* XFORMS MODEL.

xforms:submit element *See* FORM CONTROLS.

XForms action attribute *See* XFORMS MODEL.

XForms caption element *See* FORM CONTROLS.

XForms controls *See* FORM CONTROLS.

XForms input element *See* FORM CONTROLS.

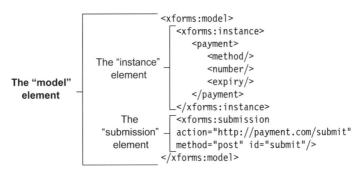

```
                              ┌<xforms:model>
                              │  ┌<xforms:instance>
                              │  │  <payment>
              The "instance"  │  │     <method/>
               element        ┤  │     <number/>
  The "model"               ┤  │     <expiry/>
   element                  │  │  </payment>
                              │  └</xforms:instance>
              The           │  ┌<xforms:submission
             "submission"   ┤  │ action="http://payment.com/submit"
              element       │  └ method="post" id="submit"/>
                              └</xforms:model>
```

Figure X.4 An example of an XForm model.

XForms instance data *See* INSTANCE DATA.

XForms instance element *See* INSTANCE DATA.

XForms model An XFORMS SECTION that is used to define the STRUCTURAL CONSTRUCTS of a form. The "model" ELEMENT is used as a container for the XForms model components. Figure X.4 shows a sample XForms model that defines that this form is used to collect three pieces of information and submit them to the URL specified in the "action" ATTRIBUTE.

XForms processor Part of a WEB BROWSER that is responsible for submitting the XFORMS data to a target using XML as the data format.

XForms sections Three parts into which XForms are divided: (1) XFORMS MODEL; (2) INSTANCE DATA; (3) USER INTERFACE. This division allows to implement the principle of SEPARATION OF FORM FROM CONTENT.

XForms submit element *See* FORM CONTROLS.

XGF (XML Game Format) An XML-BASED MARKUP LANGUAGE for describing turn-based games. More details about XGF can be obtained from http://www.red-bean.com/sgf/xml/.

XGL (Extensible Graphics Library) An XML-BASED MARKUP LANGUAGE that is intended to represent 3D information for the purpose of visualization. For more details, see the information at http://www.xglspec.org/.

XGMML (Extensible Graph Markup and Modeling Language) An XML-BASED MARKUP LANGUAGE for describing nodes and edges of a graph. It facilitates the exchange of graphs between different tools. For more details, see the information at http://www.cs.rpi.edu/~puninj/XGMML/.

xhtml The FILENAME EXTENSION of a Web page written in XHTML. For example, "Catalog.xhtml".

XHTML (Extensible Hypertext Markup Language) The latest version of HTML, fully compatible with XML. It includes all the HTML elements and attributes but imposes a few strict rules, such as that all ELEMENT NAMES and ATTRIBUTE NAMES must be written in lowercase, all non-empty ELEMENTS have to include proper END TAGS, and others. See Figure X.5 for a comparison of the main features of XML, HTML and XHTML. See http://www.w3.org/TR/xhtml1/ for more details. *See also* XHTML DOCUMENT.

XHTML Basic A subset of XHTML for mobile devices. More details are available at http://www.w3.org/TR/xhtml-basic/.

XHTML document An XML DOCUMENT written in XHTML. An example of an XHTML document is shown in Figure X.6. Notice that the document includes an XML DECLARATION, an XHTML-related DOCTYPE DECLARATION and a NAMESPACE DECLARATION for XHTML. It also contains examples of the compulsory use of end tags for non-empty elements and of NESTING ELEMENTS properly, without overlapping.

XML	HTML	XHTML
Metalanguage	SGML-based language	XML-based language
Intended for describing and structuring data	Intended for formatting and displaying data	Intended for formatting and displaying data
No predefined set of tags	Predefined set of tags	Predefined set of tags
Case-sensitive	Case-insensitive	Case-sensitive. Tag and attribute names must be written in lower case
XML documents must be well formed	HTML documents do not need to be well formed	XHTML documents must be well formed
All non-empty elements require end tags	Some end tags are optional	All non-empty elements require end tags
Empty elements must be terminated, e.g. `<img />`	Empty elements are not terminated, e.g. `<img >`	Empty elements must be terminated, e.g. `<img />`
Attribute values must be quoted	Unquoted attribute values are allowed	Attribute values must be quoted
No attribute minimalization is allowed	The minimal form of an attribute is allowed	No attribute minimalization is allowed
Tags must be nested properly, without overlapping	Tags may be nested with overlapping	Tags must be nested properly, without overlapping

Figure X.5 A comparison between XML, HTML and XHTML.

xi namespace prefix A commonly used NAMESPACE PREFIX for the XINCLUDE NAMESPACE.

xi:fallback element *See* FALLBACK ELEMENT.

xi:include element *See* INCLUDE ELEMENT.

XincaML (Extensible Inter-Nodes Constraint Markup Language) An XML-BASED MARKUP LANGUAGE for describing the presence or value dependencies among nodes located on different branches of an XML TREE STRUCTURE. It is intended to ensure the integrity of data by specifying constraints that cannot be expressed by the XML SCHEMA language.

More details are available at http://alphaworks.ibm.com/tech/xincaml/.

XInclude (XML Inclusions) An XML-BASED LANGUAGE that specifies a generic inclusion mechanism for merging XML DOCUMENTS (mostly to facilitate modularity). If an ELEMENT in an XML document has an ATTRIBUTE that is the XInclude NAMESPACE DECLARATION, it can be used as a container for the INCLUDE ELEMENT and FALLBACK ELEMENT. See Figure X.7. More details about XInclude can be obtained from http://www.w3.org/TR/xinclude/.

XInclude fallback element *See* FALLBACK ELEMENT.

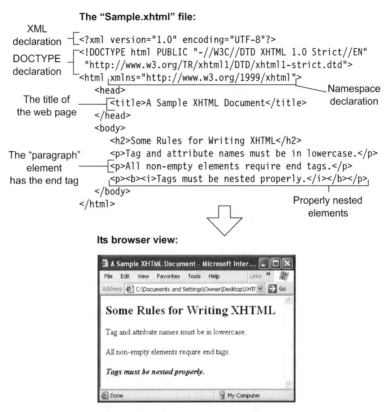

The "Sample.xhtml" file:

XML declaration ⎯

DOCTYPE declaration ⎯

The title of the web page ⎯

The "paragraph" element has the end tag ⎯

```
<?xml version="1.0" encoding="UTF-8"?>
<!DOCTYPE html PUBLIC "-//W3C//DTD XHTML 1.0 Strict//EN"
    "http://www.w3.org/TR/xhtml1/DTD/xhtml1-strict.dtd">
<html xmlns="http://www.w3.org/1999/xhtml">
    <head>
        <title>A Sample XHTML Document</title>
    </head>
    <body>
        <h2>Some Rules for Writing XHTML</h2>
        <p>Tag and attribute names must be in lowercase.</p>
        <p>All non-empty elements require end tags.</p>
        <p><b><i>Tags must be nested properly.</i></b></p>
    </body>
</html>
```

Namespace declaration

Properly nested elements

Its browser view:

Figure X.6 A sample XHTML document.

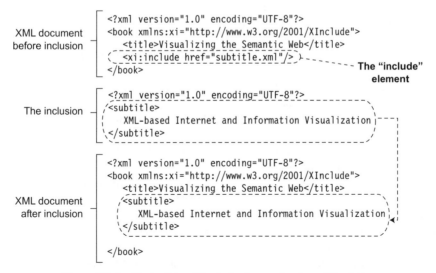

XML document before inclusion —
```
<?xml version="1.0" encoding="UTF-8"?>
<book xmlns:xi="http://www.w3.org/2001/XInclude">
    <title>Visualizing the Semantic Web</title>
    <xi:include href="subtitle.xml"/>
</book>
```
The "include" element

The inclusion —
```
<?xml version="1.0" encoding="UTF-8"?>
<subtitle>
    XML-based Internet and Information Visualization
</subtitle>
```

XML document after inclusion —
```
<?xml version="1.0" encoding="UTF-8"?>
<book xmlns:xi="http://www.w3.org/2001/XInclude">
    <title>Visualizing the Semantic Web</title>
    <subtitle>
        XML-based Internet and Information Visualization
    </subtitle>

</book>
```

Figure X.7 An illustration of the inclusion mechanism of XInclude.

193

The start tag of the
"book" element
with the XInclude
namespace declaration

Namespace
prefix

```
<?xml version="1.0" encoding="UTF-8"?>
<book xmlns:xi="http://www.w3.org/2001/XInclude">
    <title>Visualizing the Semantic Web</title>
    <xi:include href="subtitle.xml"/>
</book>
```

Figure X.8 The XInclude namespace declaration.

XInclude include element *See* INCLUDE ELEMENT.

XInclude namespace The NAMESPACE of XINCLUDE. The use of XInclude within an ELEMENT requires a NAMESPACE DECLARATION for the XInclude namespace to be specified as one of its ATTRIBUTES. See Figure X.8. Notice that the NAMESPACE PREFIX of the XInclude namespace is usually "xi".

XL (XML programming language) A high-level XML programming language for the implementation of Web services. XL is not an XML-BASED MARKUP LANGUAGE, but it is compliant with the relevant W3C STANDARDS. XL allows programmers to concentrate on the logic of their application by providing them with high-level and declarative constructs for actions typical for the implementation of a Web service, such as logging, workload management and error handling. More information about XL is available at http://xl.in.tum.de/index2.html.

XLIFF (XML Localization Interchange File Format) An XML-BASED MARKUP LANGUAGE for describing and interchanging LOCALIZATION information. It supports the localization-related aspects of INTERNATIONALIZATION and the entire localization process. Details of XLIFF can be found at http://www.oasis-open.org/committees/xliff/.

XLink (XML Linking Language) An XML-BASED LANGUAGE for describing and creating a variety of different kinds of LINKS within and between XML DOCUMENTS. It enables both basic unidirectional SIMPLE LINKS between RESOURCES (similar to HTML

links) and more complex and sophisticated linking structures, such as EXTENDED LINKS. More details about XLink can be obtained from http://www.w3.org/TR/xlink/. *See also* TRAVERSAL; TYPE ATTRIBUTE; XLINK NAMESPACE.

xlink:actuate attribute *See* ACTUATE ATTRIBUTE.

xlink:show attribute *See* SHOW ATTRIBUTE.

xlink:type attribute *See* TYPE ATTRIBUTE.

XLink actuate attribute *See* ACTUATE ATTRIBUTE.

XLink arc *See* ARC.

XLink ending resource *See* TRAVERSAL.

XLink extended link *See* EXTENDED LINK.

XLink inbound arc *See* INBOUND ARC.

XLink link *See* LINK.

XLink linkbase *See* LINKBASE.

XLink link database *See* LINKBASE.

XLink local ending resource *See* LOCAL ENDING RESOURCE.

XLink local resource *See* LOCAL RESOURCE.

XLink local starting resource *See* LOCAL STARTING RESOURCE.

```
XLink          <spc:cover_image xmlns:spc="http://www.springer.de/spc"
namespace ──┌─ xmlns:xlink="http://www.w3.org/1999/xlink"
declaration    xlink:type="simple"
               xlink:href="VSW.gif"
               />
```

Figure X.9 The XLink namespace declaration.

XLink locator *See* LOCATOR.

XLink namespace A NAMESPACE of the XML Linking Language (XLINK). The use of XLink ELEMENTS and ATTRIBUTES requires a NAMESPACE DECLARATION of the XLink namespace, as shown in Figure X.9. Notice that the NAMESPACE PREFIX of the XLink namespace is usually "xlink".

XLink outbound arc *See* OUTBOUND ARC.

XLink remote ending resource *See* REMOTE ENDING RESOURCE.

XLink remote resource *See* REMOTE RESOURCE.

XLink remote starting resource *See* REMOTE STARTING RESOURCE.

XLink show attribute *See* SHOW ATTRIBUTE.

XLink simple link *See* SIMPLE LINK.

XLink starting resource *See* TRAVERSAL.

XLink third-party arc *See* THIRD-PARTY ARC.

XLink type attribute *See* TYPE ATTRIBUTE.

XLL (Extensible Linking Language) The name under which the development of XLINK and XPOINTER started. No longer in use.

XMCL (Extensible Media Commerce Language) An XML-BASED MARKUP LANGUAGE for describing and interchanging rules that apply to multi-media content. More information about XMCL is available at http://www.xmcl.org/specification.html/.

XMI (XML Metadata Interchange Format) An XML-based format for interchanging METADATA and information between UML-based modeling tools and between tools and metadata repositories. XMI is intended to integrate XML, UML and MOF (Meta Objects Facility). More details are available at http://www.omg.org/technology/documents/formal/xmi.htm.

xml A FILENAME EXTENSION that indicates that the file is an XML DOCUMENT. For example, "Catalog.xml". Note that a document written in XML may have many other FILENAME EXTENSIONS, such as "rdf" or "x3d".

XML (Extensible Markup Language) A METALANGUAGE for creating other XML-BASED MARKUP LANGUAGES. The group of languages derived from XML is known the XML FAMILY OF TECHNOLOGIES. XML is intended to form a technological basis for the transformation the WWW from the FIRST-GENERATION WEB into the SEMANTIC WEB. Most of the SEMANTIC WEB TECHNOLOGIES are based on XML.

XML was introduced in 1998 as a subset of SGML. Like HTML, it uses TAGS to mark up the data, but it is marking up the MEANING of data not the presentation of data (*see* METADATA; PRESENTATIONAL MARKUP; SEPARATION OF FORM FROM CONTENT; STRUCTURAL MARKUP). Unlike HTML, XML has no predefined set of tags. Being a metalanguage, it is just a set of syntactic rules (*see* XML SYNTAX) that allow anyone to create custom XML-BASED MARKUP LANGUAGES for describing any specific DOMAINS.

The main STRUCTURAL CONSTRUCTS of XML include: (1) ANGLE BRACKETS and other DELIMITERS; (2) TAGS; (3) ELEMENTS comprised of START TAGS and END TAGS; (4) EMPTY-ELEMENT TAGS; (5) ATTRIBUTES; (6) PROCESSING INSTRUCTIONS; (7) ENTITY REFERENCES; (8) XML DECLARATION;

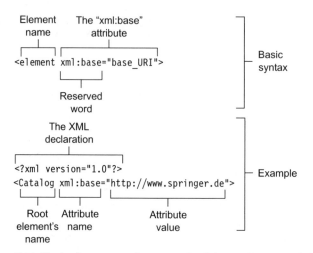

Figure X.10 The basic syntax and an example of the "xml:base" attribute.

(9) XML COMMENTS. *See also* XML DOCUMENT; XML DOCUMENT STRUCTURE. More details about http://www.w3.org/XML/.

xml:base attribute A special ATTRIBUTE defined by the W3C in the XML BASE SPECIFICATION. It is intended to allow authors to explicitly specify a base URI of an XML DOCUMENT in order to resolve relative URIs in links to external Internet resources. Unlike most attributes, its value applied to all children of the ELEMENT that includes the xml:base attribute. It can be overridden by a subsequent xml:base attribute. In example shown in Figure X.10, the xml:base is an attribute of the ROOT ELEMENT "Catalog", and therefore its value is applied to the entire XML document.

xml:lang attribute One of two XML RESERVED ATTRIBUTES that specify the language in which the content of an XML DOCUMENT or its particular ELEMENTS is written. Language codes may consist of two characters (such as "en" for English and "de" for German) and can also have a sub-code attached by a hyphen (such as "en-US" for English in the USA). Note that the xml:lang attribute is applied not only to the element including the attribute but also to all its CHILD ELEMENTS and their ATTRIBUTES. If used, this attribute must be declared in the XML SCHEMA or DTD. See Figure X.11. *See also* XML:SPACE ATTRIBUTE.

xml:space attribute One of two XML RESERVED ATTRIBUTES that specify how an XML PROCESSOR should

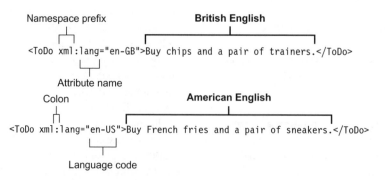

Figure X.11 An example of the use of the "xml:lang" attribute.

handle WHITE SPACE within specified ELEMENTS of an XML DOCUMENT. This attribute can take one of two ATTRIBUTE VALUES: (1) the "preserve" value means that the XML processor should preserve all white space; (2) the "default" value means that the XML processor may use its own default processing rules. Note that the xml:space attribute is applied not only to the element including the attribute but also to all its CHILD ELEMENTS and their ATTRIBUTES. If used, this attribute must be declared in the XML SCHEMA or DTD. *See also* XML:LANG ATTRIBUTE.

XML 1.0 Non-normative References *See* NON-NORMATIVE REFERENCES.

XML 1.0 Normative References *See* NORMATIVE REFERENCES.

XML 1.0 REC An abbreviation that is sometimes used for XML 1.0 RECOMMENDATION.

XML 1.0 Recommendation XML version 1.0, which became a W3C RECOMMENDATION in February 1998. The Second Edition of the XML 1.0 Recommendation was published in October 2000. It does not change XML itself (it is not a new version of XML), but just corrects some minor errors and updates the documentation related to underlying standards. The XML 1.0 Recommendation is sometimes abbreviated as XML 1.0 REC. An annotated version of the First Edition of the XML 1.0 Recommendation is available at http://www.w3.org/TR/REC-xml/.

XML 1.0 References References to non-W3C standards and specifications given in the Appendices of the XML 1.0 RECOMMENDATION. They include NORMATIVE REFERENCES and NON-NORMATIVE REFERENCES.

XML 1.0 Second Edition *See* XML 1.0 RECOMMENDATION.

XML 1.0 syntax The basic SYNTAX of the XML language that is documented in the XML 1.0 RECOMMENDATION, the Second Edition of which was

published by the W3C in October 2000. For more details, see the information at http://www.w3.org/TR/REC-xml/.

XML 1.1 (Extensible Markup Language 1.1) A W3C CANDIDATE RECOMMENDATION that specifies a new version of XML which fixes synchronization problems with the UNICODE character database, as well as problems with WHITE SPACE characters on certain platforms. XML 1.1 was formerly known as XML Blueberry. The XML 1.1 specification is available at http://www.w3.org/TR/2002/CR-xml11-20021015/. More information about XML Blueberry can be found at http://www.w3.org/TR/xml-blueberry-req/.

XML Access Control Language *See* XACL.

XML application An official term for XML-BASED MARKUP LANGUAGE. Many consider this term misleading, because an application is a full-blow program such as XMLSpy rather that a domain-specific markup language written in XML, such as SVG, XHTML or NEWSML.

XMLBase *See* XML:BASE ATTRIBUTE; XML BASE SPECIFICATION.

XML-based language *See* XML-BASED MARKUP LANGUAGE.

XML-based markup language A computer language that is derived from XML as a METALANGUAGE, i.e. written using XML SYNTAX. Every document of such a MARKUP LANGUAGE must be a WELL-FORMED XML DOCUMENT and can be a VALID XML DOCUMENT (if there is an XML SCHEMA or a DTD that defines the VOCABULARY and structural relationships of this particular XML-based language). All XML-based markup languages can be divided into two big groups: (1) the languages that are intended mainly for functional use. These are often called "XML-technologies" and include, for example, RDF, XML SCHEMA, XSL and SVG. (2) The languages that are intended for describing, storing and exchanging domain-specific data, such as ARCHAEOML (Archaeological Markup Language) or SML (Spacecraft Markup Language). In other words, the languages of the first group serve mainly as technological tools, and those of the second group are chiefly used as self-describing databases. *See also* SELF-DESCRIBING DATA.

XML-based multimedia A new generation of multimedia that uses XML as a METALANGUAGE for defining specialist multimedia-related languages. This type of multimedia will play a central role on the SECOND-GENERATION WEB. At the moment, XML-based multimedia includes SVG, X3D, SMIL, XHTML, VOICEXML and WML. All of them are XML-BASED MARKUP LANGUAGES. Since XML-based multimedia can easily be integrated with SEMANTIC WEB TECHNOLOGIES (for example, by embedding RDF STATEMENTS into multimedia-related files), this emerging technology will also contribute to the SEMANTIC WEB.

XML-based technology *See* XML FAMILY OF TECHNOLOGIES.

XML-based Web *See* SEMANTIC WEB.

XML-based Web services *See* XML WEB SERVICES.

XML Base specification A W3C RECOMMENDATION that specifies the use of the XML:BASE ATTRIBUTE for defining base URIS for parts of XML DOCUMENTS in a way similar to that of HTML Base. This SPECIFICATION was developed primarily to provide base URI services to XLINK. But it can also be used by many other specifications, because is created in a modular fashion. The XML Base

recommendation is available at http://www.w3.org/TR/xmlbase/.

XML Blueberry *See* XML 1.1.

XML Bookmark Exchange Language *See* XBEL.

XML building block A term that is sometimes used to refer to the main STRUCTURAL CONSTRUCTS of an XML DOCUMENT, such as ELEMENTS, ATTRIBUTES and ATTRIBUTE VALUES.

XML character reference *See* CHARACTER REFERENCE.

XML comment A COMMENT that can be inserted into an XML DOCUMENT using the syntax, shown in Figure X.12. Comments can contain any text and characters, can be placed anywhere in an XML file, and can span as many lines of text as needed to annotate the XML document or any of its parts. XML comments: (1) cannot contain a double hyphen (--); (2) cannot be placed before the XML DECLARATION or inside an XML TAG; (3) cannot be NESTED. Comments are ignored by an XML PARSER and therefore are not displayed in a Web browser. They are intended only for human readers of the source XML code. Note that although XML is considered to be a SELF-DESCRIBING LANGUAGE with an easy-to-follow structure, it is still very useful to comment XML documents, especially when the programmer begins a document, or adds new building blocks whose names and structure are not intuitively obvious. Comments can also be used to hide ("to comment out") a section of code from the software program during the development or debugging of a complex project.

Figure X.12 The syntax for XML comments.

Figure X.13 An example of XML data and metadata.

XML Common Business Library *See* XCBL.

XML core *See* CORE XML TECHNOLOGIES.

XML data A term that is occasionally used to refer to CHARACTER DATA (i.e. the content) of an XML DOCUMENT. The use of this term is sometimes ambiguous because it can also refer the special type of data contained within MARKUP TAGS and known as METADATA. See Figure X.13.

XML-Data One of the early SCHEMA language proposals that led to the current XML SCHEMA language. For more details, see the information at http://www.w3.org/TR/1998/NOTE-XML-data-0105/. *See also* DDML; DT4DTD; SOX.

XML Data-Reduced Schema *See* XDR SCHEMA.

XML declaration A special kind of PROCESSING INSTRUCTION that identifies to the processor the version of the XML SPECIFICATION the document was developed with. The XML declaration is optional (a program recognizes an XML file by its .xml FILENAME EXTENSION) but it is a good programming practice to begin every XML DOCUMENT with it. The XML declaration must be the very first characters of the document – no white space, comments etc. should appear before it. Since the XML declaration is a PROCESSING INSTRUCTION rather than an ELEMENT, it has no matching closing part, similar to an END TAG.

An XML declaration can be written either using the complete syntax or its minimal form, as shown in Figure X.14. The complete syntax of the XML declaration includes a compulsory VERSION ATTRIBUTE, an optional ENCODING ATTRIBUTE and an optional STANDALONE ATTRIBUTE. Note that if an XML declaration is included, the use of its minimal form is compulsory.

XML-DEV The XML developers' mailing list, available at http://www.xml.org/xml/xmldev.shtml.

XMLDSig *See* XML DIGITAL SIGNATURE.

XML dialect A term that is sometimes used to refer to an XML-BASED MARKUP LANGUAGE such as SVG, XSLT or MATHML. This term is rather misleading. Strictly speaking, XML cannot have any dialects because it is not a language but a METALANGUAGE

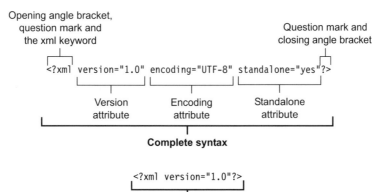

Figure X.14 The anatomy of the XML declaration.

that can be used for defining domain-specific languages. Sometimes another misleading term, "XML flavor", is also used in the sense of "XML dialect".

XML Digital Signature *See* XML SIGNATURE.

XML document A PLAIN TEXT document written in XML. There are two main types of XML document: (1) VALID XML DOCUMENTS; and (2) WELL-FORMED XML DOCUMENTS.

XML can be used for: (1) creating custom domain-specific languages (for example, "Book Catalog Markup Language"); and (2) developing members of the XML FAMILY OF TECHNOLOGIES. Thus, all the documents that are written using XML SYNTAX are XML documents, including, for example, XML SCHEMA documents, RDF and RDF SCHEMA documents, OWL documents, and so on. Some of these documents have the "xml" FILENAME EXTENSION; others have specialist extensions, such as "rdf" or "owl".

Note that practically all of these XML documents start with an XML DECLARATION. Figure X.15 shows a sample XML document and its main STRUCTURAL CONSTRUCTS. *See also* ATTRIBUTE; ELEMENT; ELEMENT CONTENT; ELEMENT NAME; EMPTY ELEMENT; END TAG; NESTING ELEMENTS; ROOT ELEMENT; START TAG; XML DOCUMENT SECTIONS; XML DOCUMENT STRUCTURE.

XML document fragment *See* FRAGMENT.

XML document sections A WELL-FORMED XML DOCUMENT may have three sections: (1) an optional PROLOG; (2) the BODY of the XML DOCUMENT; (3) an optional EPILOG. See Figure X.16.

XML document structure An abstract structure in the form of a HIERARCHICAL TREE on which any WELL-FORMED XML DOCUMENT must be based. It consists of the following hierarchical levels and its structural constructs, shown in Figure X.17: (Level 1) one and only one root node called the

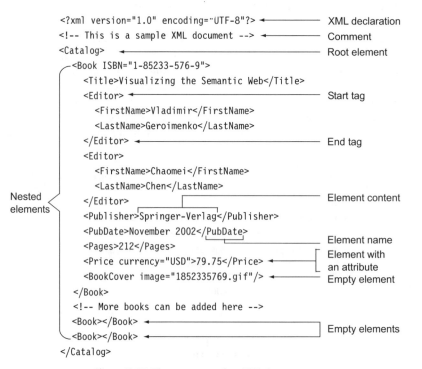

Figure X.15 The anatomy of an XML document.

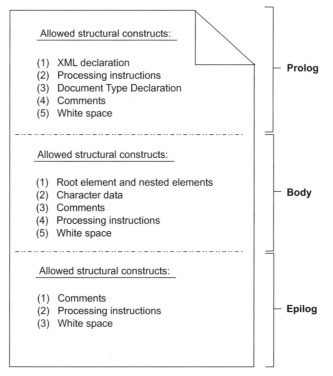

Figure X.16 XML document sections and their building blocks.

DOCUMENT ROOT or the Document entity; (Level 2) the three XML DOCUMENT SECTIONS: an optional PROLOG, a BODY and an optional EPILOG; (Level 3) one and only one root node called the ROOT ELEMENT or the Document element; (Level 4, Level 5 and so on) any number of NESTED ELEMENTS. *See also* HIERARCHICAL TREE STRUCTURE; XML DOCUMENT; XML DOCUMENT SECTIONS.

XML document tree *See* XML DOCUMENT STRUCTURE.

XML DOM A data model and application interface used to programmatically assess and manipulate the content and structure of XML DOCUMENTS. In XML DOM, a document is being stored in the computer memory in the form of a tree-like structure (called a "DOM tree"), as shown in Figure X.18. This allows random access to document content. Details of XML DOM can be found at http://www.w3.org/DOM/. *See also* DOM; SAX.

XML DTD *See* DTD.

XML editor Software specially intended for writing and editing XML DOCUMENTS. Such tools allow explicit control over XML markup and vary from simple editors for small documents to full-featured IDEs, such as XMLSpy.

XML element *See* ELEMENT.

XMLEnc *See* XML ENCRYPTION.

XML encoding rules *See* XER.

XML Encryption (XML Encryption Syntax and Processing) A W3C SPECIFICATION that outlines the ENCRYPTION process for data and the representation of the result in XML. It facilitates encrypting sections of XML DOCUMENTS. More details are available at http://ww.w3.org/TR/xmlen-core/.

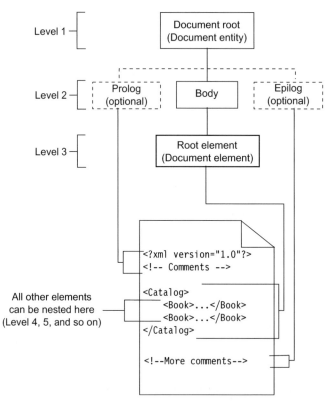

Figure X.17 The structure of a well-formed XML document.

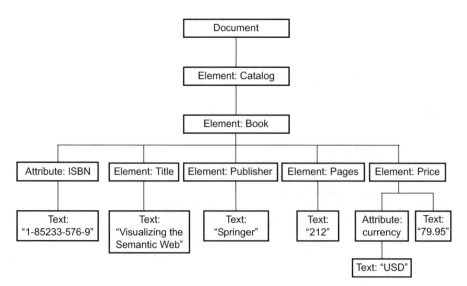

Figure X.18 The DOM representation of an XML document.

XML family of languages *See* XML FAMILY OF TECHNOLOGIES.

XML family of standards *See* XML FAMILY OF TECHNOLOGIES.

XML family of technologies A big group of XML-related technologies (also known as languages), most of which are W3C SPECIFICATIONS written in XML. Different classifications of the XML family of languages are possible, such as dividing them into four groups: XML, XML Accessories, XML Transducers and XML Applications. Considering the XML family as a technological basis of the SEMANTIC WEB, it is possible to arrange the major family members into the following three groups in accordance with their functions: (1) XML technologies for designing and creating XML-BASED MARKUP LANGUAGES and their documents: XML itself as a METALANGUAGE, NAMESPACES, XML SCHEMAS, XPATH, XPOINTER, XLINK, XFORMS, XML SIGNATURE etc.; (2) XML technologies for accessing, manipulating, transforming and rendering XML DOCUMENTS: XML DOM, XSLT, XSL-FO, XQUERY, CSS, XHTML, SVG, SMIL, X3D, WML, MATHML etc.; (3) XML technologies for adding METADATA and ONTOLOGIES to Web data and RESOURCES: RDF, RDF SCHEMA, DAML+OIL, TOPIC MAPS, OWL etc. *See also* SEMANTIC WEB ARCHITECTURE; XML-BASED MARKUP LANGUAGES.

XML FAQ (XML Frequently Asked Questions) A Web site that contains Frequently Asked Questions about the Extensible Markup Language. For more details, see http://www.ucc.ie/xml/.

XML file A textual file in PLAIN TEXT format that is written using XML SYNTAX. XML files can have other the "xml" FILENAME EXTENSION or other language-specific extensions, such as "rdf" or "owl". Almost always, an XML file begins with an XML DECLARATION. *See also* XML DOCUMENT.

XML flavor *See* XML DIALECT.

XML for Life Insurance *See* XMLLIFE.

XML for Transportation-Related Transactions *See* TRANXML.

XML Fragment Interchange *See* XFI.

XML Game Format *See* XGF.

XML hierarchical tree structure *See* HIERARCHICAL TREE STRUCTURE.

XML hierarchy *See* HIERARCHICAL TREE STRUCTURE; XML DOM.

XML Industry Portal A term that refers to the "xml.org" Web site that is hosted by OASIS and is an independent resource for news and information about the industrial and commercial applications of XML. More details are available at http://www.xml.org/.

XML Information Set *See* INFORMATION SET.

XML Infoset (XML Information Set) *See* INFORMATION SET.

XML language *See* XML-BASED MARKUP LANGUAGE.

XMLife (XML for Life Insurance) A family of XML-based standards for the life insurance industry. For more details, see http://www.acord.org/standards/lifexml.aspx.

XML Linking Language *See* XLINK.

XMLLiteral class In an RDF SCHEMA, the CLASS of WELL-FORMED XML strings.

XML Localization Interchange File Format *See* XLIFF.

XML markup The type of MARKUP that is used in XML. The specifics of XML markup are: (1) it is METADATA markup (or STRUCTURAL MARKUP), i.e. it is used to mark up the MEANING of data and their structural organization (in contrast with HTML,

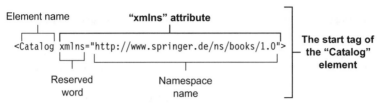

Figure X.19 The "xmlns" attribute.

which is PRESENTATIONAL MARKUP); (2) unlike HTML, XML has no predefined set of MARKUP TAGS, since XML is a METALANGUAGE that is intended for creating special-purpose XML-BASED MARKUP LANGUAGES. These languages specify a set of XML-based markup tags, usually in an XML SCHEMA or a DTD.

XML Media Types *See* MIME.

XML Metadata Interchange Format *See* XMI.

XML name *See* VALID XML NAME.

XML Namespace *See* NAMESPACE.

XML Namespace Catalog Format *See* XNCL.

XML namespace declaration *See* NAMESPACE DECLARATION.

XML Namespace Gloss *See* XNGLOSS.

XML Namespace Related Resource Language *See* XNRL.

XMLNS *See* XML NAMESPACE.

xmlns:env attribute *See* ENVELOPE.

xmlns:f attribute *See* XFI NAMESPACE.

xmlns:fo attribute *See* XSL-FO.

xmlns:owl attribute *See* OWL NAMESPACE.

xmlns:xi attribute An ATTRIBUTE used for declaring an XINCLUDE NAMESPACE.

xmlns:xs attribute *See* XS ATTRIBUTE.

xmlns:xsi attribute *See* XML SCHEMA REFERENCE.

xmlns:xsl attribute *See* XSLT NAMESPACE DECLARATION.

xmlns attribute A reserved attribute used for declaring a NAMESPACE. Notice that "xmlns" is actually an abbreviation of XML NAMESPACE. See Figure X.19. *See also* DEFAULT NAMESPACE; NAMESPACE DECLARATION; PREFIXED NAMESPACE; UNPREFIXED NAMESPACE.

XML parser A software module that reads an XML DOCUMENT, usually on behalf of another module, called the application. There are two classes of XML parser behavior: (1) VALIDATING PARSERS; and (2) NON-VALIDATING PARSERS. Each of them can have two different implementations as (1) an EVENT-DRIVEN PARSER or (2) a TREE-BASED PARSER. Also known as an XML processor.

XML Path Language *See* XPATH.

XMLPay (XML Payment Specification) An XML-based framework for sending payment requests and responses through financial networks. Details of XMLPay are available at http://www.verisign.com/developer/xml/xmlpay.html.

XML Payment Specification *See* XMLPAY.

XML Pointer Language *See* XPOINTER.

XML processing instruction *See* PROCESSING INSTRUCTION.

XML processor A software module that reads an XML DOCUMENT and usually provides access to its structure and content to another module called the application. Also known as the XML PARSER.

XML programming A term that usually refers to using an API to manipulate XML DATA. Standard APIs are implemented in many programming languages.

XML programming language *See* XL.

XML Query Language *See* XQUERY.

XML-related language *See* XML-BASED MARKUP LANGUAGE.

XML Remote Procedure Calls *See* XML-RPC.

XML reserved attributes A pair of attributes ("xml:lang" and "xml:space") that have special meaning in XML as in the XML 1.0 RECOMMENDATION. *See* XML:LANG ATTRIBUTE; XML:SPACE ATTRIBUTE.

XML reserved characters *See* SPECIAL SYMBOLS.

XML result tree *See* TRANSFORMATION.

XML Résumé Library An XML-based language for marking and formatting résumés and CVs. More details are available at http://xmlresume.sourceforge.net/.

XML root element *See* ROOT ELEMENT.

XML-RPC (XML Remote Procedure Calls) A SPECIFICATION that allows software belonging to different operating systems and environments to make remote procedure calls over the Internet. As a result, complex data structures can be transmitted, processed and returned. XML-RPC is a predecessor of SOAP that utilizes HTTP for the transport and XML for the encoding. Also known as "RPC over XML". More details are available at http://www.xmlrpc.com/.

XML Schema 1. Also known as W3C XML Schema, XSD (XML Schema Definition), XML Schema language and XSDL (XML Schema definition language). An XML-BASED MARKUP LANGUAGE for describing the structure and constraining the contents of XML DOCUMENTS. An XML Schema is a set of SCHEMA COMPONENTS, such as TYPE DEFINITIONS and ELEMENT DECLARATIONS.

An XML Schema allows its authors to define legal STRUCTURAL CONSTRUCTS of a particular class of XML documents (also known as DOCUMENT TYPE). An XML Schema provides mechanisms for defining, for example: (1) ELEMENTS and ATTRIBUTES that may appear in XML documents; (2) the number and order of CHILD ELEMENTS; (3) EMPTY ELEMENTS; (4) DATA TYPES for elements and attributes; (5) DEFAULT VALUES and FIXED VALUES for elements and attributes.

The XML Schema language developed by the W3C is used as the main "schema" (or the SCHEMA OF SCHEMAS) for all specific XML Schemas that can be developed by anyone. The language is described in three W3C RECOMMENDATIONS, available at http://www.w3.org/XML/Schema/.

2. Any XML SCHEMA DOCUMENT, i.e. a particular XML DOCUMENT written in the XML Schema language.

XML Schema abstract data model The abstract data model of the XML SCHEMA that is based on an INFORMATION SET and is comprised of XML SCHEMA COMPONENTS.

XML Schema annotation *See* ANNOTATION ELEMENT.

XML Schema comment A COMMENT that can be inserted into an XML SCHEMA using the DOCUMENTATION ELEMENT. This ELEMENT must be NESTED within the ANNOTATION ELEMENT, as shown in Figure X.20.

XML Schema component The generic term for abstract STRUCTURAL CONSTRUCTS of the XML SCHEMA. There are 13 components, divided into three groups: (1) the primary components: SIMPLE TYPE DEFINITION, COMPLEX TYPE DEFINITION, ELEMENT DECLARATION, ATTRIBUTE DECLARATION; (2) the secondary components: attribute group definition,

Figure X.20 An example of XML Schema comments.

identity-constrain definition, model group defini-tion; and (3) the helper components: annotation, model group, particle, wildcard, attribute use.

XML Schema Definition *See* XSD.

XML Schema Definition Language An official term, often abbreviated as XSDL, used to refer to XML SCHEMAS.

XML Schema document An XML DOCUMENT that specifies an XML SCHEMA and therefore has the XS:SCHEMA ELEMENT as its ROOT ELEMENT. The document file is in PLAIN TEXT format (like any other XML doc-ument) and has a FILENAME EXTENSION "xsd" (for example, "MyBooks.xsd"). The "xsd" extension can be considered as a lower-cased acronym for "XML Schema Definition" or "XML Schema Document".

XML Schema instance namespace *See* XML SCHEMA REFERENCE.

XML Schema Language *See* XML SCHEMA.

XML Schema namespace declaration A NAMESPACE DECLARATION for the SCHEMA OF SCHEMAS using the "xmnls:xs" attribute or "xmlns:xsd" attribute of the SCHEMA ELEMENT. The NAMESPACE NAME of the declaration is the URI of the W3C XML SCHEMA

language. This indicates that the specific XML SCHEMA document conforms to the syntax and rules that are specified in the W3C RECOMMENDATIONS for the XML Schema. The NAMESPACE PREFIX of this NAMESPACE DECLARATION can be either "xs" (recently more often in use) or "xsd". See Figure X.21.

XML Schema reference Special attributes of the ROOT ELEMENT of an XML DOCUMENT that are used for making a reference to a corresponding XML SCHEMA, as shown in Figure X.22. The xmlns:xsi attribute specifies the XML Schema Instance NAMESPACE and its NAMESPACE PREFIX "xsi". The xsi attribute uses this prefix with the LOCAL PART "schemaLocation" and takes an ATTRIBUTE VALUE that is the URL of the actual XML SCHEMA file.

XML Scripture Encoding Model *See* XSEM.

XML server A WEB SERVER that is able to handle XML documents specifically.

XML Signature A COMMUNICATION PROTOCOL that describes the signing of digital content, including sections of XML DOCUMENTS. Also known as an "XML Digital Signature". More information about XML Signature is available at http://www.w3.org/TR/xmldsig-core/.

XML source tree *See* TRANSFORMATION.

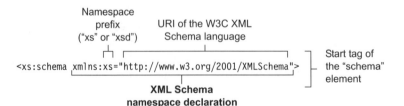

Figure X.21 The namespace declaration for the W3C XML Schema.

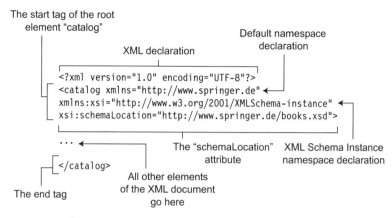

The start tag of the root element "catalog"

XML declaration

Default namespace declaration

```
<?xml version="1.0" encoding="UTF-8"?>
<catalog xmlns="http://www.springer.de"
xmlns:xsi="http://www.w3.org/2001/XMLSchema-instance"
xsi:schemaLocation="http://www.springer.de/books.xsd">
```

```
...
</catalog>
```

The "schemaLocation" attribute

XML Schema Instance namespace declaration

The end tag

All other elements of the XML document go here

Figure X.22 Referencing a Schema in an XML document.

XML special attributes *See* XML RESERVED ATTRIBUTES.

XML Specification An unofficial term used to refer to XML 1.0 RECOMMENDATION by the W3C.

XML-specified language *See* XML-BASED MARKUP LANGUAGE.

XML standard *See* W3C STANDARD; W3C SPECIFICATION; W3C TECHNICAL REPORT; XML SPECIFICATION.

XML structural construct *See* STRUCTURAL CONSTRUCT.

XML structure *See* XML DOCUMENT STRUCTURE.

XML sub-language A term that is sometimes used to refer to an XML-BASED MARKUP LANGUAGE.

XML syntax The SYNTAX of the Extensible Markup Language as defined in the XML 1.0 RECOMMENDATION. Since XML is actually not a language but a METALANGUAGE, it has no predefined set of MARKUP TAGS at all. XML is a set of rules for writing special-purpose XML-BASED MARKUP LANGUAGES. An XML DOCUMENT that adheres to general XML syntax rules is called a WELL-FORMED XML DOCUMENT.

The main STRUCTURAL CONSTRUCTS of the XML syntax include: (1) ANGLE BRACKETS and other DELIMITERS; (2) TAGS; (3) ELEMENTS comprised of START TAGS and END TAGS; (4) EMPTY-ELEMENT TAGS; (5) ATTRIBUTES; (6) PROCESSING INSTRUCTIONS; (7) ENTITY REFERENCES; (8) XML DECLARATION; (9) XML COMMENTS.

The major XML syntax rules are: (1) any XML document should start with an optional XML declaration; (2) any XML document must have one and only one ROOT ELEMENT; (3) all elements that do not use empty-element tags must have end tags; (4) all start tags must match end tags (Note that XML is CASE-SENSITIVE); (5) all elements must be properly NESTED (*see* NESTING ELEMENTS); (6) all attributes must be enclosed in matching quotes; (7) SPECIAL SYMBOLS must be replaced with their ENTITY REFERENCES.

XML syntax rules *See* XML SYNTAX.

XML System for Textual and Archaeological Research *See* XSTAR.

XML tag *See* TAG.

XML technologies *See* XML FAMILY OF TECHNOLOGIES.

XML tree structure *See* HIERARCHICAL TREE STRUCTURE. *See also* NODE TREE; XML DOCUMENT STRUCTURE; XML DOM; XPATH DATA MODEL.

XML vocabulary *See* VOCABULARY.

XML Web services *See* WEB SERVICES.

xml-stylesheet processing instruction A term that is sometimes used to refer to a CSS STYLE SHEET REFERENCE as a special PROCESSING INSTRUCTION with a TARGET of xml-stylesheet.

XMML (Exploration and Mining Markup Language) An XML-BASED MARKUP LANGUAGE for describing geoscience features such as ore-bodies, boreholes, geophysics and samples. More details about XMML can be obtained from http://www.ned.dem.csiro.au/XMML/.

XMP (Extensible Metadata Platform) An XML-based framework for embedding data about a file (METADATA) inside an application file itself. This metadata can include XML schemas described in RDF syntax. Details of XMP can be found at http://www.adobe.com/products/xmp/.

xNAL (Extensible Name and Address Language) An XML-BASED MARKUP LANGUAGE for describing and managing customer name and address data. It consists of two XML-based languages: XNL (Extensible Name Language that defines the name components) and XAL (Extensible Address Language that defines the address components). xNAL is a sub-language of XCIL. More details about xNAL can be obtained from http://www.oasis-open.org/committees/ciq/.

XNCL (XML Namespace Catalog Format) An XML-based data markup language for describing an XML Namespace Catalog superseded by RDDL. For more details, see http://www.openhealth.org/XMLCatalog/.

XNGloss (XML Namespace Gloss) An XML/XHTML-based language that is intended to be used as a "dereferencable" resource for namespace. More information is available at http://infomesh.net/2001/01/xngloss/.

xNL (Extensible Name Language) An XML-BASED MARKUP LANGUAGE for describing customer name data. It is part of XNAL (Extensible Name and Address Language) and is referenced by XCIL. More details of xNL may be obtained from http://www.oasis-open.org/committees/ciq/. *See also* XAL; XNAL; XCIL.

XNRL (XML Namespace Related Resource Language) An HTML-based markup language that enables the use of a human-readable description of an XML NAMESPACE, and also pointers to multiple resources related to that namespace. More details about XNRL can be obtained from http://www.textuality.com/xml/xnrl.html.

XNS (Extensible Name Service) An XML-based COMMUNICATION PROTOCOL for digital identity and relationship management. It is intended for identifying and linking any resource participating in any kind of digital transaction. Details of XNS can be found at http://www.xns.org/.

XPath (XML Path Language) A NON-XML-BASED LANGUAGE for defining parts of an XML DOCUMENT using path-based navigation through the NODE TREE of the document. XPath is part of XSL. The main structural components of the XML Path language are path EXPRESSIONS and especially LOCATION PATHS. XPath is used for addressing ELEMENTS in XPOINTER and for matching elements in XSLT and XQUERY. XPath is a set of syntax rules that uses two kinds of SYNTAX: (1) UNABBREVIATED SYNTAX; (2) ABBREVIATED SYNTAX. XPath is a W3C RECOMMENDATION, available at http://www.w3.org/TR/xpath/. *See also* NODE TYPE.

XPath data model An abstract DATA MODEL on which the XML Path Language is based. According to the model, an XML DOCUMENT is considered as a NODE TREE, as shown in Figure X.23. Each XML document has one and only one root of the node tree, called the ROOT NODE. This node is actually representing the DOCUMENT ROOT and is the PARENT of the special ELEMENT NODE that represents

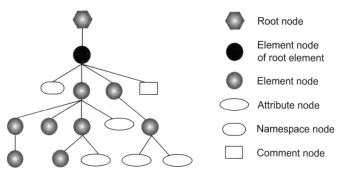

Figure X.23 An example of the XPath data model.

the ROOT ELEMENT. This NODE is sometimes called "the element root". The descendants of the root element node can be a set of nodes that includes different NODE TYPES. Note that in XPath, an element node is the PARENT of an ATTRIBUTE NODE, but an attribute node is *not* the CHILD of its parent element node.

XPath expression *See* EXPRESSION.

XPath function One of a set of functions in the XPATH function library for converting and translating data. The result returned by a function and its arguments can be of four types: (1) NODE SET; (2) Boolean; (3) Number; or (4) STRING. For example, the name() function retunes a QUALIFIED NAME that represent the name of a NODE.

XPath location path *See* LOCATION PATH.

XPath node tree *See* NODE TREE.

XPath predicate *See* PREDICATE.

XPath tree *See* XPATH DATA MODEL.

XPointer (XML Pointer Language) An XPATH-based language that is intended for addressing of parts of an XML DOCUMENT, including not only its NODES but also points, ranges etc. See Figure X.24. For more details, see http://www.w3.org/XML/Linking/.

URI

```
http://www.springer.de/catalog.xml#xpointer(book1)
```

Fragment
identifier

Figure X.24 An example of a simple XPointer.

XPointer processor A software component that that is able to identify parts of an XML DOCUMENT by applying an XPOINTER to it.

XQuery (XML Query Language) A non-XML functional language that make it possible to access XML DOCUMENTS like a database. It is based on the ABBREVIATED SYNTAX of XPATH. More information about XQuery is available at http://www.w3.org/TR/xquery/.

XRL (Exchangeable Routing Language) An XML-BASED MARKUP LANGUAGE for supporting cross-organizational processes. It uses XML for the representation of process and workflow definitions and Petri nets for its semantics. More information about XRL is available at http://tmitwww.tm.tue.nl/staff/wvdaalst/Workflow/xrl/.

XrML (Extensible Rights Markup Language) An XML-BASED MARKUP LANGUAGE for expressing rights and conditions associated with digital content, services or any digital resource. See http://www.xrml.org/ for more details.

xs attribute (XML Schema attribute) A special ATTRIBUTE of the SCHEMA ELEMENT that is currently very often used to declare the NAMESPACE for the W3C XML SCHEMA language as the SCHEMA OF SCHEMAS. The ATTRIBUTE NAME "xmlns:xs" stands actually for "XML Namespace: XML Schema". *See also* XSD ATTRIBUTE.

xs:all element *See* ALL ELEMENT.

xs:boolean data type *See* BOOLEAN DATA TYPE.

xs:choice element *See* CHOICE ELEMENT.

xs:complexType element *See* COMPLEXTYPE ELEMENT.

xs:complexType element *See* COMPLEX TYPE DEFINITION.

XS element (XML Schema element) A term that is sometimes used to refer to ELEMENTS that are STRUCTURAL CONSTRUCTS of an XML SCHEMA. The ELEMENT NAME of an XS element is usually a QUALIFIED NAME with the "xs" NAMESPACE PREFIX, such as "xs:complexType" or "xs:element". Note that the "xs:element" element is used for declaring XML DOCUMENT elements and is just one of many XS elements.

If the "xsd" namespace prefix is used instead of the "xs" namespace prefix, the term "XSD element" (stands for "XML Schema Definition element") can be used instead of "XS element". Note that both namespace prefixes are legal, but recently the "xs" PREFIX is more commonly used. See also XML SCHEMA NAMESPACE DECLARATION.

xs namespace prefix A NAMESPACE PREFIX declared in the XML SCHEMA NAMESPACE DECLARATION. It is used in QUALIFIED NAMES of XML SCHEMA elements (XS ELEMENTS) to indicate that they belong to the NAMESPACE of the W3C XML SCHEMA language (SCHEMA OF SCHEMAS). This prefix is currently used more often then the other alternative – the "xsd" namespace prefix.

xs:restriction element *See* FACET; RESTRICTION ELEMENT.

xs:restriction element *See* RESTRICTION ELEMENT.

xs:schema element *See* SCHEMA ELEMENT.

xs:sequence element *See* SEQUENCE ELEMENT.

xs:simpleType element *See* SIMPLETYPE ELEMENT.

XSchema The former name for DDML.

xsd A FILENAME EXTENSION that indicates that the file is an XML SCHEMA DOCUMENT (i.e. it is written in XSD). For example, "Catalog.xsd".

XSD (XML Schema Definition) A term that is used to refer to XML SCHEMA. Note that "xsd" is the FILENAME EXTENSION of an XML SCHEMA DOCUMENT.

xsd:schema element *See* SCHEMA ELEMENT.

xsd attribute (XML Schema Definition attribute) A special ATTRIBUTE of the SCHEMA ELEMENT that is still sometimes used to declare the NAMESPACE for the W3C XML SCHEMA language as the SCHEMA OF SCHEMAS. The ATTRIBUTE NAME "xmlns:xsd" stands actually for "XML Namespace: XML Schema Definition". *See also* XS ATTRIBUTE.

XSD element (XML Schema Definition element) *See* XS ELEMENT.

XSDL (XML Schema Definition Language) An official term used to refer to XML SCHEMA.

xsd namespace prefix *See* XS NAMESPACE PREFIX.

XSEM (XML Scripture Encoding Model) An XML-BASED MARKUP LANGUAGE for describing Scripture as a particular type of literature. It allows the text of the Bible to be encoded in a standard way regardless of the language the text may be written in. Details of XSEM can be found at http://www.sil.org/computing/xsem/documentation/Documentation.html.

xsi namespace prefix *See* XML SCHEMA REFERENCE.

xsi:schemaLocation attribute *See* XML SCHEMA REFERENCE.

XSIL (Extensible Scientific Interchange Language) An XML-BASED MARKUP LANGUAGE for describing and interchanging scientific data objects. Details of XSIL can be found at http://www.cacr.caltech.edu/SDA/xsil/.

xsl The FILENAME EXTENSION of a file that is an XSL (Extensible Style Sheet Language) style sheet. For example, "Catalog.xsl".

XSL (Extensible Style Sheet Language) A family of W3C RECOMMENDATIONS for defining XML DOCUMENT transformations and presentations that consists of three parts: (1) XSLT; (2) XPATH; (3) XSL-FO. Also known as "The Extensible Style Sheet Language Family". More details about XSL are available at http://www.w3.org/Style/XSL/.

xsl:comment element *See* XSLT COMMENT ELEMENT.

xsl:for-each element *See* FOR-EACH ELEMENT.

xsl:sort element *See* SORT ELEMENT.

xsl:stylesheet element *See* STYLE SHEET ELEMENT.

xsl:template element *See* TEMPLATE.

xsl:transform element *See* TRANSFORM ELEMENT.

xsl:value-of element *See* VALUE-OF ELEMENT.

XSL comment element *See* XSLT COMMENT ELEMENT.

XSL-FO (XSL Formatting Objects) An XML-BASED LANGUAGE for the presentation of XML on screen or on paper. An XSL-FO document contains not only the content of an XML DOCUMENT but also the complete layout information for the XML document. The combination of XSL-FO with SVG graphics and SMIL multimedia is a very promising direction in the development of efficient GUIS for XML documents. Figure X.25 shows a skeleton XSL-FO document. Like any XML document, it begins with an XML DECLARATION. The ROOT ELEMENT of every XSL-FO document is the fo:root ELEMENT with a special xmls:fo ATTRIBUTE used as the NAMESPACE DECLARATION of the NAMESPACE for the XSL-FO language. The fo:layout-master-set CHILD ELEMENT of the

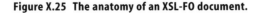

```
                                    XML declaration        Namespace
                                                           declaration
  The start tag
   of the root     ┌─ <?xml version="1.0" encoding="UTF-8"?>
     element    ╲ ─┤  <fo:root xmlns:fo="http://www.w3.org/1999/XSL/Format">
                   ┌─ <fo:layout-master-set>
 Element that      │     <fo:simple-page-master>
   specifies    ───┤        <fo:region-body></fo:region-body>
     page          │     </fo:simple-page-master>
    layout         └─ </fo:layout-master-set>
                   ┌─ <fo:page-sequence>
                   │     <fo:sequence-specification>
 Element that      │        <fo:sequence-specifier-single>
   specifies    ───┤        </fo:sequence-specifier-single>
     page          │     </fo:sequence-specification>
   content         │     <fo:flow>
                   │        <fo:block></fo:block>
                   │     </fo:flow>
                   └─ </fo:page-sequence>
                      </fo:root>
```

Figure X.25 The anatomy of an XSL-FO document.

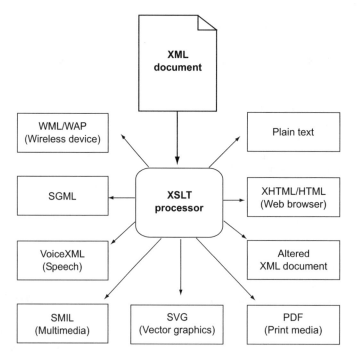

Figure X.26 The use of XSLT for transforming an XML document into a variety of formats.

fo:root element is used to define one or more page layouts in the document. The fo:page-sequence element is used as a container for the actual page content.

XSL-FO document *See* XSL-FO.

XSL-FO namespace *See* XSL-FO.

XSL for-each element *See* FOR-EACH ELEMENT.

XSL Formatting Objects *See* XSL-FO.

XSL-FO root element *See* XSL-FO.

XSL match attribute *See* MATCH ATTRIBUTE.

XSL select attribute *See* SELECT ATTRIBUTE.

XSL sort element *See* SORT ELEMENT.

XSL style sheet *See* XSLT STYLE SHEET.

XSL style sheet element *See* STYLE SHEET ELEMENT.

XSL style sheet reference *See* XSLT STYLE SHEET. *See also* ASSOCIATING STYLE SHEETS WITH XML DOCUMENTS.

xslt A FILENAME EXTENSION that shows that the file is an XSLT document (or transformation). For example, "Catalog.xslt".

XSLT (XSL Transformations) An XML-BASED LANGUAGE for transforming XML DOCUMENTS into a variety of formats, as shown in Figure X.26. XSLT is part of XSL. XSLT can also be used for formatting XML documents as a styling language that is much more powerful than CSS. XML documents written in XSLT are called XSLT STYLE SHEETS. More details about XSLT can be found at http://www.w3.org/TR/xslt/. *See also* TEMPLATE; TRANSFORMATION; XSLT STYLE SHEET.

XSLT comment element The ELEMENT of an XSLT STYLE SHEET that is used to add comments to the

```
                        <?xml version="1.0" encoding="UTF-8"?>
The start tag          <xsl:stylesheet version="1.0"
of the root            xmlns:xsl="http://www.w3.org/1999/XSL/Transform">
element                   ...
                        </xsl:stylesheet>        The XSLT namespace
                                                 declaration
```

Figure X.27 The namespace declaration for the XSLT namespace.

resulting XML DOCUMENT, using the following syntax: `<xsl:comment>Comment text goes here!</ xsl:comment>`.

XSLT construction rule A term that is sometimes used to refer to a TEMPLATE.

XSLT document *See* XSLT STYLE SHEET.

XSL template *See* TEMPLATE.

XSL template rule A term that is sometimes used to refer to a TEMPLATE.

XSLT for-each element *See* FOR-EACH ELEMENT.

XSLT match attribute *See* MATCH ATTRIBUTE.

XSLT namespace declaration The NAMESPACE DECLARATION of a NAMESPACE for XSLT specified in an XSLT STYLE SHEET using the `xmlns:xsl` ATTRIBUTE, as shown in Figure X.27. This attribute is an attribute of the XSLT ROOT ELEMENT that can be either the STYLE SHEET ELEMENT or the TRANSFORM ELEMENT. The NAMESPACE PREFIX of the namespace of XSLT is usually "xsl".

XSLT pattern A term that is often used to refer to the ATTRIBUTE VALUE of the MATCH ATTRIBUTE.

XSLT processing model *See* TRANSFORMATION.

XSLT processor In XSLT, a software component or standalone application that performs the actual TRANSFORMATION of an XML-based document into a variety of other XML-based document formats in

The use of the "xsl:stylesheet" element

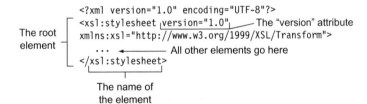

The use of the "xsl:transform" element

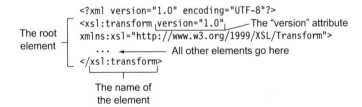

Figure X.28 The use of two synonymous XSLT root elements.

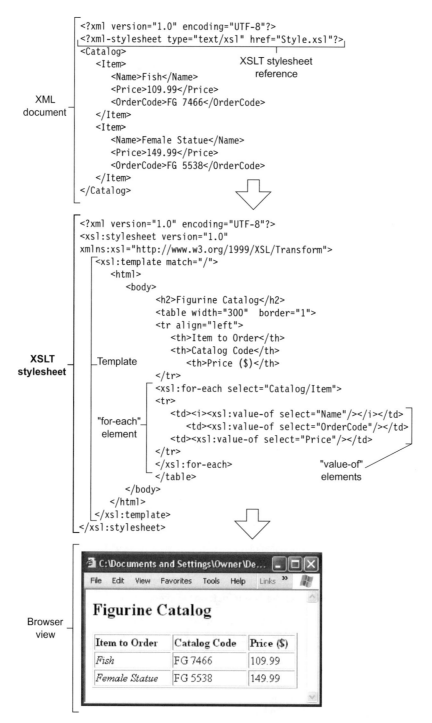

```
<?xml version="1.0" encoding="UTF-8"?>
<?xml-stylesheet type="text/xsl" href="Style.xsl"?>
<Catalog>
    <Item>                          XSLT stylesheet
        <Name>Fish</Name>              reference
        <Price>109.99</Price>
        <OrderCode>FG 7466</OrderCode>
    </Item>
    <Item>
        <Name>Female Statue</Name>
        <Price>149.99</Price>
        <OrderCode>FG 5538</OrderCode>
    </Item>
</Catalog>
```

XML document

```
<?xml version="1.0" encoding="UTF-8"?>
<xsl:stylesheet version="1.0"
xmlns:xsl="http://www.w3.org/1999/XSL/Transform">
    <xsl:template match="/">
        <html>
            <body>
                <h2>Figurine Catalog</h2>
                <table width="300"  border="1">
                <tr align="left">
                    <th>Item to Order</th>
                    <th>Catalog Code</th>
                        <th>Price ($)</th>
                </tr>
                <xsl:for-each select="Catalog/Item">
                <tr>
                    <td><i><xsl:value-of select="Name"/></i></td>
                        <td><xsl:value-of select="OrderCode"/></td>
                    <td><xsl:value-of select="Price"/></td>
                </tr>
                </xsl:for-each>
                </table>
            </body>
        </html>
    </xsl:template>
</xsl:stylesheet>
```

XSLT stylesheet

Template

"for-each" element

"value-of" elements

Browser view

Figurine Catalog

Item to Order	Catalog Code	Price ($)
Fish	FG 7466	109.99
Female Statue	FG 5538	149.99

Figure X.29 An example of the use of an XSLT style sheet.

accordance with the rules specified in an XSLT STYLE SHEET.

XSL transform element *See* TRANSFORM ELEMENT.

XSL transformation *See* TRANSFORMATION; XSLT.

XSLT root element The ROOT ELEMENT of an XSLT STYLE SHEET. It can be one of the two completely synonymous elements: either the xsl:stylesheet ELEMENT or the xsl:transform element, as shown in Figure X.28.

XSLT select attribute *See* SELECT ATTRIBUTE.

XSLT sort element *See* SORT ELEMENT.

XSLT style sheet A term commonly used to refer to an XSLT document. An XSLT style sheet consists of a set of rules called TEMPLATES that define how an XML DOCUMENT should be transformed and/or formatted. Figure X.29 shows an example of an XSLT style sheet and its use for formatting an XML document. Note that the XML document contains a special PROCESSING INSTRUCTION that is used as an XSLT style sheet reference (*see* ASSOCIATING STYLE SHEETS WITH XML DOCUMENTS). The associated XSLT style sheet consists of a template that includes one FOR-EACH ELEMENT and three VALUE-OF ELEMENTS. The XSLT-formatted XML document is rendered in a WEB BROWSER as a table. *See also* CSS; CSS STYLE SHEET; STYLE SHEET.

XSLT style sheet element *See* STYLE SHEET ELEMENT.

XSLT style sheet reference *See* XSLT STYLE SHEET. *See also* ASSOCIATING STYLE SHEETS WITH XML DOCUMENTS.

XSLT template *See* TEMPLATE.

XSLT template rule A term that is sometimes used to refer to a TEMPLATE.

XSLT transform element *See* TRANSFORM ELEMENT.

XSLT transformation *See* TRANSFORMATION.

XSLT value-of element *See* VALUE-OF ELEMENT.

XSL value-of element *See* VALUE-OF ELEMENT.

XSTAR (XML System for Textual and Archaeological Research) A long-term initiative to create XML-BASED MARKUP LANGUAGES for researchers and specialists in textual and archaeological studies such as archaeologists, philologists, historians, and historical geographers. More details about XSTAR are available at http://www.oi.uchicago.edu/OI/PROJ/XSTAR/XSTAR.html. *See also* ARCHAEOML.

XTML (Extensible Telephony Markup Language) An XML-BASED MARKUP LANGUAGE that is intended for creating and delivering enhanced communication services over any next-generation network using any protocol or API. Details of XTML can be found at http://www.pactolus.com/pcs-xtml.pdf.

X-VRML (Extensible Virtual Reality Modeling Language) A high-level XML-BASED MARKUP LANGUAGE that extends virtual reality standards such as VRML, X3D and MPEG-4 with dynamical modeling capabilities. Details of X-VRML can be found at http://xvrml.kti.ae.poznan.pl/. *See also* X3D.

Y

Year data type In an XML SCHEMA, a DATA TYPE that is used for specifying a value that is a particular calendar year, as shown in Figure Y.1.

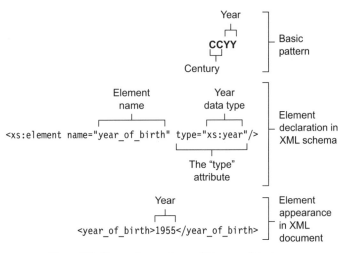

Figure Y.1 The syntax and use of the year data type.

z dimension *See* Z-INDEX PROPERTY.

z-index property In CSS, a property that is used for positioning ELEMENTS in the third dimension (also known as *z* dimension or depth). Just as the *x* and *y* dimensions are used to positioning elements in two dimensions, the *z* dimension is used to position elements in front of or behind other elements. The *z* dimension of an element can be specified using the z-index property, as shown in Figure Z.1.

The *n* value of the z-index property can be any integer (..., −2, −1, 0, 1, 2, ...). The higher is the *n* value, the higher up is the staking level of an element. See Figure Z.1.

z-order *See* Z-INDEX PROPERTY.

Basic syntax

```
z-index:n
```
Property   Property
value

Example

The "z-index"
property

```
Element3 {display:block; position:absolute; left:50px; z-index:4}
Element2 {display:block; position:absolute; left:30px; z-index:2}
Element1 {display:block; position:absolute; left:10px; z-index:1}
```

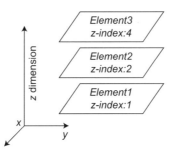

Figure Z.1 The z-index property.

Appendix A

Main Web Resources

Many entries in this dictionary include addresses of Web sites from which more information about specific technologies, languages, concepts etc. can be found. The list below comprises only the major Web sites, several of which can serve as portals to further online resources.

http://www.w3.org/
The Web site of the World Wide Web Consortium (W3C) contains all the latest W3C standards, related to XML technologies and the Semantic Web.

http://www.xml.org/
The XML Industry Portal, hosted by OASIS, provides an independent resource for news and information about the industrial and commercial applications of XML.

http://www.oasis-open.org/cover/
The XML Cover Pages is a comprehensive Web-accessible reference collection.

http://www.xml.com/
Articles, tutorials, software and other XML-related information hosted by O'Reilly.

http://www.semanticweb.org/
The portal of the Semantic Web community.

http://www.garshol.priv.no/download/xmltools/
A comprehensive list of free XML tools and software by Lars Marius Garshol.

http://wdvl.com/Authoring/Languages/XML/
The XML section of the Web Developer's Virtual Library (WDVL), which contains links to major XML sites and specifications.

http://www.ucc.ie/xml/
A list of Frequently Asked Questions (FAQ) about XML.

http://msdn.microsoft.com/xml/
Microsoft Developer Network's XML developer center, which aggregates content and resources about XML.

http://www.w3schools.com/
Free tutorials on XML, XSL, XPath and other XML technologies.

http://www.xmlbooks.com/
Charles F. Goldfarb's "All the XML Books in Print" Web site.

http://www.oasis-open.org/
The Web site of OASIS (the Organization for the Advancement of Structured Information Standards).

http://xml.apache.org/
The Apache XML Project (part of the Apache Software Foundation).

http://java.sun.com/xml/
Java technology and XML.

http://metalab.unc.edu/xml/
Cafe con Leche's XML news and resources.

http://www.alphaworks.ibm.com/xml/
IBM's XML Web site for early adopter developers.

http://www.idealliance.org/XMLRoadmap/
WEB/TOC/xmlrotoc.htm
The "XML Road Map" – a guide to XML standards.

http://www.ontoweb.org/
The Web site of a European Union-funded project about ontology-based information exchange for knowledge management and electronic commerce.

http://www.perfectxml.com/
A collection of information on different aspects of XML.

http://www.xml-acronym-demystifier.org/
A project that is intended to collect and published information about the various acronyms prevalent within the XML technology.

http://www.xmlfiles.com/
XML-related resources.

http://www.xmlhack.com/
A news Web site for XML developers.

http://www.xmlmag.com/
An online XML magazine.

http://www.xmlsoftware.com/
An index of XML-related software resources.

http://www.egroups.com/group/xml-dev/
An informal unmoderated list to support those who are interested in the implementation and development of XML.

http://www.xml.org/xml-dev/
The XML developers' mailing list.

Appendix B

Bibliography: Books

CSS

Cascading Style Sheets (CSS) by Example by Steve Callihan. Que, 2001

Cascading Style Sheets: Separating Content from Presentation by Owen Briggs, Steve Champeon, Eric Costello and Matthew Patterson. Glasshaus, 2002

Cascading Style Sheets: The Definitive Guide by Eric A. Meyer. O'Reilly & Associates, 2000

CSS Pocket Reference by Eric A. Meyer. O'Reilly & Associates, 2001

HTML for the World Wide Web with XHTML and CSS: Visual QuickStart Guide by Elizabeth Castro. Peachpit Press, 2002

Professional Style Sheets for HTML and XML by Frank Boumphrey. Wrox, 1998

Sams Teach Yourself CSS in 24 Hours by Kynn Bartlett. Sams, 2002

Web Design with XML: Generating Web pages with XML, CSS, and XSLT by Manfred Knobloch and Matthias Kopp. John Wiley & Sons, 2002

DirXML

Novell's Guide to DirXML by Peter Kuo. John Wiley & Sons, 2002

ebXML

Business Process Integration with Service Oriented Architectures: ebXML by NEIMAN. Sams, 2003

ebXML Simplified – a Guide to the New Standard for Global E-commerce by Eric Chiu. John Wiley & Sons Inc, 2002

ebXML: Concepts and Application by Brian Gibb and Suresh Damodaran. John Wiley & Sons Inc, 2002

ebXML: Developing Global E-business Solutions by Klaus Deiter-Naujok. Sams, 2002

ebXML: The Technical Reports by Aaron Walsh. Prentice Hall PTR, 2002

ebXML: the New Global Standard by Alan Kotok and David Webber. Prentice Hall, 2001

Professional ebXML Foundations by Pim van der Eijk, Duane Nickull, J.J. Dubray *et al*. Wrox, 2001

MathML

The MathML Handbook by Pavi Sandhu. Charles River Media, 2002

Metadata

Creating the Semantic Web with RDF: Professional Developer's Guide by Johan Hjelm. John Wiley & Sons, 2001

Digital Preservation and Metadata: History, Theory, Practice by Susan S. Lazinger. Libraries Unlimited, 2001

Introduction to Metadata: Pathways to Digital Information by Murtha Baca (Editor). Getty Information Inst, 2000

Managing Metadata with XML and RDF: Improving Workflow for Web Applications by Jeffrey Ricker. John Wiley & Sons, 1999

Metadata Fundamentals for All Librarians by Priscilla Caplan. Amer Library Assn Editions, 2003

Metadata Management for Information Control and Business Success by Guy V. Tozer. Artech House, 1999

Metadata Solutions: Using Metamodels, Repositories, XML, and Enterprise Portals to Generate Information on Demand by Adrienne Tannenbaum. Addison Wesley Professional, 2001

Metadata and Organizing Educational Resources on the Internet by Jane Greenberg (Editor). Haworth Press, 2001

Online GIS and Metadata by Terry Bossomaier and David R. Green. Taylor & Francis, 2002

Ontology Learning for the Semantic Web by Alexander Maedche. Kluwer Academic Publishers, 2002

Professional XML Meta Data by David Dodds, Andrew Watt, Mark Birbeck et al. Wrox, 2001

XML Topic Maps: Creating and Using Topic Maps for the Web by Jack Park, Sam Hunting and Douglas C. Engelbart (eds.). Addison Wesley Professional, 2002

RDF

Creating the Semantic Web with RDF by Johan Hjelm. John Wiley & Sons, 2001

Managing Metadata with XML and RDF: Improving Workflow for Web Applications by J. Ricker. John Wiley & Sons, 2002

Practical RDF by Shelley Powers. O'Reilly UK, 2003

RDF Specifications: Containing Resource Description Framework RDF Schema and Resource Description Framework RDF Model and Syntax Specification. Iuniverse.Com, 2000

Semantic Web

Building Semantic Web Applications by Ernesto Damiani. Addison Wesley, 2003

Creating the Semantic Web with RDF by Johan Hjelm. John Wiley & Sons, 2001

The Emerging Semantic Web: Selected Papers from the First Semantic Web Working Symposium by I.F. Cruz (ed.) et al. IOS Press, 2002

Internet-based Workflow Management: Toward a Semantic Web by Marinescu. John Wiley & Sons, 2002

Knowledge Engineering and Knowledge Management. Ontologies and the Semantic Web (Lecture Notes in Artificial Intelligence.) by V.R. Benjamins and A. Gomez-Perez (eds.). Springer-Verlag, 2003

Ontologies: a Silver Bullet for Knowledge Management and Electronic Commerce by D. Fensel. Springer-Verlag, 2001

Ontology Learning for the Semantic Web by R. Studer (Foreword), Alexander Maedche. Kluwer Academic Publishers, 2002

Semantic Web Field Guide by Thomas B. Passin. Manning, 2003

The Semantic Web: A Guide to the Future of XML, Web Services, and Knowledge Management by Michael C. Daconta, Leo J. Obrst and Kevin T. Smith. John Wiley & Sons, 2003

The Semantic Web: ISWC 2002: First International Semantic Web Conference, Sardinia, Italy, 9–12 June 2002: Proceedings by Ian Horrocks, James Hendler (eds.). Springer-Verlag, 2002

Spinning the Semantic Web: Bringing the World Wide Web to Its Full Potential by Dieter Fensel, James Hendler, Henry Lieberman and Wolfgang Wahlster. MIT Press, 2003

The Unfinished Revolution: Human-Centered Computers and What They Can Do for Us by Michael L. Dertouzos and Tim Berners-Lee (Foreword). HarperBusiness, 2002

Towards the Semantic Web: Ontology-driven Knowledge Management by John Davies. John Wiley & Sons Ltd, 2003

Visualizing the Semantic Web: XML-based Internet and Information Visualization by Vladimir Geroimenko and Chaomei Chen (eds.). Springer-Verlag, 2002

Weaving the Web: The Past, Present and Future of the World Wide Web by Its Inventor by Tim Berners-Lee. Texere Publishing, 2000

Web Services, E-Business, and the Semantic Web: Caise 2002 International Workshop, Wes 2002, Toronto, Canada, 27–28 May 2002: Revised Papers (Lecture Notes in Computer Science, 2512) by Christoph Bussler, Rick Hull, Sheila McIlraith, Maria E. Orlowska, Barbara Pernici and Jian Yang. Springer-Verlag, 2002

XML Semi-structured Databases and the Semantic Web by Bhavani Thuraisingham. CRC Press, 2001

SGML

The Concise SGML Companion by Neil Bradley. Addison Wesley, 1996

Developing SGML DTDs: From Text to Model to Markup by Eve Maler and Jeanne El Andaloussi. Prentice Hall PTR, 1995

SGML: The Billion Dollar Secret by Chet Ensign. Prentice Hall, 1996

The SGML FAQ Book: Understanding the Foundation of HTML and XML by Steven J. Derose. Kluwer Academic Publishers, 1997

The SGML Handbook by Charles F. Goldfarb and Yuri Rubinsky. Clarendon Press, 1991

SGML on the Web: Small Steps Beyond HTML (Charles F. Goldfarb Series on Open Information Management) by Yuri Rubinsky and Murray Maloney. Prentice Hall Computer Books, 1997

SMIL

SMIL for Dummies by Heather Williamson. John Wiley & Sons, 2001

SMIL: Adding Multimedia to the Web by Tim Kennedy and Mary Slowinski. Sams, 2001

SMIL: Interactive Multimedia on the Web by Lloyd Rutledge and Dick Bulterman. Addison Wesley, 2003

Synchronized Multimedia Integration Language SMIL 1.0 Specification. Iuniverse.Com, 2000

SVG

Data Visualization on the Web With SVG and PHP by Jacek Artymiak. Wordware Publishing, 2002

Designing SVG Web Graphics: Visual Components for Graphics in the Internet Age by Andrew H. Watt. New Rider, 2001

Developing SVG-based Web Applications by Lorien House and Ellen Pearlman. Prentice Hall, 2002

Foundation SVG by Jon Frost, Stefan Goessner and Ian Tindale. Friends of ED, 2001

Inside SVG: Mastering the Use of Scalable Vector Graphics for the Web by Kas Thomas. Random House, 2000

Motion Graphics Studio: Web Design with Flash, Shockwave, LiveMotion, SVG, and Streaming Audio/Video by Peter Holm. Friends of Ed, 2001

Professional PHP4 XML by Luis Argerich, Chris Lea, Ken Egervari, Matt Anton, Chris Hubbard and James Fuller. Wrox, 2002

SVG Design Classroom: Using Scalable Vector Graphics in Next-generation Web Sites by Bill Trippe and Kate Binder. Osborne McGraw-Hill, 2002

SVG Essentials by J. David Eisenberg. O'Reilly UK, 2002

SVG Programming: The Graphical Web by Kurt Cagle. Apress, 2002

SVG Unleashed by Chris Lilley and Andrew Watt. Sams, 2002

SVG for Web Designers by J.Teague and Marc Campbell. John Wiley & Sons, 2003

Sams Teach Yourself SVG in 24 Hours by Micah Laaker. Sams, 2002

Scalable Vector Graphics SVG 1.0 Specification by Jon Ferraiolo. Iuniverse.Com, 2000

Visualizing the Semantic Web: XML-based Internet and Information Visualization by Vladimir Geroimenko and Chaomei Chen (Editors). Springer-Verlag, 2002

Topic Maps

XML Topic Maps: Creating and Using Topic Maps for the Web by Jack Park and Sam Hunting (eds.). Addison Wesley, 2002

UML

Building Web Applications with UML (2nd Edition) by Jim Conallen. Addison Wesley Professional, 2002

Developing Web Systems with UML by Jake Sturm. Addison Wesley, 2004

Essential UML Fast by Aladdin Ayesh. Springer-Verlag, 2002

Learning UML by Sinan Si Alhir and Jonathan Gennick. O'Reilly & Associates, 2003

Mastering XMI: Java Programming with XMI, XML and UML by Timothy J. Grose, Stephen A. Brodsky and Gary C. Doney. John Wiley, 2002

Mobile UML: Developing Wireless and Voice Applications by Reza Behravanfar. Cambridge University Press, 2003

Modeling XML Applications with UML: Practical e-Business Applications by David Carlson. Addison Wesley, 2001

Professional UML with VS.NET: Unmasking Visio for Enterprise Architects by Tony Loton, Kevin McNeish et al. Wrox, 2002

UML Applied: A .Net Perspective by Martin Shoemaker. APress, 2003

UML: A Beginner's Guide by Jason T. Roff, Michael Mueller (Illustrator), Melinda Lytle (Illustrator). McGraw-Hill Osborne Media, 2002

UML Bible by Tom Pender. Hungry Minds, Inc, 2003

UML 2002 - The Unified Modeling Language by Jean-Marc Jezequel, Heinrich Hussmann and Stephen Cook (eds.). Springer-Verlag, 2002

Visual Modeling with Rational Rose and UML by Terry Quatrani. Addison Wesley Professional, 1997

VoiceXML

Definitive VoiceXML by Adam Hocek and David Cuddihy. Prentice Hall PTR, 2002

Early Adopter VoiceXML by Eve Astrid Andersson, Stephen Breitenbach, Tyler Burd et al. Wrox, 2001

Voice Application Development with VoiceXML by Rick Beasley, Veta Bonnewell, Mike Farley et al. Sams, 2001

Voice Enabling Web Applications: VoiceXML and Beyond by Kenneth R. Abbott. APress, 2001

The Voice XML Handbook: Understanding and Building the Phone-enabled Web by Bob Edgar. McGraw-Hill Education, 2001

VoiceXML by Rick Parfitt. Manning, 2002

VoiceXML 2.0 Developer's Guide by Dream Tech Software India Inc. McGraw-Hill, 2002

VoiceXML 2.0: Building Professional Voice-enabled Applications with JSP, ASP & ColdFusion by Dream Tech. McGraw-Hill, 2002

VoiceXML: Professional Developer's Guide with CD-ROM by Chetan Sharma and Jeff Kunins. John Wiley & Sons, 2001

VoiceXML: 10 Projects to Voice Enable Your Website by Mark Miller. John Wiley & Sons, 2002

VoiceXML: Introduction to Developing Speech Applications by James A. Larson. Prentice Hall, 2002

VoiceXML: Strategies and Techniques for Effective Voice Application Development with VoiceXML 2.0 by Chetan Sharma. John Wiley & Sons, 2001

WML

Beginning WAP: WML and WMLScript by Mee Soo Foo, Meng Wei Lee, Karli Watson and Ted Wugofski. Wrox, 2000

The Book of WAP: Developing Wireless Applications with WML and WMLScript by Masum Huq. No Starch Press, 2001

Getting Started with WAP and WML by Huw Evans and Paul Ashworth. Sybex International, 2001

Inside WAP: Programming Applications with WML and WML Script by Pekka Niskanen. Addison Wesley, 2000

Learning WML & WMLScript by Martin Frost. O'Reilly UK, 2000

The Net-Works Guide to WAP and WML: An Introduction to the mobile Internet, and to creating your own WAP site by Pete Smith. Net Works, 2000

Professional JSP: Using JavaServer Pages, Servlets, EJB, JNDI, JDBC, XML, XSLT, and WML to create dynamic and customizable web content by Karl Avedal, Sing Li, Tom Myers et al. Wrox, 2000

WAP Development with WML and WMLScript by Ben Forta, Paul Fonte and Ronan Mandel. Sams, 2000

Wireless XML Developer's Guide by Mikael Hillborg. McGraw-Hill Osborne Media, 2002

WML and WMLScript Fast and Easy Web Development by Candace Garrod. Premier Press, 2001

WML and WMLScript: a Beginner's Guide by Kris Jamsa. Osborne McGraw-Hill, 2001

X3D

Core Web3D by Aaron E. Walsh and Mikaël Bourges-Sévenier. Prentice Hall PTP, 2001

Visualizing the Semantic Web: XML-based Internet and Information Visualization by Vladimir Geroimenko and Chaomei Chen (eds.). Springer-Verlag, 2002

XHTML

Beginning XHTML by Frank Boumphrey (ed.), Dave Raggett, Jenny Raggett, Ted Wugofski, Cassandra Greer and Sebastian Schnitzenbaumer. Wrox, 2000

Essential XHTML Fast by John Cowell. Springer-Verlag, 2002

Mastering XHTML Premium Edition by Ed Tittel (ed.), Chelsea Valentine, Mary Burmeister and Lucinda Dykes. Sybex, 2001

Platinum Edition Using XHTML, XML and Java 2 by Eric Ladd (ed.), Jim O'Donnell, Mike Morgan and Andrew H. Watt. Que, 2000

Understanding XHTML by Jeremy Kurtz and Stephen Morosko. OnWord Press, 2003

Web Design & Development Using XHTML by Jeffrey Griffin, Carlos Morales and John Finnegan. Franklin Beedle & Assoc, 2002

XHTML by Chelsea Valentine and Chris Minnick. New Riders Publishing, 2001

XHTML 1.0 Language and Design Sourcebook: The Next Generation HTML by Ian S. Graham. John Wiley & Sons, 2000

XHTML Black Book: A Complete Guide to Mastering XHTML by Steven Holzner. The Coriolis Group, 2000

XHTML Complete by Kurt Cagle and Joseph A. Webb (eds.), Sybex Inc., 2001

XHTML Essentials by Michael Sauers and R. Allen Wyke. John Wiley & Sons, 2001

XHTML Example By Example by Aaron E. Walsh and Dave Raggett. Prentice Hall PTR, 2001

XHTML Fast & Easy Web Development by Brian Proffitt and Ann Zupan (ed.). Premier Press, 2000

XHTML by Example by Ann Navarro. Que, 2000

XHTML: Moving Toward XML by Simon St. Laurent and B.K. DeLong. John Wiley & Sons, 2000

XML, HTML, XHTML Magic by Molly E. Holzschlag. New Riders Publishing, 2001

XLink

XLink Essentials by Andrew Watt and R. Allen Wyke. John Wiley, 2002

XPath, XLink, XPointer, and XML: A Practical Guide to Web Hyperlinking and Transclusion by Erik Wilde and David Lowe. Addison Wesley, 2002

XMI

Mastering XMI: Java Programming with XMI, XML, and UML by Timothy J. Grose, Gary C. Doney and Stephen A. Brodsky. John Wiley & Sons, 2002

XML

Applied XML Solutions by Benoit Marchal. Sams, 2000

Applied XML: A Toolkit for Programmers by Alex Ceponkus and Faraz Hoodbhoy. John Wiley & Sons, 1999

Beginning XML by David Hunter (ed.), Jeff Rafter, Jon Pinnock, Chris Dix, Kurt Cagle and Roger Kovack. Wrox, 2001

Building Web Sites with XML by Michael Floyd. Prentice Hall, 1999

Charles F. Goldfarb's XML Handbook (4th Edition) by Charles F. Goldfarb and Paul Prescod. Prentice Hall, 2001

Data on the Web: From Relations to Semistructured Data and XML by Serge Abiteboul, Dan Suciu and Peter Buneman. Morgan Kaufmann, 2000

The Essential Guide to XML Technologies by Ronald Turner. Prentice Hall PTR, 2002

Essential XML: Beyond MarkUp by Don Box, Aaron Skonnard and John Lam. Addison Wesley, 2000

Essential XML Quick Reference: A Programmer's Reference to XML, XPath, XSLT, XML Schema, SOAP, and More by Aaron Skonnard and Martin Gudgin. Addison Wesley, 2001

Essential XML for Web Professionals by Dan Livingston. Prentice Hall, 2002

Extending Content Technologies through XML: The Advantage, Trends, and Opportunities by IDC. IDC, 2002

Extensible Markup Language (XML) by Faulkner Information Services. Faulkner Information Services, 2001

Inside XML by Steven Holzner. New Riders Publishing, 2000

Introduction to XML and its Family of Technologies by Scott L. Bain and Alan Shalloway. Net Objectives, 2001

Just XML by John E. Simpson. Prentice Hall PTR, 2000

Learning XML by Erik T. Ray. O'Reilly & Associates, 2001

Mastering XML Premium Edition by Chuck White, Liam Quin and Linda Burman. Sybex, 2001

Nitty Gritty XML by Ingo Dellwig and Magnus Stein. Addison Wesley Professional, 2001

Practical XML for the Web by Chris Auld, Paul Spencer, Jeff Rafter, Jon James, Dave Addey, Oli Gauti Gudmundsson, Allan Kent, Alex Schiell and Inigo Surguy. Glasshaus, 2002

Professional XML by Mark Birbeck, Michael Kay, Stephen F. Mohr, Jonathan Pinnock, Brian Loesgen, Steven Livingston, Didier Martin, Nikola Ozu, Mark Seabourne and David Baliles. Wrox, 2000

Professional XML Databases by Kevin Williams (ed.), Michael Brundage, Patrick Dengler, Jeff Gabriel, Andy Hoskinson, Michael Kay, Thomas Maxwell, Marcelo Ochoa, Johnny Papa and Mohan Vanmane. Wrox, 2000

Sams Teach Yourself XML in 21 Days by Devan Shepherd. Sams, 2001

The Semantic Web: A Guide to the Future of XML, Web Services, and Knowledge Management by Michael C. Daconta, Leo J. Obrst and Kevin T. Smith. John Wiley & Sons, 2003

Special Edition Using XML by David Gulbransen. Que, 2002

Step by Step XML by Michael J. Young. Microsoft Press, 2000

Strategic XML by W. Scott Means. Sams, 2001

System Architecture with XML by Berthold Daum and Udo Merten. Morgan Kaufmann, 2002

XML Bible by Elliotte Rusty Harold. Hungry Minds, Inc., 1999

XML Black Book, 2nd Edition: The Complete Reference for XML Designers and Content Developers by Ted Wugofski and Natanya Pitts. The Coriolis Group, 2000

XML by Stealth: A Manager's Guide to Strategic Implementation by Peter Pappamikail. John Wiley & Sons, 2002

The XML Companion (2nd Edition) by Neil Bradley. Addison Wesley Pub Co, 2000

XML Complete by Pat Coleman (ed.), Sybex Inc., 2001

XML Developer's Guide by Fabio Arciniegas A. McGraw-Hill Osborne Media, 2000

XML Elements of Style by Simon St. Laurent. McGraw-Hill Professional, 1999

XML Family of Specifications Reference and Guide by Dan Vint. Manning Publications, 2001

XML Family of Specifications: A Practical Guide by Kenneth B. Sall. Addison Wesley Professional, 2002

XML How to Program by Harvey M. Deitel, Paul J. Deitel, T. R. Nieto, Ted Lin and Praveen Sadhu. Prentice Hall, 2000

XML Pocket Consultant by William R. Stanek. Microsoft Press, 2002

XML Pocket Reference by Robert Eckstein. O'Reilly & Associates, Inc., 2001

XML Primer Plus by Nicholas Chase. Sams, 2002

XML Step by Step by Michael J. Young. Microsoft Press, 2001

XML Unleashed by Michael Morrison (ed.), David Brownell and Frank Boumphrey. Sams, 1999

XML Weekend Crash Course by Kay Ethier and Alan Houser. John Wiley & Sons, 2001

XML by Example (2nd Edition) by Benoit Marchal. Que, 2001

XML for Real Programmers by Reaz Hoque. Morgan Kaufmann, 2000

XML from A to Z: A Quick Reference of More Than 300 XML Tasks, Terms and Tricks by Heather A. Williamson. Redmond Technology, Inc., 2001

XML in Theory & Practice by Chris Bates. John Wiley & Sons, 2003

XML in a Nutshell: A Desktop Quick Reference by Elliotte Rusty Harold and W. Scott Means. O'Reilly & Associates, 2001

XML: A Manager's Guide (2nd Edition) by Kevin Dick. Addison Wesley Professional, 2002

XML: Content and Data by Kelly Carey and Stanko Blatnik. Prentice Hall, 2002

XML: Introduction to Applied XML – Technologies in Business by Ralph Hilken, Aaron E. Walsh and William Wagner. Prentice Hall, 2002

XML: Opportunities, Pitfalls & Areas to Watch by Aspatore Books. Aspatore Books, 2003

XML: The Complete Reference by Heather Williamson. McGraw-Hill Osborne Media, 2001

XML: Your Visual Blueprint for Building Expert Web Pages by Emily A. Vander Veer and Rev Mengle. John Wiley & Sons, 2000

XML – Illustrated Introductory. Course Technology, 2003

XML & .NET
ADO.NET and XML: ASP.NET On The Edge by Gregory A. Beamer. John Wiley & Sons, 2002

Applied XML Programming for Microsoft .NET by Dino Esposito. Microsoft Press, 2002

Beginning VB.NET XML: Essential XML Skills for VB.NET Programmers by Steven Livingstone and Stewart Fraser. Wrox, 2002

Building XML Web Services for the Microsoft .NET Platform by Scott Short. Microsoft Press, 2002

Developing .Net Web Services with XML by David Jorgensen. Syngress Media Inc, 2002

Fundamentals of Web Applications Using .Net and XML by Eric Bell, Hao Howard Feng, Edward L.W. Soong, David Zhang and Shijia Sam Zhu. Prentice Hall, 2002

Microsoft .NET XML Web Services by Robert Tabor. Sams, 2002

Microsoft .NET XML Web Services Step by Step by Allen Jones and Adam Freeman. Microsoft Press, 2002

.NET and XML by Niel M. Bornstein, Kim Topley and John Osborn. O'Reilly & Associates, 2003

Professional XML for .NET Developers by Dinar Dalvi, Darshan Singh, Kevin Williams, Andy Olsen, J. Michael Palermo IV, John Slater, Bipin Joshi, Joe Gray, Fredrik Normén and Francis Norton. Wrox, 2001

Programming Directory Services with Microsoft .Net and XML by Charles Oppermann. Microsoft Press, 2003

Programming Microsoft .Net XML Web Services by Damien Foggon, Dan Maharry and Chris Ullman. Microsoft Press, 2003

Visual Basic.NET and XML: Harness the Power of XML in VB.NET Applications by Rod Stephens and Brian Hochgurtel. John Wiley & Sons, 2002

XML and ASP.NET by Kirk Allen Evans, Ashwin Kamanna and Joel Mueller. New Riders Publishing, 2002

XML.NET Developer's Guide by Henk-Evert Sonder, Jonothon Ortiz and Adam Sills. Syngress Media Inc, 2002

XML & ASP

ADO.NET and XML: ASP.NET On The Edge by Gregory A. Beamer. John Wiley & Sons, 2002

ASP, ADO, and XML Complete by Sybex Inc. Sybex, 2001

Interactive Programming on the Internet: Using Perl, CGI, ASP, PHP and XML by Craig D. Knuckles and David Yuen. John Wiley & Sons, 2003

Professional ASP XML by Mark Baartse (ed.), Steven Hahn, Stephen Mohr, Brian Loesgen, Richard Blair, Alex Homer, Corey Haines, Dinar Dalvi, John Slater, Mario Zucca, Luca Bolognese, Kevin Williams, Bill Kropog and Mario Zuccar. Wrox, 2000

XML Programming with VB and ASP by Mark Wilson and Tracey Wilson. Manning Publications, 1999

XML Web Services for ASP.NET by Bill Evjen. John Wiley & Sons, 2002

XML and ASP.NET by Kirk Allen Evans, Ashwin Kamanna and Joel Mueller. New Riders Publishing, 2002

XML for ASP.NET Developers by Dan Wahlin. Sams, 2001

XML and C#

Beginning C# XML: Essential XML Skills for C# Programmers by Steven Livingstone and Stewart Fraser. Wrox, 2002

C# Developer's Guide to ASP.NET, XML, and ADO.NET by Chris Kinsman and Jeffrey P. McManus. Addison Wesley Professional, 2002

Professional ASP.NET 1.0 XML with C# by Michael Palermo, Darshan Singh, Steve Mohr, Pieter Siegers and Chris Knowles. Wrox, 2002

XML and C++
C++ XML by Fabio Arciniegas. New Riders Publishing, 2001

XML and Delphi
Delphi Developer's Guide to XML by Keith Wood. Wordware Publishing, 2001

XML and Flash
Flash XML StudioLab by Ian Tindale, Paul McDonald and James Rowley. Friends of ED, 2001

Flash and XML: A Developer's Guide by Dov Jacobson and Jesse Jacobson. Addison Wesley, 2002

Object-oriented Macromedia Flash MX by William Drol. Springer-Verlag, 2002

XML in Flash by Craig Swann and Gregg Caines. SAMS, 2001

XML and Java
The Book of SAX: The Simple API for XML by W. Scott Means and Michael A. Bodie. No Starch Press, 2002

Building Wired and Wireless Services with Java and XML: Integration-Ready Architecture and Design by Jeff Zhuk. Cambridge Univ Press, 2002

Cocoon 2 Programming: Web Publishing with XML and Java by Bill Brogden, Conrad D'Cruz and Mark Gaither. Sybex, 2002

Enterprise Applications Integration with XML and Java by J.P. Morgenthal. Prentice Hall PTR, 2000

JAX: Java APIs for XML Kick Start by Aoyon Chowdhury and Parag Choudhary. Sams, 2002

JSP and XML: Integrating XML and Web Services in Your JSP Application by Casey Kochmer and Erica Frandsen. Addison Wesley Professional, 2002

Java & XML for Dummies by Barry Burd. John Wiley & Sons, 2002

Java & XML, 2nd Edition: Solutions to Real-World Problems by Brett McLaughlin. O'Reilly & Associates, 2001

Java XML Programmer's Reference by Eric Jung, Andrei Cioroianu, Dave Writz, Mohammad Akif, Steven Brodhead and James Hart. Wrox, 2001

Java XML Programming by Nazmul Idris and Nazmul Adris. Independent Publishers Group, 2000

Java XML and Web Services Bible by Mike Jasnowski. John Wiley & Sons, 2002

Java and XML by Brett McLaughlin and Mike Loukides. O'Reilly & Associates, 2000

Java and XML Data Binding by Brett McLaughlin. O'Reilly & Associates, 2002

Java and XML: Your visual blueprint for creating Java-enhanced Web programs by Paul Whitehead, Ernest Friedman-Hill and Emily A. Vander Veer. John Wiley & Sons, 2002

Java, XML, and the JAXP by Arthur Griffith. John Wiley & Sons, 2002

Processing XML with Java: A Guide to SAX, DOM, JDOM, JAXP, and TrAX by Elliotte Rusty Harold. Addison Wesley Professional, 2002

Professional JSP: Using Java Server Pages, Servlets, EJB, JNDI, JDBC, XML, XSLT, and WML by Karl Avedal, Danny Ayers, Timothy Briggs *et al.* Wrox, 2000

Professional Java XML by Kal Ahmed, Sudhir Ancha, Andrei Cioroianu *et al.* Wrox, 2001

Professional Java XML Programming with servlets and JSP by Alexander Nakhimovsky and Thomas J. Myers. Wrox, 1999

Program Generators with XML and Java by J. Craig Cleaveland. Prentice Hall, 2001

XML Development with Java 2 by Michael C. Daconta and Al Saganich. Sams, 2000

XML and Java from Scratch by Nicholas Chase, Jesse Liberty. Que, 2001

XML and Java: Developing Web Applications by Hiroshi Maruyama, Kent Tamura and Naohiko Uramoto. Addison Wesley, 1999

XML and Oracle

Building Oracle XML Applications by Steve Muench. O'Reilly & Associates, 2000

Oracle XML Handbook by Ben Chang, Mark Scardina, K. Karun, Stefan Kiritzov, Ian Macky and Niranjan Ramakrishnan. McGraw-Hill Osborne Media, 2000

Oracle9i XML Handbook by Ben Chang, Mark Scardina and Stefan Kiritzov. McGraw-Hill Osborne Media, 2001

Professional Oracle 8i Application Programming with Java, PL/SQL and XML by Michael Awai (ed.), Matthew Bortniker, John Carnell *et al.* Wrox, 2000

XML & Oracle: A Practical Guide by Roger Hipperson. John Wiley & Sons, 2003

XML and Perl

Interactive Programming on the Internet: Using Perl, CGI, ASP, PHP and XML by Craig D. Knuckles and David Yuen. John Wiley & Sons, 2003

Perl & XML by Erik T. Ray and Jason McIntosh. O'Reilly & Associates, 2002

XML Processing with Perl, Python, and PHP by Martin C. Brown. Sybex, 2001

XML and Perl by Mark Riehl, Ilya Sterin and Llya Sterin. New Riders Publishing, 2002

XML and PHP

Interactive Programming on the Internet: Using Perl, CGI, ASP, PHP and XML by Craig D. Knuckles and David Yuen. John Wiley & Sons, 2003

Professional PHP4 XML by Luis Argerich, Chris Lea, Ken Egervari, Matt Anton, Chris Hubbard, James Fuller and Charlie Killian. Wrox, 2002

XML Processing with Perl, Python, and PHP by Martin C. Brown. Sybex, 2001

XML and PHP by Vikram Vaswani. New Riders Publishing, 2002

XML and Python

Python & XML by Christopher A. Jones and Fred L. Jr. Drake. O'Reilly & Associates, 2001

XML Processing with Perl, Python, and PHP by Martin C. Brown. Sybex, 2001

XML Processing with Python by Sean McGrath. Prentice Hall, 2000

XML and Visual Basic

Professional Visual Basic 6 XML by James G. Britt and Teun Duynstee. Wrox, 2000

Visual Basic.NET Developer's Guide to ASP .NET, XML and ADO.NET by Chris Kinsman and Jeffrey P. McManus. Addison Wesley Professional, 2002

Visual Basic.NET XML Web Services Developer's Guide by Roger Jennings. McGraw-Hill Osborne Media, 2002

Visual Basic.NET and XML: Harness the Power of XML in VB.NET Applications by Rod Stephens and Brian Hochgurtel. John Wiley & Sons, 2002

XML Programming with VB and ASP by Mark Wilson and Tracey Wilson. Manning Publications, 1999

XML Applications

Building B2B Applications with XML: A Resource Guide by Mike Fitzgerald. John Wiley, 2001

Building Commercial XML Web Applications: Problem - Design - Solution by Wrox Author Team. Wrox, 2003

Building Oracle XML Applications by Steve Muench. O'Reilly & Associates, 2000

Building XML Applications by Simon St. Laurent and Ethan Cerami. McGraw-Hill, 2000

Cocoon: Building XML Applications by Carsten Ziegeler and Matthew Langham. New Riders Publishing, 2002

Definitive XML Application Development by Lars Marius Garshol. Prentice Hall PTR, 2002

Designing XML Internet Applications by Michael Leventhal, David Lewis, Matthew Fuchs and Michael Fuchs. Prentice Hall PTR, 1998

Modeling XML Applications with UML: Practical e-Business Applications by David Carlson. Addison Wesley, 2001

XML Application Development with MSXML 4.0 by Danny Ayers, Steven Livingstone, Stephen Mohr, Darshan Singh and Michael Corning. Wrox, 2002

XML Applications by Frank Boumphrey. Wrox, 1998

XML Databases

Beginning Java Databases: JDBC, SQL, J2EE, EJB, JSP, XML by Kevin Mukhar, Todd Lauinger and John Carnell. Wrox, 2001

Data on the Web: from Relations to Semistructured Data and XML by Serge Abiteboul, Peter Buneman and Dan Suciu. Morgan Kaufmann, 1999

Designing XML Databases by Mark Graves. Prentice Hall, 2001

Distributed Data Exchange with XML, ASP, IE5, LDAP and MSMQ by Stephen T. Mohr. Wrox, 1999

Domino 5 Web Programming with XML, Java, and JavaScript by Randy Tamura. Que, 2000

Open Source XML Database Toolkit: Resources and Techniques for Improved Development by Liam Quin. John Wiley & Sons, 2000

Oracle XML Handbook by Ben Chang, Mark Scardina *et al*. Osborne McGraw-Hill, 2000

Professional Oracle 8i Application Programming with Java, PL/SQL and XML by Michael Awai, Matthew Bortniker, John Carnell *et al*. Wrox, 2000

Professional XML Databases by Kevin Williams, Patrick Dengler, Jeff Gabriel *et al*. Wrox, 2000

SQL Server 2000 and Business Intelligence in an XML/ .NET World by Joseph Valiaveedu. Apress, 2002

Succeeding with Object Databases: A Practical Look at Today's Implementations with Java and XML by Akmal Chaudhri and Roberto Zicari. John Wiley & Sons, 2000

XML Data Management: Native XML and XML-enabled Database Systems by Akmal B. Chaudhri, Awais Rashid and Roberto Zicari. Addison Wesley, 2003

XML Semi-structured Databases and the Semantic Web by Bhavani Thuraisingham. CRC Press, 2001

XML and SQL Server 2000 by John Griffin. New Riders, 2001

XML-Based Data Management and Multimedia Engineering - EDBT 2002 Workshops: EDBT 2002 Workshops XMLDM, MDDE, and YRWS, Prague, Czech Republic, 24–28 March 2002, Revised Papers (Lecture Notes in Computer Science). Springer-Verlag, 2003

XML Database Techniques by Jeroen Van Rotterdam. Addison Wesley, 2004

XML Schema

Definitive XML Schema by Priscilla Walmsley. Prentice Hall, 2001

Essential XML Quick Reference: A Programmer's Reference to XML, XPath, XSLT, XML Schema, SOAP and More by Aaron Skonnard and Martin Gudgin. Addison Wesley, 2001

Inside XML DTDs: Scientific and Technical by Simon St. Laurent and Robert J. Biggar. McGraw-Hill Osborne Media, 1999

Professional XML Schemas by Jon Duckett (Editor), Nik Ozu, Kevin Williams, Stephen Mohr, Kurt Cagle, Oliver Griffin, Francis Norton, Ian Stokes-Rees and Jeni Tennison. Wrox, 2001

XML Schema by Neil Bradley. Addison Wesley, 2002

XML Schema by Eric van der Vlist. O'Reilly UK, 2002

XML Schemas by Lucinda Dykes, Ed Tittel and Chelsea Valentine. Sybex, 2002

XML Schema Book by Berthold Daum. Morgan Kaufmann, 2003

The XML Schema Complete Reference by Cliff Binstock, David Peterson, Mitchell Smith, Mike Wooding and Chris Dix. Sams, 2002

XML Schema Definition (XSD) by Shruti Gupti and Sonal Mukhi. BPB Publications, 2002

XML Schema Developer's Guide by Ron Pronk. Osborne McGraw-Hill, 2002

XML Schema Development: An Object-oriented Approach by Peter Brauer. Sams, 2002

XML Schema Elucidated by Jeff Lowery. Manning, 2002

XML Schema Essentials by R. Allen Wyke and Andrew Watt. John Wiley, 2002

XML Schema Interlinear by Rick Jelliffe. Manning Publications, 2002

XML Security

Hack Proofing XML by Larry Loeb, Everett F. Carter, Ken Ftu et al. (eds.). Syngress Media Inc, 2002

Mastering Web Services Security by Bret Hartman, Donald J. Flinn, Konstantin Beznosov and Shirley Kawamoto. John Wiley & Sons, 2003

Secure XML: The New Syntax for Signatures and Encryption by Donald E. Eastlake and Kitty Niles. Addison Wesley Professional, 2002

XML Tools

HTML-to-XML Conversion Tools Market Trends by Faulkner Information Services. Faulkner Information Services, 2001

Worldwide XML Development Tools Software Forecast 2002–2006 by IDC. IDC, 2002

XML Development Tools by Faulkner Information Services. Faulkner Information Services, 2001

XMLSPY Handbook by Larry Kim. John Wiley & Sons, 2003

XMLSPY 5 User & Reference Manual by Altova Inc., 2002

XML Web Services

Architecting Web Services by William L. Oellermann Jr. APress, 2001

Building Web Applications with ADO.NET and XML Web Services by Richard Hundhausen, Steven Borg, Cole Francis and Kenneth Wilcox. John Wiley & Sons, 2002

Building Web Services with Java: Making Sense of XML, SOAP, WSDL and UDDI by Steve Graham, Simeon Simeonov, Toufic Boubez, Glen Daniels, Doug Davis, Yuichi Nakamura and Ryo Neyama. Sams, 2001

Building XML Web Services for the Microsoft .NET Platform by Scott Short. Microsoft Press, 2002

Developing .Net Web Services with XML by David Jorgensen. Syngress Media Inc, 2002

Java XML and Web Services Bible by Mike Jasnowski. John Wiley & Sons, 2002

Microsoft .NET XML Web Services by Robert Tabor. Sams, 2002

Microsoft .NET XML Web Services Step by Step by Adam Freeman and Allen Jones. Microsoft Press, 2002

Professional XML Web Services by Vivek Chopra, Zaev Zoran, Gary Damschen, Chris Dix, Patrick Cauldwell, Rajesh Chawla, Kristy Saunders, Glenn Olander, Francis Norton, Tony Hong, Uche Ogbuji and Mark A. Richman. Wrox, 2001

Programming Microsoft .Net XML Web Services by Damien Foggon, Dan Maharry and Chris Ullman. Microsoft Press, 2003

Programming Web Services with XML-RPC by Simon St. Laurent, Edd Dumbill and Joe Johnston. O'Reilly & Associates, 2001

The Semantic Web: A Guide to the Future of XML, Web Services, and Knowledge Management by Michael C. Daconta, Leo J. Obrst and Kevin T. Smith. John Wiley & Sons, 2003

Understanding Web Services: XML, WSDL, SOAP, and UDDI by Eric Newcomer. Addison Wesley Professional, 2002

Water: Simplified Web Services and XML Programming by Mike Plusch. John Wiley & Sons, 2002

Web Services Essentials by Ethan Cerami. O'Reilly & Associates, 2002

XML Web Services Professional Projects by Geetanjali Arora and Sai Kishore. Premier Press, 2002

XML Web Services for ASP.NET by Bill Evjen. John Wiley & Sons, 2002

XML Web Services in the Organization by Chris Boar. Microsoft Press, 2003

XML and Web Services Unleashed by Ron Schmelzer, Travis Vandersypen, Jason Bloomberg et al. Diane Kennedy. Sams, 2002

XML, Web Services, and the Data Revolution by Frank P. Coyle. Addison Wesley Professional, 2002

XPath

Definitive XSLT and XPath (The Charles F. Goldfarb Definitive XML Series) by G. Ken Holman. Prentice Hall PTR, 2001

Essential XML Quick Reference: A Programmer's Reference to XML, Xpath, XSLT, XML Schema, SOAP and More by Aaron Skonnard and Martin Gudgin. Addison Wesley, 2001

XPath & XPointer by John E. Simpson. O'Reilly UK, 2002

XSLT & XPath on the Edge by Jeni Tennison. John Wiley & Sons Inc, 2001

XSLT and XPath: Guide to XML Transformations by Zarella L. Rendon and John Robert Gardner. Prentice Hall, 2001

XPath Essentials by Andrew Watt. John Wiley & Sons Inc, 2002

XPath, XLink, XPointer, and XML: A Practical Guide to Web Hyperlinking and Transclusion by Erik Wilde and David Lowe. Addison Wesley, 2002

XPath: Navigating XML Documents by Steven Holzner. Sams, 2003

XPointer

XPath & XPointer by John E. Simpson. O'Reilly UK, 2002

XPath, XLink, XPointer, and XML: A Practical Guide to Web Hyperlinking and Transclusion by Erik Wilde and David Lowe. Addison Wesley, 2002

XQuery

Early Adopter XQuery by Dan Maharry, Kurt Cagle, Rogerio Saran, Mark Fussell and Nalleli Lopez. Wrox, 2002

XQuery Kick Start by James McGovern, Per Bothner, Kurt Cagle, James Linn and Vaidyanathan Nagarajan. Sams, 2003

XSL and XSL-FO

Definitive XSL-FO by G. Ken Holman. Prentice Hall, 2003

Introduction to XML/XSL Programming. Course Technology, 2003

Just XSL by John E. Simpson. Prentice Hall, 2001

Professional XSL by Kurt Cagle, Michael Corning, Jason Diamond, Teun Duynstee, Oli Gudmundsson, Jirka

Jirat, Mike Mason, Jon Pinnock, Paul Spencer, Jeff Tang, Paul Tchistopolskii, Jeni Tennison and Andrew Watt. Wrox, 2001

The XSL Companion by Neil Bradley. Addison Wesley Professional, 2002

XML Elements of Style by Simon St. Laurent. McGraw-Hill Professional, 1999

XSL Essentials by Michael Fitzgerald. John Wiley & Sons, 2001

XSL FO by Dave Pawson. O'Reilly & Associates, 2002

XSL Formatting Objects Developer's Handbook by Douglas Lovell. Sams, 2002

XSLT

Beginning XSLT by Jeni Tennison. Wrox, 2002

Definitive XSLT and XPath by G. Ken Holman. Prentice Hall, 2001

Inside XSLT by Steven Holzner. New Riders Publishing, 2001

Mastering XSLT by Chuck White. Sybex, 2002

Special Edition Using XSLT by Michael Floyd, David Gulbransen, Joe Hinder, Alaric B. Snell and Mark Wutka. Que, 2002

XSLT by Doug Tidwell. O'Reilly & Associates, 2001

XSLT Developer's Guide by Chris Von See and Nitin Keskar. McGraw-Hill Osborne Media, 2002

XSLT Programmer's Reference by Michael Kay. Wrox, 2000

XSLT Quickly by Bob Ducharme. Manning Publications Company, 2001

XSLT and XPath: A Guide to XML Transformations by John Robert Gardner and Zarella L. Rendon. Prentice Hall, 2001

XSLT and XPath on the Edge, Unlimited Edition by Jeni Tennison. John Wiley & Sons, 2001

XSLT: Professional Developer's Guide by Johan Hjelm and Peter Stark. John Wiley & Sons, 2001

XSLT: Working with XML and HTML by Khun Yee Fung. Addison Wesley, 2000

Bibliography: Journal Articles and Conference Proceedings

CSS

Lurching toward Babel: HTML, CSS and XML by Korpela, J. *Computer*, **31**(7), 103–4, 106 (1998)

Multipurpose Web publishing using HTML, XML, and CSS by Lie, H.W. and Saarela, *J. Communications of the ACM*, **42**(10), 95–101 (1999)

ebXML

E-business technology: ebXML for the energy market by Marz, W. *Elektrizitaetswirtschaft*, **101**(5), 36–41 (2002)

ebXML: status, research issues, and obstacles by Hofreiter, B., Huemer, C. and Klas, W. *Proceedings Twelfth International Workshop on Research Issues in Data Engineering: Engineering E-Commerce/E-Business Systems* RIDE-2EC 2002, pp. 7–16. IEEE Computer Society, Los Alamitos, CA, 2002

ebXML gets ready for prime time by McGarr, M.S. *Electronic Commerce World*, **11**(5), 38–41(2001)

Extending support for contracts in ebXML by Cole, J. and Milosevic, Z. *Proceedings Workshop on Information Technology for Virtual Enterprises*. ITVE 2001, pp. 119–27. IEEE Computer Society, Los Alamitos, CA, 2001

MathML

Examples of MathML by Watt, S.M. and Xuehong Li. *SIGSAM Bulletin*, **33**(1), 1–4 (1999)

FIGUE: mathematical formula layout with interaction and MathML support by Naciri, H. and Rideau, L. *Computer Mathematics. Proceedings of the Fifth Asian Symposium (ASCM 2001)*, pp. 112–21. World Scientific, Singapore

Future scientific digital documents with MathML, XML, and SVG by Landau, R.H., Vediner, D., Wattanakasiwich, P. and Kyle, K.R. *Computing in Science & Engineering*, **4**(2), 77–85 (2002)

Interactive mathematics via the Web using MathML by Wright, F.J. *SIGSAM Bulletin*, **34**(2), 49–57 (2000)

The interchange of mathematics in XML: MathML, OpenMath and their application by Buswell, S. *XML Europe '99 Conference Proceedings*, pp. 379–85. Graphic Communications Association, Alexandria, VA, 1999

MathML – markup language for mathematical documents on the World Wide Web by Sroczynski, Z. *Studia Informatica*, **21**(3), 25–45 (2000)

OpenMath, MathML and XSL by Carlisle, D. *SIGSAM Bulletin*, **34**(2), 6–11 (2000)

Metadata

A conceptual metadata schema for representing and cataloguing images for semantic attribute retrieval by de Carvalho Moura, A.M., de Souza Garcia, S. and Campos, M.L.M. *Proceedings of the International Conference on Imaging Science, Systems, and Technology, CISST'2000*, pp. 583–9, Vol. 2. CSREA Press/Univ. Georgia, Athens, GA, 2000

Deployment of personalized e-catalogues: an agent-based framework integrated with XML metadata and user models by Duen-Ren Liu, Yuh-Jaan Lin, Chung-

Min Chen and Ya-Wen Huang. *Journal of Network and Computer Applications*, 24(3), 201–28 (2001)

Embedding knowledge in Web documents: CGs versus XML-based metadata languages by Martin, P. and Eklund, P. *Conceptual Structures: Standards and Practices. 7th International Conference on Conceptual Structures, ICCS'99, Proceedings* (Lecture Notes in Computer Science 1640), pp. 230–46. Springer-Verlag, Berlin, 1999

Enabling flexible services using XML metadata by Velasco, L. and Marshall, L. *Multimedia Applications, Services and Techniques – ECMAST'99. 4th European Conference, Proceedings*, pp. 332–47 Springer-Verlag, Berlin, 1999

The EOR toolkit: an open source solution for RDF metadata by Wagner, H.R. *Information Technology and Libraries*, 21(1), 27–31 (2002)

A framework for personalized e-catalogs: an integration of XML-based metadata, user models and agents by Duen-Ren Liu, Yuh-Jaan Lin, Ya-Wen Huang and Chung-Min Chen. *Proceedings of the 34th Annual Hawaii International Conference on System Sciences*, p. 10. IEEE Computer Society, Los Alamitos, CA, 2001

Integrating ontologies and thesauri for RDF schema creation and metadata querying by Amann, B., Fundulaki, I. and Scholl, M. *International Journal on Digital Libraries*, 3(3), 221–36 (2000)

Knowledge management with ontologies and metadata by Staab, S. *Informatik Spektrum*, 25(3), 194–6 (2002)

Managing scientific metadata using XML by Ruixin Yang, Kafatos, M. and Wang, X.S. *IEEE Internet Computing*, 6(4), 52–9 (2002)

Managing metadata over the WWW using eXtensible markup language (XML) [for electric power industry] by Bin Qiu, Yilu Liu, Yew Soon Ong, Hoay Beng Gooi and Shiun Chen *2002 IEEE Power Engineering Society Winter Meeting. Conference Proceedings*, pp. 678–83. IEEE, Piscataway, NJ, 2002

MARC metadata description approach based on XML/RDF by Huang Weihong and Zhang Fuyan. *Journal of the China Society for Scientific and Technical Information*, 19(4), 326–32 (2000)

Metadata design for Chinese medicine digital library using XML by Yang, C.C. and Chan, W.W.M. *Proceedings of the 33rd Annual Hawaii International Conference on System Sciences*, p. 10, Vol. 1. IEEE Computer Society, Los Alamitos, CA, 2000

Metadata encoded in XML: enabling complex query formulation in distributed statistical databases by Bi, Y. and Lamb, J. *Third International Conference on Information Integration and Web-based Applications and Services. (IIWAS 2001)*, pp. 477–9. Osterreichische Comput. Gesellschaft, Wien, 2001

Metadata representation in XML for Internet-based electronic XML application from business to government by Imamura, M., Nagahama, R., Suzuki, K., Watabe, A. and Tsuji, H. *Proceedings Seventh International Conference on Parallel and Distributed Systems: Workshops*, pp. 387–92. IEEE Computer Society, Los Alamitos, CA, 2000

Metadata, a "semantic" approach by Zarri, G.P. Database and Expert Systems Applications. *10th International Conference, DEXA'99* (Lecture Notes in Computer Science 1677), pp. 646–55. Springer-Verlag, Berlin, 1999

A metadata repository system for an efficient description of visual multimedia documents by Ye Sun Joung, Jae Houng Lim, Hyun, S.J. and Yong Man Ro. *Concurrent Engineering: Research and Applications*, 9(2), 93–104 (2001)

Modeling, metadata, and XML by North, K. *WEB Techniques*, 4(6), 18, 20–2 (1999)

Open metadata formats: efficient XML-based communication for heterogeneous distributed systems by Widener, P., Schwan, K. and Eisenhauer, G. *Proceedings 21st International Conference on Distributed Computing Systems*, pp. 739–42. IEEE Computer Society, Los Alamitos, CA, 2001

Open metadata formats: efficient XML-based communication for high performance computing by Widener, P., Eisenhauer, G. and Schwan, K. *Proceedings 10th IEEE International Symposium on High Performance Distributed Computing*, pp. 371–80. IEEE Computer Society, Los Alamitos, CA, 2001

Open metadata formats: efficient XML-based communication for high performance computing by Widener, P., Eisenhauer, G., Schwan, K. and Bustamante, F.E. *Cluster Computing*, 5(3), 315–24 (2002)

A quantitative categorical analysis of metadata elements in image-applicable metadata schemas by Greenberg, J. *Journal of the American Society for Information Science and Technology*, 52(11), 917–24 (2001)

RDF Declarative Description (RDD): a language for metadata by Anutariya, C., Wuwongse, V., Akama, K. and Nantajeewarawat, E. *JoDI – Journal of Digital Information*, 2(2) (2001)

The RDF metadata generation system for Web site management by Mi Kyung Lee, Yan Ha and Yong Sung Kim. *Journal of KISS: Software and Applications*, **28**(4), 346–57. (2001)

Resource Description Framework – metadata for Internet in the future by Kronman, U. and Parnefjord, J. *Tidskrift for Dokumentation*, **56**(1), 15–25 (2001)

Semantic metadata for the integration of Web-based data for electronic commerce by Bornhovd, C. *Proceedings of International Workshop on Advance Issues of E-Commerce and Web-Based Information Systems*, pp.137–45 IEEE, Piscataway, NJ, 1999

A semantic modeling approach to metadata by Brasethvik, T. *Internet Research: Electronic Networking Applications and Policy*, **8**(5), 377–86 (1998)

Simultaneous topic maps and RDF metadata structures in SVG by Dodds, D. *Conference Proceedings. Extreme Markup Languages 2000. Expanding XML/SGML Universe*, pp. 45–53. Graphic Communications Association, Alexandria, VA, 2000

Structured Graph Format: XML metadata for describing Web site structure by Liechti, O., Sifer, M.J. and Ichikawa, T. *Computer Networks and ISDN Systems*, **30**(1–7), 11–21 (1998)

Visual interaction with XML metadata by Geroimenko, V. and Geroimenko, L. *Proceedings Fifth International Conference on Information Visualisation*, pp. 539–45. IEEE Computer Society, Los Alamitos, CA, 2001

Web metadata: a matter of semantics by Lassila, O. *Journal: IEEE Internet Computing*, **2**(4), 30–7 (1998)

Web metadata semantics-on the road to well formed topic maps by Widhalm, R. and Mueck, T.A. *Proceedings of the Second International Conference on Web Information Systems Engineering*, pp. 141–50, Vol. 2. IEEE Computer Society, Los Alamitos, CA, 2002

Who will create the metadata for the Internet? by Thomas, C.F. and Griffin, L.S. *First Monday*, **3**(12) (1998)

An XML-based distributed metadata server (DIMES) supporting Earth science metadata by Ruixin Yang, Xinhua Deng, Kafatos, M., Changzhou Wang and Wang, X.S. *Proceedings Thirteenth International Conference on Scientific and Statistical Database Management, SSDBM 2001*, pp. 251–6. IEEE Computer Society, Los Alamitos, CA, 2001

An XML-based metadata interchange among relational database systems by Wol-Young Lee and Kiho Lee. *Proceedings of the IASTED International Conference.*

Internet and Multimedia Systems and Applications, pp. 251–5. IASTED, Anaheim, CA, 2000

XML metadata and efficient knowledge discovery by Lang, K. and Burnett, M. *Knowledge-Based Systems*, **13**(5), 321–31 (2000)

RDF

Annotea: an open RDF infrastructure for shared Web annotations by Kahan, J., Koivunen, M.-R., Prud'Hommeaux, E. and Swick, R.R. *Computer Networks*, **39**(5), 589–608 (2002)

Aspects of the development of information systems on the basis of XML and RDF by Hirsch, S. *NFD Information – Wissenschaft und Praxis*, **51**(2), 75–82 (2000)

Automatic RDF metadata generation for resource discovery by Jenkins, C., Jackson, M., Burden, P. and Wallis, J. *Computer Networks*, **31**(11–16), 1305–20 (1999)

Automatic generation of Java/SQL based inference engines from RDF Schema and RuleML by Eberhart, A. *The Semantic Web – ISWC 2002. First International Web Conference, Proceedings* (Lecture Notes in Computer Science 2342), pp. 102–16. Springer-Verlag, Berlin, 2002

Benchmarking RDF schemas for the Semantic Web by Magkanaraki, A., Alexaki, S., Christophides, V. and Plexousakis, D. *The Semantic Web – ISWC 2002. First International Web Conference, Proceedings* (Lecture Notes in Computer Science 2342), pp. 132–46. Springer-Verlag, Berlin, 2002

Distributed meta data objects using RDF by Bebee, B.R., Mack, G.A. and Shafi, I. *Proceedings IEEE 8th International Workshops on Enabling Technologies: Infrastructure for Collaborative Enterprises (WET ICE'99)*, pp. 325–9. IEEE Computer Society, Los Alamitos, CA, 1999

Empirical study on location based Web service based on CC/PP and RDF by Kitagawa, K., Okada, W. and Kato, F. *Proceedings of the SPIE – The International Society for Optical Engineering*, pp. 20–7. SPIE-Int. Soc. Opt. Eng., 2001

Enabling knowledge representation on the Web by extending RDF Schema by Broekstra, J., Klein, M., Decker, S., Fensel, D., van Harmelen, F. and Horrocks, I. *Computer Networks*, **39**(5), 609–34 (2002)

Framework for the semantic Web: an RDF tutorial by Decker, S., Mitra, P. and Melnik, S. *IEEE Internet Computing*, **4**(6), 68–73 (2000)

Integrated object modeling for SMIL, RDF, WIDL documents by Sang-Eun Kim, Yan Ha and Yong-Sung Kim.

Journal of KISS: Software and Applications, 28(1), 14–25 (2001)

Integrating ontologies and thesauri to build RDF schemas by Amann, B. and Fundulaki, I. *Research and Advanced Technology for Digital Libraries. Third European Conference, ECDL'99, Proceedings* (Lecture Notes in Computer Science 1696), pp. 234–53. Springer-Verlag, Berlin, 1999

Integrating ontologies and thesauri for RDF schema creation and metadata querying by Amann, B., Fundulaki, I. and Scholl, M. *International Journal on Digital Libraries*, 3(3), 221–36 (2000)

Managing RDF metadata for community Webs by Alexaki, S., Christophides, V., Karvounarakis, G., Plexousakis, D., Tolle, K., Amann, B., Fundulaki, I., Scholl, M. and Vercoustre, A.-M. *Conceptual Modeling for E-Business and the Web. ER 2000 Workshops on Conceptual Modeling Approaches for E-Business and the World Wide Web and Conceptual Modeling, Proceedings* (Lecture Notes in Computer Science 1921), pp. 140–51. Springer-Verlag, Berlin, 2000

Metadata for the Web: RDF and the Dublin Core by Powell, A. *New Networks, Old Information: UKOLUG98. UKOLUG's 20th Birthday Conference*, pp. 99–108. Inst. Inf. Sci, London, 1998

Networked knowledge representation and exchange using UML and RDF by Cranefield, S. *JoDI – Journal of Digital Information*, 1(8) (2001)

Pattern-based design and implementation of an XML and RDF parser and interpreter: a case study by Neumann, G. and Zdun, U. *ECOOP 2002 – Object Oriented Programming. 16th European Conference, Proceedings* (Lecture Notes in Computer Science 2374), pp. 392–414. Springer-Verlag, Berlin, 2002

Performance improvement of municipal solid waste drying in RDF production process by Tatemoto, Y., Bando, Y., Yasuda, K., Nakamura, M. and Azegami, M. *Proceedings First International Symposium on Environmentally Conscious Design and Inverse Manufacturing*, pp. 656–61. IEEE Computer Society, Los Alamitos, CA, 1999

RDF Declarative Description (RDD): a language for metadata by Anutariya, C., Wuwongse, V., Akama, K. and Nantajeewarawat, E. *JoDI – Journal of Digital Information*, 2(2) (2001)

The RDF metadata generation system for Web site management by Mi Kyung Lee, Yan Ha and Yong Sung Kim. *Journal of KISS: Software and Applications*, 28(4), 346–57 (2001)

RDF and Topic Maps: an exercise in convergence by Moore, G.D. *Interchange*, 7(2), 11–20 (2001)

RDF, topic maps, and the semantic Web by Lacher, M.S. and Decker, S. *Markup Languages: Theory & Practice*, 3(3), 313–31 (2001)

Resource description framework (RDF) for organised searching on Internet by Tripathi, A. *DESIDOC Bulletin of Information Technology*, 21(4–5), 3–7 (2001)

The Semantic Web: the roles of XML and RDF by Decker, S., Melnik, S., van Harmelen, F., Fensel, D., Klein, M., Broekstra, J., Erdmann, M. and Horrocks, I. *IEEE Internet Computing*, 4(5), 63–73 (2000)

Sesame: a generic architecture for storing and querying RDF and RDF schema by Broekstra, J., Kampman, A. and van Harmelen, F. *The Semantic Web – ISWC 2002. First International Web Conference, Proceedings* (Lecture Notes in Computer Science 2342), pp. 54–68. Springer-Verlag, Berlin, 2002

Server-side automatic metadata generation using qualified Dublin Core and RDF by Jenkins, C. and Inman, D. *Proceedings 2000 Kyoto International Conference on Digital Libraries: Research and Practice*, pp. 262–9. IEEE Computer Society, Los Alamitos, CA, 2000

Simultaneous topic maps and RDF metadata structures in SVG by Dodds, D. *Conference Proceedings. Extreme Markup Languages 2000. Expanding XML/SGML Universe*, pp. 45–53. Graphic Communications Association, Alexandria, VA, 2000

Topic Maps and RDF by Freese, E. *Interchange*, 7(3), 14–16 (2001)

Topic maps vs. RDF by Freese, E. *Conference Proceedings. Extreme Markup Languages 2000. Expanding XML/SGML Universe*, pp. 79–85. Graphic Communications Association, Alexandria, VA, 2000

Towards a unified version model using the resource description framework (RDF) by Kitcharoensakkul, S. and Wuwongse, V. *International Journal of Software Engineering and Knowledge Engineering*, 11(6), 675–701 (2001)

What is RDF? [Resource Description Framework] by Bray, T. *Interchange*, 6(4), 5–9 (2000)

XML, RDF, and relatives by Klein, M. *IEEE Intelligent Systems*, 16(2), 26–8 (2001)

XML topic maps through RDF glasses by Ogievetsky, N. *Markup Languages: Theory & Practice*, 3(3), 333–64 (2001)

Semantic Web

Agents and the Semantic Web by Hendler, J. *IEEE Intelligent Systems*, **16**(2), 30–7 (2001)

Benchmarking RDF schemas for the Semantic Web by Magkanaraki, A., Alexaki, S., Christophides, V. and Plexousakis, D. *The Semantic Web – ISWC 2002. First International Web Conference, Proceedings* (Lecture Notes in Computer Science 2342), pp. 132–46. Springer-Verlag, Berlin, 2002

Bringing together semantic Web and Web services by Peer, J. *The Semantic Web – ISWC 2002. First International Web Conference, Proceedings* (Lecture Notes in Computer Science 2342), pp. 279–91. Springer-Verlag, Berlin, 2002

The Briefing Associate: easing authors into the Semantic Web by Tallis, M., Goldman, N.M. and Balzer, R.M. *IEEE Intelligent Systems*, **17**(1), 26–32 (2002)

Building the Semantic Web on XML by Patel-Schneider, P.F. and Simeon, J. *The Semantic Web – ISWC 2002. First International Web Conference, Proceedings* (Lecture Notes in Computer Science 2342), pp. 147–61. Springer-Verlag, Berlin, 2002

Calendar agents on the Semantic Web by Payne, T.R., Singh, R. and Sycara, K. *IEEE Intelligent Systems*, **17**(3), 84–6 (2002)

Creating a Semantic-Web interface with Virtual Reality by Cleary, D. and O'Donoghue, D. *Proceedings of the SPIE – The International Society for Optical Engineering*, Vol. 4528, pp.138–46. SPIE-Int. Soc. Opt. Eng., 2001

DAML-S: Web Service description for the Semantic Web by Ankolekar, A., Burstein, M., Hobbs, J.R., Lassila, O., Martin, D., McDermott, D. and McIlraith, S.A. *The Semantic Web – ISWC 2002. First International Web Conference, Proceedings* (Lecture Notes in Computer Science 2342), pp. 348–63. Springer-Verlag, Berlin, 2002

Dependable Semantic Web by Thuraisingham, B., Hughes, E. and Allen, D. *Proceedings of the Seventh IEEE International Workshop on Object-Oriented Real-Time Dependable Systems (WORDS 2002)*, pp. 305–8. IEEE Computer Society, Los Alamitos, CA, 2002

Eight questions about Semantic Web annotations by Euzenat, J. *IEEE Intelligent Systems*, **17**(2), 55–62 (2002)

Extracting focused knowledge from the Semantic Web by Crow, L. and Shadbolt, N. *International Journal of Human–Computer Studies*, **54**(1), 155–84 (2001)

Four steps towards the widespread adoption of a semantic web by McBride, B. *The Semantic Web – ISWC 2002. First International Web Conference, Proceedings* (Lecture Notes in Computer Science 2342), pp. 419–22. Springer-Verlag, Berlin, 2002

Framework for the semantic Web: an RDF tutorial by Decker, S., Mitra, P. and Melnik, S. *IEEE Internet Computing*, **4**(6), 68–73 (2000)

Hypermedia presentation adaptation on the Semantic Web by Frasincar, F. and Houben, G.-J. *Adaptive Hypermedia and Adaptive Web-Based Systems. Second International Conference, AH 2002, Proceedings* (Lecture Notes in Computer Science 2347), pp. 133–42. Springer-Verlag, Berlin, 2002

ITTALKS: an application of agents in the Semantic Web by Perich, F., Kagal, L., Chen, H., Tolia, S., Youyong Zou, Finin, T., Joshi, A., Yun Peng, Cost, R.S. and Nicholas, C. *Engineering Societies in the Agents World II. Second International Workshop, ESAW 2001. Revised Papers* (Lecture Notes in Artificial Intelligence 2203), pp. 175–93. Springer-Verlag, Berlin, 2001

ITtalks: a case study in the Semantic Web and DAML+OIL by Cost, R.S., Finin, T., Joshi, A., Yun Peng, Nicholas, C., Soboroff, I., Chen, H., Kagal, L., Perich, F., Youyong Zou and Tolia, S. *IEEE Intelligent Systems*, **17**(1), 40–7 (2002)

The languages of the Semantic Web by Ogbuji, U. *New.Architect*, **7**(6), 30–3 (2002)

Multilingual terminologies and ontologies for the Semantic Web by Budin, G. *OEGAI-Journal*, **20**(1), 22–8 (2001)

OIL: an ontology infrastructure for the Semantic Web by Fensel, D., van Harmelen, F., Horrocks, I., McGuinness, D.L. and Patel-Schneider, P.F. *IEEE Intelligent Systems*, **16**(2), 38–45 (2001)

OntoEdit: collaborative ontology development for the Semantic Web by Sure, Y., Erdmann, M., Angele, J., Staab, S., Studer, R. and Wenke, D. *The Semantic Web – ISWC 2002. First International Web Conference, Proceedings* (Lecture Notes in Computer Science 2342), pp. 221–35. Springer-Verlag, Berlin, 2002

Ontology languages for the Semantic Web by Gomez-Perez, A. and Corcho, O. *IEEE Intelligent Systems*, **17**(1), 54–60 (2002)

Ontology learning for the Semantic Web by Maedche, A. and Staab, S. *IEEE Intelligent Systems*, **16**(2), 72–9 (2001)

A portrait of the Semantic Web in action by Heflin, J. and Hendler, J. *IEEE Intelligent Systems*, **16**(2), 54–9 (2001)

Predicting how ontologies for the Semantic Web will evolve by Kim, H. *Communications of the ACM*, **45**(2), 48–54 (2002)

Querying the Semantic Web: a formal approach by Horrocks, I. and Tessaris, S. *The Semantic Web – ISWC 2002. First International Web Conference, Proceedings* (Lecture Notes in Computer Science 2342), pp. 177–91. Springer-Verlag, Berlin, 2002

RDF, topic maps, and the Semantic Web by Lacher, M.S. and Decker, S. *Markup Languages: Theory & Practice*, **3**(3), 313–31 (2001)

A review of ontologies with the Semantic Web in view by Ying Ding. *Journal of Information Science*, **27**(6), 377–84 (2001)

SEAL – a framework for developing Semantic Web portals by Maedche, A., Staab, S., Stojanovic, N., Studer, R. and Sure, Y. *Advances in Databases. 18th British National Conference on Databases, BNCOD 18, Proceedings* (Lecture Notes in Computer Science 2097), pp. 1–22. Springer-Verlag, Berlin, 2001

Semantic matching of web services capabilities by Paolucci, M., Kawamura, T., Payne, T.R. and Sycara, K. *The Semantic Web – ISWC 2002. First International Web Conference, Proceedings* (Lecture Notes in Computer Science 2342), pp. 333–47. Springer-Verlag, Berlin, 2002

The Semantic Web and its languages by Lassila, O., van Harmelen, F., Horrocks, I., Hendler, J. and McGuinness, D.L. *IEEE Intelligent Systems*, **15**(6), 67–73 (2000)

Semantic Web enabled Web Services by Fensel, D., Bussler, C. and Maedche, A. *The Semantic Web – ISWC 2002. First International Web Conference, Proceedings* (Lecture Notes in Computer Science 2342), pp. 1–2. Springer-Verlag, Berlin, 2002

The Semantic Web: the roles of XML and RDF by Decker, S., Melnik, S., van Harmelen, F., Fensel, D., Klein, M., Broekstra, J., Erdmann, M. and Horrocks, I. *IEEE Internet Computing*, **4**(5), 63–73 (2000)

Semantic Web services by McIlraith, S.A., Son, T.C. and Honglei Zeng. *IEEE Intelligent Systems*, **16**(2), 46–53 (2001)

The semantic web: yet another hip? by Ying Ding, Fensel, D., Klein, M. and Omelayenko, B. *Data & Knowledge Engineering*, **41**(2–3), 205–27.

Supporting user-profiled semantic Web-oriented search by Palopoli, L., Rosaci, D., Terracina, G. and Ursino, D. *Cooperative Information Agents V. 5th International Workshop, CIA 2001, Proceedings* (Lecture Notes in Computer Science 2182), pp. 26–31. Springer-Verlag, Berlin, 2001

SWAD-Europe: Semantic Web advanced development in Europe: a position paper by Brickley, D., Buswell, S., Matthews, B.M., Miller, L., Reynolds, D. and Wilson, M.D. *The Semantic Web – ISWC 2002. First International Web Conference, Proceedings* (Lecture Notes in Computer Science 2342), pp. 409–13. Springer-Verlag, Berlin, 2002

Syntactic and semantic interoperability: new approaches to knowledge and the semantic web by Veltman, K.H. *New Review of Information Networking*, **7**, 159–83 (2001)

Towards an architecture for personalization and adaptivity in the semantic Web by Aragao, V.R., Fernandes, A.A.A. and Goble, C.A. *Third International Conference on Information Integration and Web-based Applications and Services (IIWAS 2001)*, pp. 139–49. Osterreichische Comput. Gesellschaft, Wien, 2001

Towards semantic web mining by Berendt, B., Hotho, A. and Stumme, G. *The Semantic Web – ISWC 2002. First International Web Conference, Proceedings* (Lecture Notes in Computer Science 2342), pp. 264–78. Springer-Verlag, Berlin, 2002

TRIPLE – a query, inference, and transformation language for the semantic web by Sintek, M. and Decker, S. *The Semantic Web – ISWC 2002. First International Web Conference, Proceedings* (Lecture Notes in Computer Science 2342), pp. 364–78. Springer-Verlag, Berlin, 2002

WEBWATCH: the Semantic Web by Addison, C. *Information Development*, **17**(2), 83–4 (2001)

Word semantics for information retrieval: moving one step closer to the Semantic Web by Mihalcea, R.F. and Mihalcea, S.I. *Proceedings 13th IEEE International Conference on Tools with Artificial Intelligence, ICTAI 2001*, pp. 280–7. IEEE Computer Society, Los Alamitos, CA, 2001

XML Declarative Description: a language for the Semantic Web by Wuwongse, V., Anutariya, C., Akama, K. and Nantajeewarawat, E. *IEEE Intelligent Systems*, **16**(3), 54–65 (2001)

SGML

A case study for migration from SGML document to XML documents by Min Ho Cho, Sung Yul Rhew and

Si Hyoung Park. *Journal of KISS: Computing Practices*, 7(6), 653–60 (2001)

Development of SGML/XML middleware component by Ohno, K. and Beyer, M. *Proceedings of SGML/XML Europe '98. From Theory to New Practices*, pp. 373–82. Graphic Communications Association, Alexandria, VA, 1998

Hypertext linking with HTML, SGML and XML-technologies and techniques by Bradley, N. *Proceedings of SGML/XML Europe '98. From Theory to New Practices*, pp. 341–5. Graphic Communications Association, Alexandria, VA, 1998

Is XML becoming as complex as SGML? by Bradley, N. *Interchange*, 7(4), 6–8 (2001)

ML document grammars and exceptions by Kilpelainen, P. and Wood, D. *Information and Computation*, 169(2), 230–51 (2001)

Producing and using intelligent graphics in XML/SGML electronic publishing by Gaudron, M. *XML Europe '99 Conference Proceedings*, pp. 521–31. Graphic Communications Association, Alexandria, VA, 1999

SGML and schemas: from SGML DTDs to XML-data by Chahuneau, F. *Proceedings of SGML/XML Europe '98. From Theory to New Practices*, pp. 83–8. Graphic Communications Association, Alexandria, VA, 1998

SGML and XML content models by Kilpelainen, P. *Markup Languages: Theory & Practice*, 1(2), 53–76 (1999)

Sharing SGML/XML document information conformable to business standards by Imamura, M., Moriguchi, O., Suzuki, K. and Tsuji, H. *Proceedings of the 1999 ICPP Workshops on Collaboration and Mobile Computing (CMC'99). Group Communications (IWGC). Internet '99 (IWI'99). Industrial Applications on Network Computing (INDAP). Multimedia Network Systems (MMNS). Security (IWSEC). Parallel Computing '99 (IWPC'99). Parallel Execution on Reconfigurable Hardware (PERH)*, pp. 381–6. IEEE Computer Society, Los Alamitos, CA, 1999

Succession in standardization: Grafting XML onto SGML by Egyedi, T.M. and Loeffen, A.G.A.J. *Proceedings from the 2nd IEEE Conference on Standardization and Innovation in Information Technology*, pp. 38–49. IEEE, Piscataway, NJ, 2001

Techniques of SGML/XML by Kato, H. and Mizuno, M. *Journal of Information Processing and Management*, 42(9), 777–89 (1999)

Using an XML audit to move SGML data towards XML by Halpern-Hamu, C. *XML 98 Conference Proceedings*, p. 16. Graphic Communications Association, Alexandria, VA, 1998

XML: fulfilling the SGML dream by Burnard, L. *Online Information 99. Proceedings 23rd International Online Information Meeting*, pp. 43–4. Learned Inf. Europe, Woodside, 1999

XML is not just another name for SGML: XML is the vehicle to deploy structured data systems throughout an organization by Maziarka, M. *Proceedings of SGML/XML Europe '98. From Theory to New Practices*, pp. 293–6. Graphic Communications Association, Alexandria, VA, 1998

SMIL

About the semantic verification of SMIL documents by Sampaio, P.N.M., Santos, C.A.S. and Courtias, J.P. *2000 IEEE International Conference on Multimedia and Expo. ICME2000, Proceedings. Latest Advances in the Fast Changing World of Multimedia*, pp. 1675–8, Vol. 3. IEEE, Piscataway, NJ, 2000

Anticipating SMIL 2.0: the developing cooperative infrastructure for multimedia on the Web by Rutledge, L., Van Ossenbruggen, J., Hardman, L. and Bulterman, D.C.A. *Computer Networks*, 31(11–16), 1421–30 (1999)

Building and indexing a distributed multimedia presentation archive using SMIL by Hunter, J. and Little, S. *Research and Advanced Technology for Digital Libraries. 5th European Conference, ECDL 2001, Proceedings* (Lecture Notes in Computer Science 2163), pp. 415–28. Springer-Verlag, Berlin, 2001

A formal semantics of SMIL: a web standard to describe multimedia documents by Jourdan, M. *Computer Standards & Interfaces*, 23(5), 439–55 (2001)

SMIL 2.0 implementation overview by Rutledge, L. *Interchange*, 8(1), 20–24 (2002)

SMIL 2.0 part 1: overview, concepts, and structure by Bulterman, D.C.A. *IEEE Multimedia*, 8(4), 82–8 (2001)

SMIL 2.0 part 2. Examples and comparisons by Bulterman, D.C.A. *IEEE Multimedia*, 9(1), 74–84 (2002)

SMIL 2.0 – repurposing broadcast content for the Web by Bulterman, D.C.A. *EBU Technical Review*, 287 (2001)

SMIL 2.0: XML for Web multimedia by Rutledge, L. *IEEE Internet Computing*, 5(5), 78–84 (2001)

SMIL makes Web applications multimodal by Flammia, G. *IEEE Intelligent Systems*, **13**(4), 12–13 (1998)

SVG

Future scientific digital documents with MathML, XML, and SVG by Landau, R.H., Vediner, D., Wattanakasiwich, P. and Kyle, K.R. *Computing in Science & Engineering*, **4**(2), 77–85 (2002)

ML and SVG by Herlitz, J.C. *XML Europe '99 Conference Proceedings*, pp. 61–70. Graphic Communications Association, Alexandria, VA, 1999

Representation and display of geospatial information: a comparison of ArcXML and SVG by Baru, C., Behere, A. and Cowart, C. *Proceedings of the Second International Conference on Web Information Systems Engineering*, pp. 48–53, Vol. 2. IEEE Computer Society, Los Alamitos, CA, 2002

Scalable Vector Graphics (SVG): vector graphics for the Web by Duce, D. *Ariadne*, No. 28, June 2001

Simultaneous topic maps and RDF metadata structures in SVG by Dodds, D. *Conference Proceedings. Extreme Markup Languages 2000. Expanding XML/SGML Universe*, pp. 45–53. Graphic Communications Association, Alexandria, VA, 2000

Study on SVG-based and dynamical real-time data publication technology by Chen Chun-bo, Wang Jing and Deng Kai. *Mini-Micro Systems*, **23**(5), 609–12 (2002)

Topic Maps

Applying topic maps to ad hoc workflows for semantic associative navigation in process networks by Huth, C., Smolnik, S. and Nastansky, L. *Proceedings Seventh International Workshop on Groupware. CRIWG 2001*, pp. 44–9. IEEE Computer Society, Los Alamitos, CA, 2001

Automatically generated topic maps of World Wide Web resources by Godby, C.J., Miller, E.J. and Reighart, R.R. *Journal of Library Administration*, **34**(3–4), 393–405. Haworth Press, 2001

Building dynamic Web sites with Topic Maps and XSLT by Ogievetsky, N. *Conference Proceedings. Extreme Markup Languages 2000. Expanding XML/SGML Universe*, pp. 187–91. Graphic Communications Association, Alexandria, VA, 2000

A formal model for topic maps by Auillans, P., de Mendez, P.O., Rosenstiehl, P. and Vatant, B. *The Semantic Web – ISWC 2002. First International Web Conference, Proceedings* (Lecture Notes in Computer Science 2342), pp. 69–83. Springer-Verlag, Berlin, 2002

Integration of topic maps and databases: towards efficient knowledge representation and directory services by Luckeneder, T., Steiner, K. and Woss, W. Database and Expert Systems Applications. *12th International Conference, DEXA 2001, Proceedings* (Lecture Notes in Computer Science 2113), pp. 744–53. Springer-Verlag, Berlin, 2001

RDF and Topic Maps: an exercise in convergence by Moore, G.D. *Interchange*, **7**(2), 11–20 (2001)

RDF, topic maps, and the Semantic Web by Lacher, M.S. and Decker, S. *Markup Languages: Theory & Practice*, **3**(3), 313–31 (2001)

Simultaneous topic maps and RDF metadata structures in SVG by Dodds, D. *Conference Proceedings. Extreme Markup Languages 2000. Expanding XML/SGML Universe*, pp. 45–53. Graphic Communications Association, Alexandria, VA, 2000

Topic maps at a glance by Biezunski, M. *XML Europe '99 Conference Proceedings*, pp. 387–91. Graphic Communications Association, Alexandria, VA, 1999

Topic Maps and RDF by Freese, E. *Interchange*, **7**(3), 14–16 (2001)

Topic maps self-control by Holger Roth, H. *Markup Languages: Theory & Practice*, **2**(4), 367–88 (2000)

Topic maps – an enabling technology for knowledge management by Steiner, K., Essmayr, W. and Wagner, R. *12th International Workshop on Database and Expert Systems Applications*, pp. 472–6. IEEE Computer Society, Los Alamitos, CA, 2001

Topic maps: templates, topology, and type hierarchies by Rath, H.H. *Markup Languages: Theory & Practice*, **2**(1), 45–64 (2000)

Topic maps vs. RDF by Freese, E. *Conference Proceedings. Extreme Markup Languages 2000. Expanding XML/SGML Universe*, pp. 79–85. Graphic Communications Association, Alexandria, VA, 2000

Topic maps: what are they and how can I use them? by Garshol, L.M. *Interchange*, **8**(1), 16–19 (2002)

Web metadata semantics – on the road to well formed topic maps by Widhalm, R. and Mueck, T.A. *Proceedings of the Second International Conference on Web Information Systems Engineering*, pp. 141–50, Vol. 2. IEEE Computer Society, Los Alamitos, CA, 2002

XML topic maps: finding aids for the Web by Biezunski, M. and Newcomb, S.R. *IEEE Multimedia*, **8**(2), 104–8 (2001)

XML topic maps through RDF glasses by Ogievetsky, N. *Markup Languages: Theory & Practice*, **3**(3), 333–64 (2001)

UML

Agent-mediated e-commerce: agents, components, services, workflow, UML, Java, XML and games by Griss, M.L. *Proceedings 34th International Conference on Technology of Object-Oriented Languages and Systems – TOOLS 34*, pp. 3–9. IEEE Computer Society, Los Alamitos, CA, 2000

Toward the interoperable software design models: quartet of UML, XML, DOM and CORBA by Suzuki, J. and Yamamoto, Y. *Proceedings 4th IEEE International Software Engineering Standards Symposium and Forum (ISESS'99). 'Best Software Practices for the Internet Age'*, pp. 163–72. IEEE Computer Society, Los Alamitos, CA, 1999

Using UML to define XML document types by Eliot Kimber, W. and Heintz, J. *Markup Languages: Theory & Practice*, **2**(3), 295–320 (2000)

Using UML to define XML document types by Kimber, W.E. and Heintz, J. *Conference Proceedings. Extreme Markup Languages 2000. Expanding XML/SGML Universe*, pp. 137–54. Graphic Communications Association, Alexandria, VA, 2000

Using XML/XMI for tool supported evolution of UML models by Keienburg, F. and Rausch, A. *Proceedings of the 34th Annual Hawaii International Conference on System Sciences*, p. 10. IEEE Computer Society, Los Alamitos, CA, 2001

XML rule based source code generator for UML CASE tool by Dong Hyuk Park and Soo Dong Kim. *Proceedings Eighth Asia-Pacific Software Engineering Conference*, pp. 53–60. IEEE Computer Society, Los Alamitos, CA, 2001

VoiceXML

Design and implementation of a HTML to VoiceXML converter by Hoon il Choi and Young Gun Jang. *Journal of KISS: Computing Practices*, **7**(6), 559–68 (2001)

Making the VoiceWeb smarter – integrating intelligent component technologies and VoiceXML by Mittendorfer, M., Niklfeld, G. and Winiwarter, W. *Proceedings of the Second International Conference on Web Information Systems Engineering*, pp. 126–31, Vol. 2. IEEE Computer Society, Los Alamitos, CA, 2002

VoiceXML distributes voice to the masses by Cravotta, N. *EDN (US edition)*, **47**(1), 55–62 (2002)

A VoiceXML framework for reusable dialog components by Maes, S.H. *Proceedings 2002 Symposium on Applications and the Internet (SAINT 2002)*, pp. 28–30. IEEE Computer Society, Los Alamitos, CA, 2002

VoiceXML: the next generation applications by Malik, A.I., Usman, M.R. and Aziz, M.Z. *Pakistan Journal of Information and Technology*, **1**(1), 22–7 (2002)

VoiceXML and the voice-driven Internet by Houlding, D. *Dr. Dobb's Journal*, **26**(4), 88–95 (2001)

VoiceXML for Web-based distributed conversational applications by Lucas, B. *Communications of the ACM*, **43**(9), 53–7 (2000)

WML

A classification of hybrid (HTML/WML) search engines by Angelaccio, M. and Buttarazzi, B. *AICA 2000. Le Tecnologie dell'Informazione e della Comunicazione come motore di sviluppo del Paese (Information and Communication Technology as the Engine of National Development)*, pp. 573–579. AICA, Milan, 2000

Compressibility of WML and WMLScript byte code: initial results [Wireless Mark-up Language] by Ojanen, E. and Veijalainen, J. *Proceedings Tenth International Workshop on Research Issues in Data Engineering. RIDE 2000*, pp. 55–62. IEEE Computer Society, Los Alamitos, CA, 2000

A design and implementation of WML compiler for WAP gateway for wireless Internet services by Eunjeong Choi, Dong-Won Han and Kyungshik Lim. *Journal of KISS: Computing Practices*, **7**(2), 165–182 (2001)

X3D

Visualising human consciousness content using Java3D/X3D and psychological techniques by Geroimenko, V. and Geroimenko, L. *2000 IEEE Conference on Information Visualization. An International Conference on Computer Visualization and Graphics*, pp. 529–532. IEEE Computer Society, Los Alamitos, CA, 2000

X3D moving grid methods for semiconductor applications by Kuprat, A., Cartwright, D., Gammel, J.T., George, D., Kendrick, B., Kilcrease, D., Trease, H. and Walker, R. *VLSI Design*, **8**(1–4), 117–121 (1998)

XLink

An application of XML and XLink using a graph-partitioning method and a density map for information retrieval and knowledge discovery by Guillaume, D. and Murtagh, F. *Astronomical Society of the Pacific Conference Series*, **172**, 278–82 (1999)

What is XLink? by Arciniegas A., F. *Interchange*, **6**(3), 16–23 (2000)

XLink – the future of document linking by Gwiazda, K. and Kazienko, P. *Information Systems Architecture and Technology. ISAT 2001. Proceedings of the 23rd International Scientific School Digital Economy Concepts, Tools and Applications*, pp. 132–9. Oficyna Wydawnicza Politechniki Wroclawskiej, Wroclaw, 2001

XLink and open hypermedia systems: a preliminary investigation by Halsey, B. and Anderson, K.M. *ACM 2000 Hypertext. Proceedings of the Eleventh ACM Conference on Hypertext and Hypermedia*, pp. 212–13. ACM, New York, NY, 2000

XLink: the XML Linking Language by McGrath, S. *Dr. Dobb's Journal*, **23**(12), 94, 96–101 (1998)

XML

Applications of XML to location based services by Takayama, K., Ueda, Y. and Naito, H. *Fujitsu*, **53**(3), 245–9 (2002)

An automatic rating technique based on XML document by Hyeonjeong Mun, Sooho Ok and Yongtae Woo. *Adaptive Hypermedia and Adaptive Web-Based Systems. Second International Conference, AH 2002, Proceedings* (Lecture Notes in Computer Science 2347), pp. 424–7. Springer-Verlag, Berlin, 2002

Babel: an XML-based application integration framework by Huaxin Zhang and Stroulia, E. *Advanced Information Systems Engineering. 14th International Conference, CAiSE 2002, Proceedings* (Lecture Notes in Computer Science 2348), pp. 280–95. Springer-Verlag, Berlin, 2002

Building the Semantic Web on XML by Patel-Schneider, P.F. and Simeon, J. *The Semantic Web – ISWC 2002. First International Web Conference, Proceedings* (Lecture Notes in Computer Science 2342), pp. 147–61. Springer-Verlag, Berlin, 2002

Can XML change the way we work? by Beesley, K. *Computers and Law*, **13**(1), 6–9 (2002)

Converting business documents: a classification of problems and solutions using XML/XSLT by Wustner, E., Hotzel, T. and Buxmann, P. *Proceedings Fourth IEEE International Workshop on Advanced Issues of E-Commerce and Web-Based Information Systems (WECWIS 2002)*, pp. 61–8. IEEE Computer Society, Los Alamitos, CA, 2002

Current approaches to XML management by Nambiar, U., Lacroix, Z., Bressan, S., Mong Li Lee and

Yingguang Li. *IEEE Internet Computing*, **6**(4), 43–51 (2002)

Designing functional dependencies for XML by Mong Li Lee, Tok Wang Ling and Wai Lup Low. *Advances in Database Technology – EDBT 2002. 8th International Conference on Extending Database Technology, Proceedings* (Lecture Notes in Computer Science 2287), pp. 124–41. Springer-Verlag, Berlin, 2002

Effective Web data extraction with standard XML technologies by Myllymaki, J. *Computer Networks*, **39**(5), 635–44 (2002)

Efficient complex query support for multiversion XML documents by Shu-Yao Chien, Tsotras, V.J., Zaniolo, C. and Donghui Zhang. *Advances in Database Technology – EDBT 2002. 8th International Conference on Extending Database Technology, Proceedings* (Lecture Notes in Computer Science 2287), pp. 161–78. Springer-Verlag, Berlin, 2002

On efficient matching of streaming XML documents and queries by Lakshmanan, L.V.S. and Parthasarathy, S. *Advances in Database Technology – EDBT 2002. 8th International Conference on Extending Database Technology, Proceedings* (Lecture Notes in Computer Science 2287), pp. 142–60. Springer-Verlag, Berlin, 2002

How will XML impact industrial automation? by Pinceti, P. *InTech*, **49**(6), 37–40 (2002)

On implementing information system and databases interoperability with XML by Bouneffa, M., Deruelle, L. and Melab, N. *Proceedings of the ISCA 14th International Conference Parallel and Distributed Computing Systems*, pp. 517–22. International Society for Computers and their Applications, Cary, NC, 2001

Implementing XML in the finance industry by Wakabayashi, T. *Fujitsu*, **53**(3), 227–30 (2002)

Information exchange modeling (IEM) and extensible markup language (XML) technologies by Cleveland, F.M. 2002 *IEEE Power Engineering Society Winter Meeting. Conference Proceedings*, pp. 592–5, Vol. 1. IEEE, Piscataway, NJ, 2002

Institutions: integrating objects, XML and databases by Alagic, S. *Information and Software Technology*, **44**(4), 207–16 (2002)

An integrated interface based on Web and XML for interoperability between enterprises by Liu Jianxun, Zhang Shensheng and Hu Tao. *High Technology Letters*, **12**(5), 71–5 (2002)

Integrating of file systems and multidatabase systems based on XML by Lu Zheng-ding, Li Bing, Xiao Weijun, Li Rui-xuan and Hu He-ping. *Mini-Micro Systems*, **23**(5), 588–91 (2002)

An introduction to the e-XML data integration suite by Gardarin, G., Mensch, A. and Tomasic, A. *Advances in Database Technology – EDBT 2002. 8th International Conference on Extending Database Technology, Proceedings* (Lecture Notes in Computer Science 2287), pp. 297–306. Springer-Verlag, Berlin, 2002

Keys for XML by Buneman, P., Davidson, S., Wenfei Fan, Hara, C. and Wang-Chiew Tan. *Computer Networks*, **39**(5), 473–87 (2002)

A logical foundation for XML by Mengchi Liu. *Advanced Information Systems Engineering. 14th International Conference, CAiSE 2002, Proceedings* (Lecture Notes in Computer Science 2348), pp. 568–83. Springer-Verlag, Berlin, 2002

Management of XML documents without schema in relational database systems by Kudrass, T. *Information and Software Technology*, **44**(4), 269–75 (2002)

Managing scientific metadata using XML by Ruixin Yang, Kafatos, M. and Wang, X.S. *IEEE Internet Computing*, **6**(4), 52–9 (2002)

Mind your meta-language [XML] by Jackson, S. *Banking Technology*, **19**(1), 33–36 (2002)

Modeling and exchange of product classification systems using XML by Leukel, J., Schmitz, V. and Dorloff, F.-D. *Proceedings Fourth IEEE International Workshop on Advanced Issues of E-Commerce and Web-Based Information Systems (WECWIS 2002)*, pp. 242–4. IEEE Computer Society, Los Alamitos, CA, 2002

Modeling XML applications by Carlson, D. *Software Development*, **10**(6), 38–41 (2002)

New trends in XML technologies – personalization technology by Iida, I. *Fujitsu*, **53**(3), 250–4 (2002)

Open metadata formats: efficient XML-based communication for high performance computing by Widener, P., Eisenhauer, G., Schwan, K. and Bustamante, F.E. *Cluster Computing*, **5**(3), 315–24 (2002)

Ontology-based integration of XML Web resources by Amann, B., Beeri, C., Fundulaki, I. and Scholl, M. *The Semantic Web – ISWC 2002. First International Web Conference, Proceedings* (Lecture Notes in Computer Science 2342), pp. 117–31. Springer-Verlag, Berlin, 2002

Regulating access to XML documents by Gabillon, A. and Bruno, E. *Database and Application Security XV. IFIP TC11/WG11.3 Fifteenth Annual Working Conference on Database and Application Security*, pp.

299–314. Kluwer Academic Publishers, Norwell, MA, 2002

A unified constraint model for XML by Wenfei Fan, Kuper, G.M. and Simeon, J. *Computer Networks*, **39**(5), 489–505 (2002)

Using XML for supplemental hypertext support by Chao-Min Chiu and Bieber, M. *Information Technology & Management*, **3**(3), 271–90 (2002)

Web services and XML good news: the difficult issues are still open by Devin, M. *Proceedings Fourth IEEE International Workshop on Advanced Issues of E-Commerce and Web-Based Information Systems (WECWIS 2002)*, p. 3. IEEE Computer Society, Los Alamitos, CA, 2002

Who will be your expert? [XML] by Trippe, B. *Transform Magazine*, **11**(6), 23 (2002)

An XML approach for assessment in education by Manso, V., Raga, J.M., Romero, R., Palau, C.E., Guerri, J.C. and Esteve, M. *Proceedings of the IASTED International Conference Applied Informatics. International Symposium on Artificial Intelligence and Applications*, pp. 442–7. ACTA Press, Anaheim, CA, 2001

An XML-based architecture for distributed real-time multimedia systems by Tsang, T. *GLOBECOM'01. IEEE Global Telecommunications Conference*, pp. 2005–8, Vol. 3. IEEE, Piscataway, NJ, 2001

XML-based manufacturing resource model for process planning by Zhong-hua Ni, Hong Yi, Wen-cheng Tang and Qing Shen. *Computer Integrated Manufacturing Systems*, **8**(6), 429–32 (2002)

An XML-based quality of service enabling language for the web by Xaohu Gu, Nahrstedt, K., Wanghong Yuan, Wichadakul, D. and Dongyan Xu. *Journal of Visual Languages and Computing*, **13**(1), 61–95 (2002)

An XML digital signature for Internet e-business applications by Woo-Yong Han, Cheon-Shu Park, Shin-Young lim and Ji-Hoon Kang. *2001 International Conferences on Info-Tech and Info-Net. Proceedings*, pp. 23–9, Vol. 6. IEEE, Piscataway, NJ, 2001

XML and global name access control by Ki-Tat Lam. *OCLC Systems & Services*, **18**(2), 88–96 (2002)

XML goes native by Wonnacott, L. *Enterprise Systems Journal*, **17**(5), 32–4 (2002)

The XML revolution by Hill, A. *Financial Technology*, **1**(14), 5–6 (2002)

XML is top of the class by Anderson, T. *Application Development Advisor*, **6**(4), 30, 32, 34, 36–7 (2002)

An XML Schema representation for the communication design of electronic negotiations by Strobel, M. *Computer Networks*, **39**(5), 661–80 (2002)

XML structures for relational data by Wenyue Du, Mong Li Lee and Tok Wang Ling. *Proceedings of the Second International Conference on Web Information Systems Engineering*, pp. 151–60, Vol. 1. IEEE Computer Society, Los Alamitos, CA, 2002

XML system development tools by Miyashita, Y., Yamamoto, R., Hara, H. and Suzuki, T. *Fujitsu*, **53**(3), 200–6 (2002)

XML/Web services bring about a new world by Morishita, T., Urano, N. and Hirosue, S. *Fujitsu*, **53**(3), 180–5 (2002)

XML and Security

Using XML security mechanisms by Selkirk, A. *BT Technology Journal*, **19**(3), 35–43 (2001)

XML Applications

Modeling XML applications by Carlson, D. *Software Development*, **10**(6), 38–41 (2002)

XML applications and XML processing model by Kato, H., Hori, N. and Mizuno, M. *Journal of Information Processing and Management*, **42**(10), 876–86 (2000)

XML Databases

Why and how to benchmark XML databases by Schmidt, A., Waas, F., Kersten, M., Florescu, D., Carey, M.J., Manolescu, I. and Busse, R. *SIGMOD Record*, **30**(3), 27–32 (2001)

XML Schemas

Comparative analysis of six XML Schema languages by Lee, D. and Chu, W.W. *SIGMOD Record*, **29**(3), 76–87 (2000)

DTDs go XML schema – a tools perspective by Schweiger, R., Hoelzer, S., Heitmann, K.U. and Dudeck, J. *Medical Informatics and the Internet in Medicine*, **26**(4), 297–308 (2001)

From XML schema to relations: a cost-based approach to XML storage by Bohannon, P., Freire, J., Roy, P. and Simeon, J. *Proceedings 18th International Conference on Data Engineering*, pp. 64–75. IEEE Computer Society, Los Alamitos, CA, 2002

A grammar based model for XML schema integration by Behrens, R. *Advances in Databases. 17th British National Conference on Databases, BNCOD 17, Proceedings* (Lecture Notes in Computer Science 1832), pp. 172–90. Springer-Verlag, Berlin, 2000

Modeling and transformation of object-oriented conceptual models into XML schema by Renguo Xiao, Dillon, T.S., Chang, E. and Ling Feng. *Database and Expert Systems Applications. 12th International Conference, DEXA 2001, Proceedings* (Lecture Notes in Computer Science 2113), pp. 795–804. Springer-Verlag, Berlin, 2001

Validation with MSXML and XML schema by Nelson, M. *Windows Developer Magazine*, **13**(1), 35–8 (2002)

XML and electronic publishing. XML schema languages: beyond DTD by Ioannides, D. *Library Hi Tech*, **18**(1), 9–14 (2000)

XML Schema Directory: a data structure for XML data processing by Kotsakis, E. and Bohm, K. *Proceedings of the First International Conference on Web Information Systems Engineering*, pp. 62–9, Vol. 1. IEEE Computer Society, Los Alamitos, CA, 2000

XML schema language: taking XML to the next level by Roy, J. and Ramanujan, A. *IT Professional*, **3**(2), 37–40 (2001)

XML schema mappings for heterogeneous database access by Collins, S.R., Navathe, S. and Mark, L. *Information and Software Technology*, **44**(4), 251–7 (2002)

XML Tools

SQL server adds XML tools by Hicks, M. and Galli, P. *IT Week*, **5**(18), 21 (2002)

XML tools and architecture for named entity recognition by Mikheev, A., Grover, C. and Moens, M. *Markup Languages: Theory & Practice*, **1**(3), 89–113 (1999)

XML tools: the tools, the categories, the leading players by Burman, L.A. *XML 98 Conference Proceedings*, p. 5. Graphic Communications Association, Alexandria, VA, 1998

XML Web Services

Bayanihan Computing .NET: grid computing with XML web services by Sarmenta, L.F.G., Chua, S.J.V., Echevarria, P., Mendoza, J.M., Santos, R.-R., Tan, S. and Lozada, R.P. *Proceedings CCGRID 2002. 2nd IEEE/ACM International Symposium on Cluster Computing and the Grid*, pp. 434–5. IEEE, Piscataway, NJ, 2002

Developing XML Web services with WebSphere Studio Application Developer by Lau, C. and Ryman, A. *IBM Systems Journal*, **41**(2), 178–97 (2002)

XML/Web services bring about a new world by Morishita, T., Urano, N. and Hirosue, S. *Fujitsu*, **53**(3), 180–5 (2002)

XPath

Efficient filtering of XML documents with XPath expressions by Chee-Yong Chan, Felber, P., Garofalakis, M. and Rastogi, R. *Proceedings 18th International Conference on Data Engineering*, pp. 235–44. IEEE Computer Society, Los Alamitos, CA, 2002

A formal semantics of patterns in XSLT and XPath by Wadler, P. *Markup Languages: Theory & Practice*, 2(2), 183–202 (2000)

OASIS XSLT/XPath conformance testing by Marston, D. *Markup Languages: Theory & Practice*, 3(1), 65–71 (2001)

A visual approach to authoring XPath expressions by Abe, M. and Hori, M. *Markup Languages: Theory & Practice*, 3(2), 191–212 (2001)

X marks the path [XPath] by Gudgin, M. *Developer Network Journal*, 25, 26–31 (2001)

XPointer

XML projects in Japan and Fujitsu's approach to XLink/XPointer by Suzuki, T. and Goto, M. *Fujitsu Scientific and Technical Journal*, 36(2), 175–84 (2000)

XQuery

Active XQuery by Bonifati, A., Braga, D., Campi, A. and Ceri, S. *Proceedings 18th International Conference on Data Engineering*, pp. 403–12. IEEE Computer Society, Los Alamitos, CA, 2002

XQuery by the book: the IPSI XQuery Demonstrator by Fankhauser, P., Groh, T. and Overhage, S. *Advances in Database Technology – EDBT 2002. 8th International Conference on Extending Database Technology, Proceedings* (Lecture Notes in Computer Science 2287), pp. 742–4. Springer-Verlag, Berlin, 2002

XQuery: a flexible query language for XML by Cheng, A. *Windows Developer Magazine*, 13(3), 22–26 (2002)

XQuery formal semantics state and challenges by Fankhaser, P. *SIGMOD Record*, 30(3), 14–19 (2001)

XSL

Building and managing XML/XSL-powered Web sites: an experience report by Kerer, C., Kirda, E., Jazayeri, M. and Kurmanowytsch, R. *25th Annual International Computer Software and Applications Conference. COMPSAC 2001*, pp. 547–54. IEEE, Piscataway, NJ, 2001

Code generation templates using XML and XSL by Georgescu, C. *C/C++ Users Journal*, 20(1), 6–19 (2002)

Evolution of an organizational Web site: migrating to XML/XSL by Kirda, E., Kerer, C., Jazayeri, M., Gall, H. and Kurmanowytsch, R. *Proceedings 3rd International Workshop on Web Site Evolution. WSE 2001*, pp. 62–9. IEEE Computer Society, Los Alamitos, CA, 2001

The Extensible Style Language: XSL by Walsh, N. *WEB Techniques*, 4(1), 49–50, 52, 54–5 (1999)

OpenMath, MathML and XSL by Carlisle, D. *SIGSAM Bulletin*, 34(2), 6–11 (2000)

Patterns in XSL by Floyd, M. *WEB Techniques*, 4(6), 36, 38–41 (1999)

Processing templates in XSL by Floyd, M. *WEB Techniques*, 4(7), 44, 46–48 (1999)

Rendering XML documents using XSL by McGrath, S. *Dr. Dobb's Journal*, 23(7), 82–5, 97–8 (1998)

Structured document transformations based on XSL by Maneth, S. and Neven, F. *Research Issues in Structured and Semistructured Database Programming. 7th International Workshop on Database Programming Languages, DBPL'99. Revised Papers* (Lecture Notes in Computer Science 1949), pp. 80–98. Springer-Verlag, Berlin, 2000

The Valid Web: an XML/XSL infrastructure for temporal management of Web documents by Grandi, F. and Mandreoli, F. *Advances in Information Systems. First International Conference, ADVIS 2000, Proceedings* (Lecture Notes in Computer Science 1909), pp. 294–303. Springer-Verlag, Berlin, 2000

An XML/XSL-based software architecture for application service providers (ASPs) by Gunther, O. and Ricou, O. *Electronic Commerce and Web Technologies. First International Conference, EC-Web 2000, Proceedings* (Lecture Notes in Computer Science 1875), pp. 334–48. Springer-Verlag, Berlin, 2000

XSL theory and practice by Bradley, N. *XML Europe '99 Conference Proceedings*, pp. 357–61. Graphic Communications Association, Alexandria, VA, 1999

XSLT

Breaking the mould [XSLT] by Gudgin, M. *Developer Network Journal*, 27, 22–8 (2001)

Building dynamic Web sites with Topic Maps and XSLT by Ogievetsky, N. Conference Proceedings. *Extreme Markup Languages 2000. Expanding XML/SGML Universe*, pp. 187–91. Graphic Communications Association, Alexandria, VA, 2000

Converting business documents: a classification of problems and solutions using XML/XSLT by Wustner, E., Hotzel, T. and Buxmann, P. *Proceedings Fourth IEEE International Workshop on Advanced Issues of E-*

Commerce and Web-Based Information Systems (WECWIS 2002), pp. 61–8. IEEE Computer Society, Los Alamitos, CA, 2002

Demonstrational interface for XSLT stylesheet generation by Koyanagi, T., Ono, K. and Hori, M. *Markup Languages: Theory & Practice*, **2**(2), 133–52 (2000)

Experimental XSLT processor for objects by Novak, U., Ojsterek, M. and Cajic, Z. *Proceedings of the IASTED International Conference Applied Informatics International Symposium on Software Engineering, Databases, and Applications*, pp. 277–82. ACTA Press, Anaheim, CA, 2001

A formal semantics of patterns in XSLT and XPath by Wadler, P. *Markup Languages: Theory & Practice*, **2**(2), 183–202 (2000)

Getting started with XSLT style sheets and Java servlets by Dumbill, E. *WEB Techniques*, **4**(12), pp. 77–80, 82–3 (1999)

Separating business process from user interaction utilizing process-aware XSLT stylesheets by Aberer, K., Datta, A. and Despotovic, Z. *Proceedings Fourth IEEE International Workshop on Advanced Issues of*

E-Commerce and Web-Based Information Systems (WECWIS 2002), pp. 69–78. IEEE Computer Society, Los Alamitos, CA, 2002

Using XML and XSLT to process and render online journals by Cole, T.W., Mischo, W.H., Habing, T.G. and Ferrer, R.H. *Library Hi Tech*, **19**(3), 210–22 (2001)

Verifying software requirements with XSLT by Duran, A., Ruiz, A., Bernardez, B. and Toro, M. *Software Engineering Notes*, **27**(1), 39–44 (2002)

XSLT design patterns by Tennison, J. *Interchange*, **7**(3), 19–29 (2001)

XSLT powers a new wave of Web applications by Laird, C. *Linux Journal*, **95**, 60–7 (2002)

XSLT stylesheet generation by example with WYSIWYG editing by Ono, K., Koyanagi, T., Abe, M. and Hori, M. *Proceedings 2002 Symposium on Applications and the Internet (SAINT 2002)*, pp. 150–9. IEEE Computer Society, Los Alamitos, CA, 2002

XTL: an XML transformation language and XSLT generator for XTL by Onizuka, M. *Markup Languages: Theory & Practice*, **3**(3), 251–84 (2001)